Mythmakers
of the American Dream

Also by Wiley Lee Umphlett

The Sporting Myth and the American Experience

Mythmakers of the American Dream

The Nostalgic Vision in Popular Culture

Wiley Lee Umphlett

Lewisburg
Bucknell University Press

New York and London
Cornwall Books

Associated University Presses
and Cornwall Books
440 Forsgate Drive
Cranbury, NJ 08512

Cornwall Books
25 Sicilian Avenue
London WC1A 2QH, England

Library of Congress Cataloging in Publication Data

Umphlett, Wiley Lee, 1931–
Mythmakers of the American dream.

Bibliography: p.
Includes index.
1. United States—Popular culture.   2. Mass
media—Social aspects—United States.   3. American
literature—History and criticism.   4. Comic books,
strips, etc.—United States—History and criticism.
I. Title.
E169.1.U52   302.2′3   78-75342
ISBN 0-8453-4739-X (Cornwall)
ISBN 0-8387-3123-6 (Bucknell)

Printed in the United States of America

Contents

For Jennifer,
who started it all

Preface

Generally speaking, *Mythmakers of the American Dream* is a book about "seeing"; but in another, more paradoxical sense it is a book that concerns itself with certain visual trends and influences of our popular culture that may have contributed to impairing our visual perception. Specifically, I intend to deal here with how four forms of our popular culture—fiction, comic-strip art, movies, and television—have imperceptibly conditioned us over the years to see ourselves in a unique relationship to the world around us—in actuality, to see for us. Thus my contention is that these four areas of our mass culture, three of which have been developed in this century but all of them characteristically visual in nature, have had a tremendous but subtle influence in training the mass eye to see what it sees and to see the way it does. In fact, this book goes so far as to suggest that the products of contemporary popular culture have induced us to view the world differently than those who lived prior to their influence.

Because of the magnitude of each of my areas of concentration, I have been compelled to select for discussion only those figures, examples, and developments which I believe to have had the most profound visual impact on American popular culture in the past seventy-five to one hundred years. The restrictiveness of my selections may annoy some readers, but I would remind them that I do not intend here a historical survey, but rather a thematic analysis of a social and cultural phenomenon peculiar to our times: the pervasive expansion throughout our society of a nostalgic mood that, in addition to being inspired by one's own private associations and feelings, is largely the influence of our popular culture. In stimulating us to see things in a special way, this mood has brought about an affectionate, self-indulgent feeling for those things.

Our nostalgic response is essentially visual in nature, engendered by a compulsive desire to relive a familiar part of our past by reexperiencing something familiar from it, usually through a facet of popular culture which in some way visually typifies or represents the dominant taste or feel of an era. Just why this predicament persists is not easily understood. Perhaps, as our society grows increasingly technological and complex as well as more impersonal, we long for simpler, more innocent times when our lifestyles seemed less encumbered with the kinds of doubts and problems that appear to overwhelm us today. Michael Novak, a perceptive observer of the contemporary scene, generally concurs with this outlook, expressing to me in a recent conversation that the nostalgic mood is too much with us today because there is a prevailing feeling that modernity has let us down, that life in a technocratic age is not all it's cracked up to be. As a result, those products of our popular culture (ironically made possible by an ever-expanding technological society) which remind us of more pleasant, harmonious times wield a predominant and persuasive power over our ability to function in the precarious present.

Of course, every age generates its own kind of nostalgia, but none, it seems, has been so obsessively prolific as our own with its technical capabilities for reproducing the myriad nostalgic forms and expressions that have appeared over the past decade or so—reprints of the popular fiction and comic strips of an earlier day, television reruns of vintage Hollywood movies on television, recordings of both the popular music and radio programs of yesterday, not to mention an astounding array of books on nostalgic subjects—weaving for many of us an almost hypnotic spell, which I, too, admit to having fallen under. To me there really was a time when the world seemed a much better place than the one I grew to know. The telling evidence for this observation lies in the affectionate feeling I still retain for those nostalgic reminders of my youth's popular pastimes, particularly the boys' series fiction and comic books I read, the movies I saw, and the radio programs I listened to during this most impressionable time of my life. Television, by the way, seemed light years away in 1940 when I was nine years old, but radio had its visual side, too, since the listener was induced to mentally picture what he heard being dramatized.

Still, for me the greatest visual inspiration during my growing-up years was contained in comic books and the movies. Two favorite sources of these visual stimuli stand out prominently in my mind. One was a corner drugstore which I always made it a point to pass on my way home from school simply because the store's display window exhibited the widest selection of newly published comic books that I ever saw in any one place during this heyday of the medium. For me a comic book was a ten-cent ticket to wondrously strange places where anything was possible, but because a dime was hard to come by in 1940, I hardly ever had the price of the fare. So the next best thing was to dally in front of the store window and saturate myself in the imaginative wealth pictured on those action cluttered, brightly colored covers. That they were forbidden by both parent and teacher made them even more appealing. Their very names conjured up worlds of magic and enchantment—*Fantastic, Marvel Mystery, Adventure, Thrilling, Wonderworld,* and so on, endlessly—but there was one in particular that I always looked for every month. Even though they all looked alike, just to gaze upon a cover of *Planet Comics* was a unique experience in itself, for it purported to depict life on other worlds in future centuries. And what a future those covers envisioned! The standard situation showed a scantily clad, shapely girl either in the clutches of a grotesque, monsterlike

creature or held hostage by some other demonic captor. Usually, an athletically handsome fellow dressed like Buck Rogers could be seen coming to her rescue, rocket guns blazing, and in the background, distant planets shone in a sea of space. Despite their romantic appeal, the covers of *Planet* always invited one big question in my mind: Was the exotically·fascinating, although fearsome, way of life they visualized as the future really the one toward which we were all moving?

Across the street from the drugstore was the other major visual stimulant of those years—the neighborhood movie theater—now long since a casualty to progress and changing lifestyles. Since the feature movie changed three times a week, I stopped regularly to fantasize over the lobby-card displays of the playing features as well as the coming attractions. On occasion I might even have the ten-cent admission price to take in a matinee, usually a B-rated film starring someone like Chester Morris as Boston Blackie, or perhaps Lon Chaney, Jr., as the Mummy, or even William Boyd as Hopalong Cassidy—all visual symbols of the kind of movie that could turn on a predominantly kid audience in this pretelevision era. Such movies were obviously a pleasant retreat for us from the world of adult authority, and it was always with a certain amount of reluctance that we departed that magic world of darkness to go blinking out into the sunlight of the real world outside.

Undoubtedly, the movies made a big impression on me, as they did on most juveniles of my day, but in looking back now from the vantage point of some thirty-five years, I can conclude that of all the popular visual influences with which I came in contact, the comic book had the greatest impact on my youth, mainly because of the fantastic dreamworld scenes that were captured on the covers of comic books like *Planet.* In fact, I now realize that my youthful fascination with the comic book was a kind of epiphany in that this colorful, tangible medium of pure escape contained the key to understanding my fantasy urges and, by extension, most people's nostalgic obsessions. In a way that no other popular medium could, the comic book played on the conflict between our present condition and our longing for a more idealized existence even while offering fantasies that embodied our fear of the unknown. Thus comic books like *Planet,* in their crude attempt to project, even in that long-ago, prespace era, what the future might be like, seemed highly aware of and sensitive to our distaste for the present and the workaday world, so they showed us a way of escaping into a fantasy world dreamed up, in most cases, by the untrained and underpaid artists of the Depression period. Created by dreamers who had cause to fantasize, the comic book was indeed the stuff that dreams are made of and, as such, generated a nostalgic mood and a following uniquely its own.

Considered in this light, the comic-book medium can be taken as a visual metaphor for the seminal idea behind this book. The basic premise of *Mythmakers of the American Dream* derives from my recognition of the psychic tension we experience when we face the dilemma of either confronting what the uncertain future seems to hold or clinging to the familiar objects, sights, and scenes of the past—of pursuing the common dream of the American experience or retreating into our private daydreams.

In the following sections, we shall examine those visually inspired areas of American popular culture that undeniably reveal us as a people torn between the lure of the past and the demands of the future —between the lure of the daydream and the demands of the dream. This conflict has fomented a type of neuroticism in the American psyche that reveals itself in both artist and audience. As a result, the popular artist—the mythmaker, if you will—has the power to transform both our daydreams and our nightmares into patterns of wishful identity, especially in the visual forms of our popular culture which, after a time, appear to reflect the nostalgic vision of both creator and audience. Thus our popular culture is a two-way proposition: both popular artist and expressive form derive as much from their milieu as they contribute to it. Finally, then, *Mythmakers of the American Dream* is about the symbiotic relationship between the popular artists and the expressive forms of our culture that have contributed most convincingly to our unique way of perceiving reality in this century.

Acknowledgments

I owe a debt of gratitude to a number of persons and organizations for assisting me in putting this book together. Without their help and cooperation my task would have been a formidable one indeed. Here, then, I would like to recognize and thank the following:

Harriet S. Adams of the Stratemeyer Syndicate; Avon Books; *The Antique Journal;* Arlington House; Professor Carlos Baker; Bantam Books; Michael Barnes; The Bodley Head Ltd; Brezny and Mauldin, Photographers; Edgar Rice Burroughs, Inc.; Campbell Soup Co.; Jonathan Cape Ltd; Capp Enterprises, Inc., Chicago Tribune-New York News Syndicate; The Condé Nast Publications, Inc.; Cox Cable TV of Pensacola; Culver Pictures; Chelsea House Publishers; Dell Books; Robert C. Dille; Walt Disney, Inc.; Dover Publications, Inc.; Elizabeth Dos Passos; Will Eisner; John Engstead; Ray Funk; Zane Grey, Inc.; Aaron Grimsley; Grosset & Dunlap, Inc.; Gulf Coast area television stations, especially WDAM-TV, Hattiesburg, Miss., and WEAR-TV, Pensacola, Fla.; Harcourt Brace Jovanovich, Inc.; William Heinemann Ltd; Mary Hemingway; Houghton Mifflin, Inc.; Robert Jennings; King Features Syndicate; Lever Brothers Co., Inc.; Alan Light, *The Buyer's Guide for Comic Fandom;* Love Romances Publications, Inc.; Rick Marschall; the Hollywood movie studios (Columbia, MGM, Paramount, RKO, 20th Century-Fox, United Artists, Universal-International, and Warner Brothers); Nostalgia Press, Inc.; Professor Michael Novak; Richard O'-Brien; Odyssey Publications, Inc.; Pack Memorial Library, Asheville, N.C.; Pepsico, Inc.; Byron Preiss Visual Publications, Inc.; Random House, Inc. (Alfred A. Knopf, Inc.); Thurman T. Scott; Simon & Schuster, Inc.;

Charles Scribner's Sons, Inc.; Jim Steranko, Supergraphics Publications; St. Martin's Press, Inc.; Street & Smith, Inc.; Superhero Enterprises, Inc.; Superlith, Inc.; the television networks: ABC-TV, CBS-TV, and NBC-TV; *TV Guide;* UPI; Marion Viccars, Pace Library, The University of West Florida; and Viking Press, Inc.

Special permission to quote from particular works referred to in this book has been generously granted as follows:

From *Tarzan the Untamed* by Edgar Rice Burroughs. First published in *Redbook* Magazine. © 1919 by the Redbook Corp. Book Edition © 1920 by Edgar Rice Burroughs. *TARZAN*—Registered Trademark owned by Edgar Rice Burroughs, Inc., and used by permission. Reproduced herein by permission of Edgar Rice Burroughs, Inc.

From *The U.P. Trail* and *The Arizona Clan* by Zane Grey. Reprinted by permission of Zane Grey, Inc.

From *Main Street* by Sinclair Lewis. Reprinted by permission of Harcourt Brace Jovanovich, Inc. and Jonathan Cape, Ltd.

From *The Maltese Falcon* by Dashiell Hammett. Reprinted by permission of Random House, Inc. and Alfred A. Knopf, Inc.

From "Winter Dreams" by F. Scott Fitzgerald. Reprinted by permission of Charles Scribner's Sons and The Bodley Head, Ltd.

From "The Story of a Novel" by Thomas Wolfe. Reprinted by permission of Charles Scribner's Sons and William Heinemann, Ltd.

From *The Grapes of Wrath* by John Steinbeck. Reprinted by permission of The Viking Press, Inc.

Introduction

There was a time when meadow, grove, and
  stream
The earth, and every common sight,
To me did seem
Apparelled in celestial light,
The glory and the freshness of a dream.
It is not now as it hath been of yore;—
Turn wheresoe'er I may,
By night or day,
The things which I have seen I now can see no more.
          —William Wordsworth,
            "Ode: Intimations of Immortality"

So we beat on, boats against the current, borne back
ceaselessly into the past.
          —F. Scott Fitzgerald,
          The Great Gatsby

We live in an age of communication through visual stimulation. With a syntax and grammar of their own, the visual media use a language that our society has come to know and depend on, one that has evolved during the hundred years or so since the major technological breakthroughs in communications began in the nineteenth century. Everywhere today we see graphic evidence of this special kind of communication, particularly in the mass-created images that the various media promulgate through advertising, styles of dress, automobile technology, household luxuries, and, of course, celebrity lifestyles. Curiously enough, though, the language of visual stimulation does not speak to us in a personalized, subjective manner but rather in an impersonal, detached sense to persuade, propagandize,

or merely publicize. The magazine advertisement, for example, appears, at first glance, to be highly personal and empathetic in visually expressing the intrinsic merits of a supposedly beneficial product. Its message may be soft or strong, usually inspired by the prevailing lifestyle of the time, but because of the potential customer's passive role—an arrangement which allows for no kind of interpersonal exchange—we cannot really be sure that communication has taken place in the basic sense of the word's meaning. A similar malfunctioning of the communication process can be observed in our relationship with other visual stimuli, the most prevalent and influential of which is television.

As the latest major development in a long line of technological advances in communications, televi-

In order to create a more personalized kind of visual stimulation to communicate with potential customers, magazine advertising of the 1930s and '40s depended on familiar images from popular culture areas like the comic strip, the movies, and radio to help sell a product. Note the pervasive use of the comic-strip balloon caption to convey speech by "real" people, a favorite device of the time.

sion has been held primarily accountable for many disorienting social attitudes and postures that have affected interpersonal understanding in contemporary life. Although there may be truth in this charge, television is not entirely at fault; it is actually the evolutionary culmination of technological and sociological trends that were developing long before the end of the nineteenth century, forces that have contributed in their own way to the gradual, almost imperceptible deterioration of interpersonal communication. A brief chronological survey of the most important developments in communications technology since the mid-nineteenth century, along with a historical awareness of a corresponding increase in psychological and sociological problems as these developments became widespread, can demonstrate what I mean.

The groundwork for bringing society closer together in a communicative sense was laid in the latter half of the last century with the introduction and development of photography, telegraphy, and the telephone, as well as experimentation with the theory of moving pictures. But the invention that had the most immediate and far-reaching impact on the masses during this time was linotype printing, which made it possible to produce uniform printed matter for rapid and wide distribution to a public that found newspaper features and magazine fiction, for example, the cheapest way to be informed or entertained. Our own century has seen the development and expansion of communications technology at flood tide with the inception of radio broadcasting, sound movies, television via network and satellite, not to mention a variety of peripheral inventions like the phonograph, the wirephoto, the tape recorder, the videophone, and computerized communications, whose further development should lead to undreamed-of methods of communicating.

Despite all these improvements in the instruments of mass communication, we have not made any proportionate improvements in the communication that occurs between individuals.[1] In fact, from the point in time that society learned mass distribution both of the printed word and of photographs of people and events, the breakdown in interpersonal communication began in full earnest. In contrast to the comparatively unaffected visual experience of those who lived prior to the advent of these inventions, the experience of people since has been to have those technological wonders see for them, subtly dictating how they should comprehend

appearance or reality. No one would deny that all these advances, each one a revolution in itself, have considerably improved the communal awareness of the masses of people. Seeing and hearing an event taking place in another part of the world practically as it happens is a marvelous achievement, but unfortunately the shared experiences that network television offers succeed mainly in creating a uniform way of reacting to them and in stifling fresh, individual interpretation. Because the viewpoint of the television audience is controlled by an impersonal attitude, it is, for example, a Howard Cosell who reminds us how we should react to triumph or failure in the televised sports event.

A central paradox of our time is that for all our exposure and sensitivity to the visual process, whether through the printed or illustrated page, through film, or through the more visually dominant medium of television, we no longer seem to be capable of *seeing* in the basic sense of the word, that is, capable of subjectively perceiving a thing or happening in its natural relationship to the world around it. Granted, this point of view touches on an argument that is as old as the philosophy of Plato, but I believe my stand to be unique in that at no time in the world's recorded history has there been such a variety of extrapersonal influences brought to bear on the visual process with the paradoxical effect of actually interfering with an individual's interpretation of what he sees. Because of the pervasive influence of these artificial means of seeing that modern technology has provided us, we may conclude that most people today, in marked contrast to their forebears, are indeed blind to subjective experience in that they have become literally "programmed" to see the world in a passive, more detached manner.

Furthermore, concomitant with the technological advances already described, the development and proliferation in this century of an increasingly visual and fantasy-inspired popular culture reflect both a gradual takeover of the individual's will to interpret for himself what he sees and the individual's impaired capability to see himself in relationship to his environment. As society has strayed further away from the less complex lifestyles of earlier times, many people have grown to depend more and more on the memories and memorabilia inherited from that which helped to dissociate them in the first place—the forms and expressions of the popular culture which function as direct links with the substance and spirit of the past. This ever-expanding affinity for nostalgic experience or whatever can visually fantasize and color over experience to make our present lives more tolerable or meaningful has been evolving in direct proportion to technological expansion. The overall effect has been an undermining of self-actualization by compelling us to retreat into our private dream worlds. This book contends that the nostalgic mood has become more prevalent in our society than ever before not only because of the multitude of visual stimuli affecting the popular mind as never before, but because modern technology has not really given us the answers we expected from it. As a result, the forms of creative expression designed for a popular audience—fiction, the comics, movies, and television—have developed over the years, each increasingly interdependent on the other, and they have conditioned us subconsciously to see things as we think we would like to see them. This interrelationship is one that may establish a buffer to the harshness of the real world as well as a nostalgic bind or visual link with the past for those who have been exposed to the popular trends of a particular period in our history.

Today's popular television programming, then, is actually the climax of a creative process that can be traced to the popular reception of the novel in the eighteenth century and that kept expanding throughout the nineteenth as key technological discoveries were made. In our own century, popular wish fulfillment has manifested itself not only in fiction, but in comic-strip art (initially in the newspaper, later in the comic book or magazine), in the movies, and in today's most popular medium, television. Ironically, the fantasy desires of today's media-conscious public have become so pronounced that we have difficulty at times in recognizing clear-cut lines of demarcation between the various forms: novels are specially written for or adapted to television, movies are publicized on the basis of the popularity of the novels that inspired them and vice versa, and talented artists like Jim Steranko have even been experimenting with something they call "illustrated" or "visual" fiction. This cutting across from one form to another can be construed as another sign of the recognition on the part of our creative specialists that popular taste, especially as it exists today, is continually searching for unique ways to satisfy itself.

Only recently has the cultural influence of popular taste and manners, particularly as expressed through our media forms, come under scrutiny as a field in itself worthy of inquiry and study. Part of the reason for this delayed interest lies in the difficulty many critics of culture have in taking seriously that which was apparently created in response to the ephemeral and faddish, in other words, that which was obviously destined to die with the period that produced it. The other part of the reason may be the snob appeal that each age subscribes to in identifying artists and works that are most acceptable as "art." The conflict within the artist or creative person—whether to divorce himself from society in a totally dedicated commitment to the cause of art or simply to give in commercially to what society dictates as art—is as old as the creative impulse itself, and the so-called classic work of art that has become acceptable to the general public today may have been totally rejected upon its introduction. In this connection, we are reminded of certain influential, but initially misunderstood, works of our own century like Igor Stravinsky's *The Rite of Spring,* Pablo Picasso's controversial paintings, and James Joyce's *Ulysses.* The creative person, obsessed by a personal commitment and singular vision of his own, produces the enduring or classic work of art, which by definition generates an appeal for the ages and denies an audience the self-indulgence that it derives from direct identification with the output of popular culture. If the nostalgic impulse stems from the individual's desire to recall what was personably memorable about his own past, then he would probably be hard pressed to strike a nostalgic mood in the presence of Michelangelo's *Pieta,* for example, or a Raphael painting, or in reading Shakespeare, or even in listening to a Mozart symphony, even though music has a way of generating its own nostalgic response.

The point I would make here is that while classic art exists on a level of universal recognition, popular art speaks to the whims and tastes of the people of a particular time and place. Even though the critics or self-appointed arbiters of taste may single out serious creative works as the best and most representative of a particular era's culture, it is, ironically enough, what the masses of people have recognized as peculiarly their own that offers us the most significant and revealing clues to understanding how an age or period of time thought and felt. Thus our debt to the medieval ballad, folk music, and the folk tale, which have provided rich fields of study and research. Paradoxically, a serious classic may tell us much about human values and emotions that is of lasting importance, yet reveal very little of the

underlying nuances and mannerisms of the period that contributed to its inspiration.

So that vast eternity of dead time—the past—which nostalgically can mean so many different things to different people seems to take on a reverential glow that only the generally forgotten things we inherit from an era's popular culture can recapture for us, since these are the things that best reflect the true sentiment and basic feel of an era. For most of us, then, the past has a nostalgic function much like Richard Armour diagnoses it in his foreword to a collection of pieces from the old *Liberty* magazine:

> It must be that things look better, and simpler, when they are safely in the past. Or perhaps our memories are selective, mercifully screening out the deplorable and the horrible and the confusingly complex. What is left is the pleasant, understandable part of human existence. . . . By remembering what we wish to remember, we shape the past into what we think it should have been.[2]

But even though nostalgic experience appears to be concerned with only those visually pleasant associations we have with our pasts, it can and does make allowance for any kind of remembered fantasy that deals with the future. Examples of this are the science fiction mode as visualized by Ray Bradbury, the pulp magazines, the *Buck Rogers* comic strip, and, of course, the movies—popular forms of expression which have endeared themselves to us since first experienced during an earlier, more innocent time. In other words, the future as subject matter can be nostalgic, provided it is personally fantasized and warmly associated with one's past experience, as, for example, the *Planet Comics* phenomenon is. The nostalgiac's perennial enemy is the real future, which threatens to undermine the familiar confines of his existence.

Over the course of the following sections dealing with (1) both major and minor strains of popular fiction, (2) comic art forms, (3) the movies, and (4) television, I hope to demonstrate how nostalgic affection, which seems to spring from whatever may

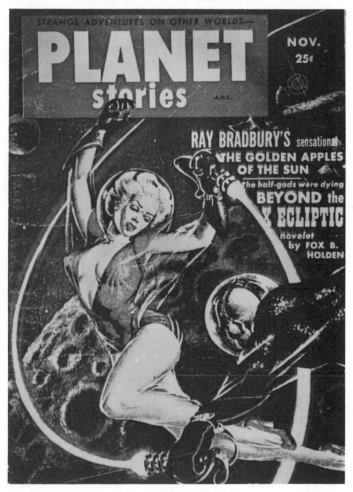

have visually appealed to popular taste during a particular time and place and which for some idiosyncratic reason now appears to be more attractive than one's present situation, is not only common to the audience for which these forms were produced, but inspires even those who create these elements of popular culture. To describe this phenomenon I use the term *nostalgia neurosis,* the implications of which will be discussed at greater length as we progress, but for now this neurosis can be understood as a state of anxiety brought on by one's realization of the wide gulf separating the uncertainty of the present from the apparent harmony of the past. To the nostalgiac, a probable solution for relieving this state is to recapture somehow the essence of the

The Nostalgia of the Past and the Future: The so-called junk culture produced by an earlier era is possessed with the power to transform itself into the precious nostalgia of a later period, as attested to by this 1926 ad publicizing the novelty wares of the Johnson Smith Co. By contrast, The Superhero Catalogue *of* 1977 *is contributing to a nostalgia of the future when the collectible objects and amusements it displays have become rare and representative of the times that produced them.*

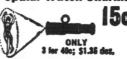

In the 1940s, the comic-book version of the science-fiction pulps was Planet Comics *with its standardized cover scene of a scantily-clad girl in the clutches of an alien captor. As one of the purest forms of American daydreaming, comic books like* Planet *contributed to a unique nostalgia identification by fantasizing our future uncertainties. As such, they are a prime metaphor for the central focus of this book.* COPYRIGHT 1941 LOVE ROMANCES PUBLICATIONS CO., INC. REPRINTED BY PERMISSION.

past itself through direct identification with an object or symbol from the past, thus improvising at least a temporary vehicle for escape. Accordingly, an individual afflicted with the neurosis because he is either bored with the present, apprehensive of the future, or both, may reread a familiar novel first encountered in his or her younger days, or view an old but favorite movie not only to identify with a past that now has a stronger semblance of order and perspective, but to be figuratively transported to a place and time, real or imaginary, that improves upon the present.

There are those, too, for whom a more material way of alleviating their nostalgic hang-ups is to collect the physical forms or products of popular cul-

ture that remind them of as well as help recreate a simpler, more secure time. A probable side effect is to slow down the inexorable fact of tomorrow becoming today. Such a quest would help explain the present obsession in our society for collecting the so-called "junk" culture of the last half-century, often even transcending the commercial fact that there is money to be made in such an enterprise. Collectibles that Marshall Fishwick calls the "Icons of America"—beverage bottles, comic books, pulp magazines, movie posters, sheet music, and toys, to name a few of the highly regarded items—really function as personalized objective correlatives, triggering fond and reassuring memories of better times, better places.[3] In fact, one of the most telling and basic symptoms of the nostalgia neurosis is the desire for visual contact with the once familiar scenes or objects that relate to personal experiences. Cherished reminders of what may now appear to be more pleasant and meaningful times, collectible "icons" acquire more status and significance with the passing of time, especially among those who may have lived during the times these things were fashionable or current. Jim Harmon, a contemporary connoisseur of nostalgia, has aptly expressed the feeling for collecting the popular artifacts of the past in his introduction to an entertaining little book that he calls the *Nostalgia Catalogue.* "Collectors," he says,

save *things* because they can't protect the past they loved from the rush of the present or from the looming engulfment of the future. Collectors are not necessarily political conservatives—they are *conservationists,* conserving the best of the past for themselves and others.

Who would want to save the breadlines of the thirties, or the newspaper headlines about Pearl Harbor? We want to preserve memories of Jimmy Cagney and Edward G. Robinson as champion gangsters, Little Orphan Annie Shake-Up Mugs, the Lone Ranger's stirring "Hi-Yo Silver!"

Nostalgia is composed of things of the past we like to remember; history is composed of things we would like to forget.[4]

This last statement gives insight not only into the collector's obsession, but into the mind of the popular artist as well; for at heart the artists or mythmakers of a popular culture afflicted by the nostalgia neurosis are great icon collectors themselves. Their output abounds with visual evidence of the right object or image in the right place so as to convey what they believe to be the right emotional feeling for an expectant audience.

Thus the mythmakers of popular culture—our fiction writers, comic-strip artists, and movie-television people—are the real masters of the unique syntax and grammar which control the language of visual stimulation. Because of this peculiar function, they are our most reliable purveyors of the moods and feelings that project the nostalgic vision. Their predicament is really one of paradox, though; for they respond to the needs of the nostalgia neurosis at the same time they feed upon it. For this reason, the artists and makers of our popular culture are probably our most pronounced nostalgiacs. Yet there is a degree of the nostalgia neurosis in us all. As Marshall McLuhan, one of our most perceptive analysts of media forms and their influence on our lives, observes, "We tend always to attach ourselves to the objects, to the flavor of the recent past. We look at the present through a rearview mirror. We march backwards into the future."[5] The ensuing sections of this book provide dramatic evidence of our obsessive love affair with the past as well as our inherent fear of what the future may portend.

Notes

1. Respecting this observation, witness the current deluge of self-help books and personal development courses designed to improve interpersonal communication and relationships.

2. Richard Armour, introduction, *Give Me Liberty* (New York: World Publishing Company, 1969), p. 1.

3. Ray B. Browne and Marshall Fishwick, eds., *Icons of America,* introduction (Bowling Green, Ohio: Popular Press, 1978.)

4. Jim Harmon, *Nostalgia Catalogue* (Los Angeles: J. P. Tarcher, Inc., 1973), p. 1.

5. David Kyle, *A Pictorial History of Science Fiction* (London: Hamlyn Publishing Group Ltd, 1976), p. 165. (source of McLuhan quote)

1

The Nostalgic Vision in Fiction

My task which I am trying to achieve is, by the power of the written word, to make you hear, to make you feel—it is, above all, to make you *see.*
—Joseph Conrad

In writing—in all writing but especially in narrative writing—you are being continually taken in. The reader . . . is asked to believe in people he knows don't exist, to be present at scenes that never occurred, to be amused or moved or instructed just as he would be in real life, only the life exists in somebody else's imagination.
—William Maxwell,
"The Writer as Illusionist"

Our storytellers are our magnificent daydreamers, characterized by the fact that we've always paid homage to them to daydream for us. It was a daydreamer, no doubt, who told the first lie when he looked around and, disappointed in what he saw, imagined a world to his own liking. When his companions heard this special kind of fabrication, they liked it too, simply because hearing the "lie" helped make life a little easier to tolerate. Sometime in a more recent and sophisticated past, an appropriate name was coined to identify these dreamers, and we began calling them fiction writers. If the root meaning of the word *fiction* is a "making," then a fiction writer may be described as a maker of stories and, by extension, a maker of myths. The public's way of

honoring those daydreamers talented enough to make myths for it is to enable them to become best-selling novelists.

To insinuate that a fiction writer deceives his reader into believing what is not true is to acknowledge that the writer's obsession is mainly the result of his *seeing* things differently than the rest of us do. In shaping reality to his own vantage point, the writer is visually motivated in either one of two polar directions—to describe reality as it appears to be or to color reality as he would like it to be. Whether the writer's task is to visualize experience in the naturalistic manner or in the pure fantasy vein is really beside the point because all fiction writers, no matter how realistic their intent, fantasize to a degree. The creative act of writing itself, or the visual process of fantasizing experience into print, implies that a writer must first daydream in order to create.

The point to consider here, then, is that since the daydreaming process is visually inspired, the one thing that all fiction writers have in common is an exceptional ability to visualize, by means of the written word, a view or interpretation of experience as either they see it or as they would have us see it. The question to ask here is whose is the more responsible function—the writer who attempts to transcribe literally what he sees as life itself, or the writer who fantasizes to the degree that he provides his readers with an instant source of daydreams? Psychiatrists now recognize the need to fantasize as a healthy universal characteristic. In Western society, this need is satisfied by a variety of stimuli, among which is the reading of popular fiction. Gore Vidal, a master of the fictional lie himself, has attributed our need to fantasize to the fact that the individual can no longer dominate his environment as he once could because

> society . . . every day grows more and more confining. Since there are few legitimate releases for the common man, he must take to daydreaming. James Bond, Mike Hammer, and Tarzan are all dream-selves, and the aim of each is to establish personal primacy in a world which in reality diminishes the individual.[1]

Today's writer of popular fiction, acutely sensitive to what is meant by the diminished self, depends upon this predicament in his effort to uncover and speak to the fantasy urges and moods of the reading public. In a sense, the history of fiction is really the history of society's response to its fantasy moods. The rage for fiction of the occult in recent years—from, for example, *Rosemary's Baby* to *The Omen*— and the production of an endless spate of novels in the gothic tradition, whose covers all appear to be adorned with the same stereotyped illustration of lonely heroine fleeing a castle-like structure in the background, mirror the psychological state of the mass mind. They also provide graphic evidence of a writer's ability to tailor his talents to the prevailing mood of the reading public and to be rewarded, in many cases, with astounding financial success.

To determine the pulse of today's mass reading audience, we can view the need to fantasize as the outgrowth of emotional anxieties created by our reaction to the uncertainties of the present and an increasingly ominous future, which every day contributes to a growing feeling of personal insecurity. The paradox of trying to "make it" in a society with a standard of living never before equaled while being simultaneously besieged on all sides by economic, sociological, and psychological doubts and perplexities has established an almost desperate need for vicarious experience or for a way to project one's self in an expanded sense. It is a situation that accounts in part for the present mania for physical thrills and sensation seeking. The result of these needs are popular media that are saturated with visually generated images of pornography, violence, and sensual stimulation—anything to remind our diluted selves that we do have feelings, even if we have to be shocked, rather than titillated, into realization of this fact. A central irony of our time, however, is that the seeker after sensation interacts in most cases, not actively, but passively with a source to obtain his kicks. Appropriately, the most popular modes of vicarious experience—those surveyed in this book—appear to have inspired an increasingly passive following in their contribution to what I call the nostalgia neurosis of our day, a state of mind that finds the fictional lie or fantasized experience more appealing and attractive than reality itself.

Fiction, which is still the creative mode that is most demanding on our visual understanding, has had a long and distinguished history of "lying," despite detractors who have predicted the demise of its most popular form, the novel, or denounced this means of literary expression as inferior to the more elevated forms like poetry and drama. The fact remains that the novelist and short story writer have never really hurt for an audience or following. Even during the early history of American literature, when so much of it was derivative and imitative of British models and when the religious zealot considered the reading of novels a frivolous waste of time as well as a tool of the devil, fictional works somehow managed to find a ready and receptive audience. As a development of the eighteenth century, the modern novel reflected the tastes and values of the growing middle-class readership for whom it was primarily designed, and although there may be more profound reasons for the acceptance of fiction as a popular vehicle for literary expression, I suspect it was the basic human need of both writer and audience to fantasize that ensured the success and popularity of both fiction writing and reading, an opinion which the remainder of this chapter will expand upon.

Some years ago, William O. Aydelotte, in discussing the uses of the detective story as a historical source, made some highly perceptive points concerning this most popular of fictional genres, and it is my contention that certain of Aydelotte's assertions about detective fiction are equally relevant to the general reception of popular fiction by a mass audience. As "wish-fulfillment fantasies designed to produce certain agreeable sensations in the reader," detective stories, according to Aydelotte, succeed popularly because (1) the people in them have simple problems in place of the complex issues of modern existence, (2) the stories make life more meaningful while glamorizing the events they describe, and (3) they introduce us to a secure universe wherein the reader is assured that the detective-hero will unravel the mystery despite temporary obstacles to this end. These points lead to the following conclusion relevant to our present discussion:

> The historical value of the detective story is that it describes daydreams. . . . A knowledge of people's daydreams may enable us to progress to an understanding of their desires. In this way, a careful study of literature of this kind may reveal popular attitudes which shed a flood of light on the motivation behind political, social, and economic history.[2]

In light of the detective story's ephemeral characteristics, some observers may feel that this is a lofty conclusion, yet I see it as an insightful deduction that is applicable to all forms of popular fiction simply because the visual implications of daydreaming are really the inspirational source for all fictional expression. The writer as daydreamer or mythmaker is merely reflecting the dream wishes or fantasies of his reader, and his degree of success as a popular writer greatly depends on his awareness of or sensitivity to the kinds of dreams his readers demand. Thus the points Aydelotte establishes about the reader of detective stories can be applied to the reader of any type of popular fiction, whether historical romance, fantasy adventure, or science fiction. Correspondingly, the popularity of a certain kind of fiction at any one time can reveal a great deal about the nature of a society that produces such writing, which is to say that a period's favorite fictional daydreams may mirror the mass obsessions and anxieties of that period.

When we consider the implications of this obser-

vation, especially in view of the proliferating nostalgia craze that has swept our society during the past decade, we detect a kind of mental frame or psychological state of mind on the part of readers of popular fiction. Throughout this work I refer to this mental state as the nostalgia neurosis, a term used both metaphorically as a convenient catchall phrase for my overall purpose and psychologically as a referent to a peculiar set of anxieties and obsessions brought about by the realization of a visualized disparity between the remote security of the past and the threatening uncertainty of both the present and the future. This feeling of dissociation may be experienced by both writer and reader, but the writer as the source of creative inspiration becomes the reader's surrogate through whose sensitivity or nostalgic vision the real world's fragmented mood may be tempered. The antithesis of the past versus the present and future affords us a key not only to analyzing the attitude of the reader as nostalgiac, but also to comprehending the mythmaking vision of the fiction writer who produces work that appeals predominantly to the nostalgic sensibility. If the neurotic condition of the fiction reader is brought on by an inner conflict fomented by what he reveres in the irrecoverable past and fears of the distasteful future, then a parallel state may be found operative in the fiction writer who writes to resolve such a conflict not only for his reader, but for himself as well.

V. S. Pritchett, in discussing the theme of cruelty in Mark Twain's *The Adventures of Huckleberry Finn* (1884), makes a particularly penetrating remark that helps us evaluate the significance of the nostalgic vision or mood in American literature. He observes that "the peculiar power of American nostalgia is that it is not only harking back to something lost in the past, but suggests also the tragedy of a lost future."[3] Mark Twain, despite his bent for the reportorial method, was something of a dreamer in his best writings, and in *Huckleberry Finn,* which was produced at a point in his life some forty to fifty years after the events the novel describes, reveals himself as overtly sensitive to America's growing industrialism and the attendant loss of a more innocent, pastoral time—indeed, the time of his own

This 1930 advertisement for the period's best-selling fiction shows that popular fiction can help us understand the tastes of the time in which it is popular. Note the forgotten romance novel that gets top billing, as well as the reference to those books "dramatized for the movies," a pervasive media influence of the day. Of all these books, only those by Edgar Rice Burroughs and Zane Grey have a popularity that has lasted. The appeal of these two writers can tell us much about contemporary fantasies and wish fulfillments.

Mark Twain's Huckleberry Finn, in his personal quest to keep his lifestyle simple and free of society's complexities, is the archetypal character of American literary nostalgia who has had an immeasurable influence on our popular culture. The pastoral scene of barefoot boy with fishing pole, like this one portrayed by Mickey Rooney for the 1939 MGM movie of Twain's novel, speaks to something elemental in the American psyche.

boyhood. Twain periodically gives himself away through passages of lyrical beauty and intensity that transcend the novel's underlying bitterness and satirical bite and that have their inspiration in his own boyhood days on the river. One of the most remarkable pieces of writing in American literature is of this order and owes much of its descriptive power to a naturalness of expression that has rarely been equaled. Here is Mark Twain's idyllic, though realistic, description of the river when Huck and Jim are on their way to what they think is a better life:

Two or three days and nights went by; I reckon I might say they swum by, they slid along so quiet and smooth and lovely. Here is the way we put in the time. It was a monstrous big river down there —sometimes a mile and half wide; we run nights, and laid up and hid daytimes; soon as night was most gone we stopped navigating and tied up— nearly always in the dead water under a towhead; and then cut young cottonwoods and willows, and hid the raft with them. Then we set out the lines. Next we slid into the river and had a swim, so as to freshen up and cool off; then we set down on the sandy bottom where the water was about knee-deep, and watched the daylight come. Not a sound anywheres—perfectly still—just like the whole world was asleep, only sometimes the bull-frogs a-cluttering, maybe. The first thing to see, looking away over the water, was a kind of dull line—that was the woods on the t'other side; you couldn't make nothing else out; then a pale place in the sky; then more paleness spreading around; then the river softened up away off, and warn't black anymore, but gray; you could see little dark spots drifting along ever so far away—trading scows, and such things; and long black streaks— rafts; sometimes you could hear a sweep screaking; or jumbled-up voices, it was so still, and sounds come so far; and by an by you could see a streak on the water which you know by the look of the streak that there's a snag there in a swift current which breaks on it and makes that streak look that way; and you see the mist curl up off of the water, and the east reddens up, and the river, and you make out a log cabin in the edge of the woods, away on the bank on t'otherside of the river, being a wood-yard, likely, and piled by them cheats so you can throw a dog through it anywheres; then the nice breeze springs up, and comes fanning you from over there, so cool and fresh and sweet to smell on account of the woods and the flowers; but sometimes not that way, because they've left dead fish laying around, gars and such, and they do get pretty rank; and next you've got the full day, and everything smiling in the sun, and the song-birds just going it![4]

The outstanding characteristic of this passage is its

visual impact which, expressed colloquially through the first-person point of view, has the overall effect of involving the reader in a startling sense of immediacy. Other senses are operative as well—hearing and smell—but the dominant effect is visual and is really what controls the nostalgic vision generated by the dream of an aging man vividly recalling a particularly fond scene from his youth. In excerpts like this, it seems evident that the wish-fulfillment or neurotically nostalgic side of Mark Twain was at war with the artist in him, for this kind of writing, like a poetic respite in the midst of a sustained, caustic statement, contrasts markedly with the major intent and plan of the novel.

Mark Twain, whose life paralleled our early developments in communications technology, is one of the most striking examples in our literature of the fiction writer stimulated by the nostalgia neurosis. His life and work reveal the influence of both the new technology and the fantasy-reality conflict that is responsible for the nostalgia hang-up. Suspicious of the formal methods and intentions of the elite among his literary forebears and contemporaries, Mark Twain forged a democratic style and attitude out of his own experience. Readers came to recognize Twain's qualities as their own, and *The Adventures of Huckleberry Finn,* written ostensibly as another boys' book, became a popular classic in the canon of American literature. This achievement makes Twain a kind of paradox in the American literary tradition: he is both popular and unique. We realize that the earthy nostalgia of Twain is the result of both the quality of his memory in recreating certain scenes and experiences of his youth as well as his personal commitment to be uniquely himself. The overall effect is a writing manner that charges the insignificant moment with significance. Even in his autobiography Twain can describe common experience in such a sensually nostalgic manner that we see and feel the experience ourselves. Observe the following:

As I have said, I spent some part of every year at the farm until I was twelve or thirteen years old. The life which I led there with my cousins was full of charm, and so is the memory of it yet. I can call back the solemn twilight and mystery of the deep woods, the earthy smells, the faint odors of the wild flowers, the sheen of rain-washed foliage, the rattling clatter of drops when the wind shook the trees, the far-off hammering of woodpeckers and the muffled drumming of wood pheasants in the remoteness of the forest, the snapshot glimpses of disturbed wild creatures scurrying through the grass—I can call it all back and make it as real as it ever was, and as blessed. I can call back the prairie, and its loneliness and peace, and a vast hawk hanging motionless in the sky, with his wings spread wide and the blue of the vault showing through the fringe of their end feathers. I can see the woods in their autumn dress, the oaks purple, the hickories washed with gold, the maples and the sumachs luminous with crimson fires, and I can hear the rustle made by the fallen leaves as we plowed through them. I can see the blue clusters of wild grapes hanging among the foliage of the saplings, and I remember the taste of them and the smell. I know how the wild blackberries looked, and how they tasted, and the same with the pawpaws, the hazelnuts, and the persimmons; and I can feel the thumping rain, upon my head, of hickory nuts and walnuts when we are out in the frosty dawn to scramble for them with the pigs, and the gusts of wind loosed them and sent them down. . . .[5]

It is this method of nostalgic recall of seemingly insignificant experience visualized as meaningful scene or act that we see surfacing frequently in American literature. This is particularly apparent in an influential writer like Ernest Hemingway, whose economy of word in describing the physically sensual experience contributes to a remarkable visual sharpness, a photographic technique of nostalgic recall. It is what Twain refers to in the passage just quoted as the "snapshot glimpse."

The point I would make here is that, like many popular writers, our so-called serious writers exhibit a marked propensity for indulging in nostalgic revelation; in fact, numerous pieces of serious fiction seem to project an underlying urgency to revel in nostalgic moods and reflections. It must be that this need—an inner compulsion on the part of the writer to "see" for us—is integral to the American writing experience. In casting a nostalgic haze over special parts of his writing, the storyteller undergoes a visual process of filtering the private emotional feelings of his experiences through his imagination—the daydreaming act. If the writer succeeds in assessing the fantasy needs of a potential reading audience, his feelings expressed in writing become *our* feelings in that we are compelled to visualize or daydream along with the writer. Thus the common response of many readers to the *Huckleberry Finn* passage quoted earlier is a nostalgic yearning for a moment lost in time and space. We might conclude, then, that the popularity of a writer is determined by his degree of success in matching his emotional feelings about experience with the emotional or fantasy needs of his audience—the more directly

the match corresponds, the more popular the writer; the more objective and controlled the writer is in verbalizing personal experience, the more likely he is to be accepted in the critical sense of adhering to the standards of classic art. Perhaps Lionel Trilling has described better than anyone else the distinction between what motivates the popular artist and the creative genius. "What," he asks,

is the difference between, on the one hand, the dream and the neurosis, and, on the other hand, art? That they have certain common elements is of course clear; that unconscious processes are at work in both would be denied by no poet or critic; they share too, though in different degrees, the element of fantasy. But there is a vital difference between them which Charles Lamb saw so clearly in his defense of the sanity of true genius: "The . . . poet dreams being awake. He is not possessed by his subject but he has dominion over it."

That is the whole difference: the poet is in command of his fantasy, while it is exactly the mark of the neurotic that he is possessed by his fantasy.[6]

Trilling's "poet" we recognize to be the pure creative genius as opposed to the "neurotic" state of the popular artist, but despite the serious intent of a creative writer and his identification with an accepted set of critical or aesthetic standards, the fact remains that the writer defines experience from his or her own private set of emotional feelings about it, and for this reason must be evaluated in terms of his or her degree of nostalgic indulgence or neuroticism. To prove my point, I could select any one of our reputably serious writers—William Dean Howells, Edith Wharton, Sherwood Anderson, Willa Cather, Theodore Dreiser, even Henry James —and build a case for classifying any one of them as a nostalgiac, according to the degree with which he or she commands subject matter. But because, like Mark Twain, Sinclair Lewis is so representatively American and because his literary attitude is close to our own day, it is useful here to examine the extent of artistic control in one of his more popular works, a "best-seller" in the modern understanding of the term.

The blurb on the cover of a paperback edition of *Main Street,* published over forty years after its initial appearance in 1920, reads,

The great American novel that set the pattern for the small-town exposé—from John O'Hara's Gibbsville to Grace Metalious' Peyton Place.

Ironically, such a commercial plug reveals a whole nostalgic undercurrent flowing through Lewis's first success, which was written with the intent of attacking and satirizing small-town life in this country, showing it up as a cultural wasteland and a concentration of the most vulgar manners. A literary sensation that made all the best-seller lists in its day, *Main Street,* when read today, still strikes the reader as an authentic, although now somewhat quaint, rendering of life in a midwestern town during the earlier part of this century. For this reason and because of its obvious fascination with and acute attention to detail, the novel has significant sociological value. Its satirical intent, though, provides us with an important clue to understanding the nostalgic preoc-

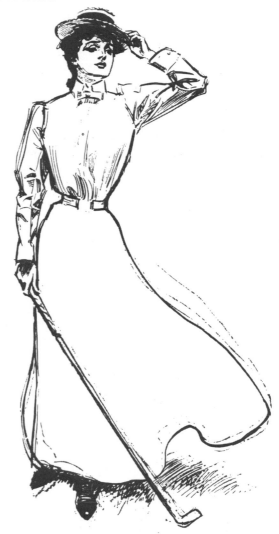

The artist's conception of the liberated woman as fictional type can be traced to around the turn of the century when Charles Dana Gibson's skillful pen was sketching the woman of his day as beginning to strain against the fetters of societal convention. Popularly known as the Gibson Girl, she was not averse to trying her hand at sport, as seen here. CULVER PICTURES

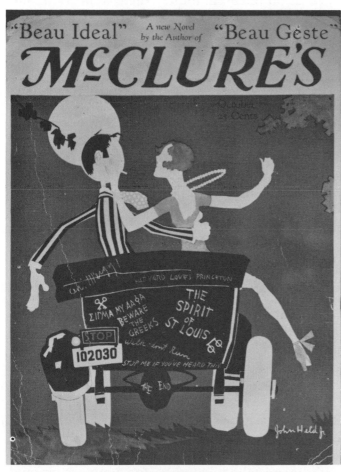

The image of the liberated woman which has pervaded the literature of this century—the kind of woman Sinclair Lewis created in Main Street's *Carol Kennicott, and F. Scott Fitzgerald portrayed in his fiction as the flapper—was visually satirized in the drawings of John Held, Jr. during the 1920s. She would later evolve into the bra-burning feminist of the 1960s and the emancipated woman of the 1970s. Here she is pictured in one of Held's popular magazine covers with one of the dominant forces contributing to her liberation—the automobile.* CULVER PICTURES

cupation of Sinclair Lewis. Even though he thought of himself essentially as a "storyteller," in reality Lewis depended on a story line that always seemed to function secondarily to the accumulation and cataloging of fact and detail to emphasize subject and theme in most of his novels. In *Main Street* his concern with exemplary detail demonstrates a powerfully keen sense of observation and recall, which in effect is the inherent sensitivity of the fictional daydreamer. As a result, the central character of the novel functions to provide the emotional reaction to Lewis's list of "objective correlatives."

When she first arrives in Gopher Prairie, Carol Kennicott takes a thirty-two-minute walk over the length and breadth of the main part of town, a theatrical device staged to dramatize her disgust and repellent feelings for her new environment. Lewis visualizes her reaction in a vividly graphic manner for his day; yet, from the perspective of well over fifty years his purpose in taking apart the area in which he had grown up and which he knew so intimately (Sauk Centre, Minnesota) takes on the flavor of a series of nostalgic pieces worthy of a magazine cover treatment by Norman Rockwell:

> She trailed down the street on one side, back on the other, glancing into the cross streets. It was a private Seeing Main Street tour. She was within ten minutes beholding not only the heart of a place called Gopher Prairie, but ten thousand towns from Albany to San Diego:
> Dyer's Drug Store, a corner building of regular and unreal blocks of artificial stone. Inside the store, a greasy marble soda-fountain with an electric lamp of red and green and curdled yellow mosaic shade. Pawed-over heaps of tooth brushes and combs and packages of shaving-soap. Shelves of soap-cartons, teething-rings, garden-seeds, and patent medicines in yellow packages—nostrums for consumption, for "women's diseases" —notorious mixtures of opium and alcohol, in the very shop to which her husband sent patients for the filling of prescriptions.
> From a second-story window the sign "W. P. Kennicott, Phys. and Surgeon," gilt on black sand.
> A small wooden motion-picture theater called "The Rosebud Movie Palace." Lithographs announcing a film called "Fatty in Love."
> Howland & Gould's Grocery. In the display window, black, overripe bananas and lettuce on which a cat was sleeping. Shelves lined with red crepe paper which was now faded and torn and concentrically spotted. Flat against the wall of the second story the signs of lodges—the Knights of Pythias, the Maccabees, the Woodmen, the Masons. . . .[7]

Carol's "seeing Main Street tour" rambles on for several more pages as the objects, places, sights, and impressions that comprise Gopher Prairie are cumulatively built up in a nostalgic description of an American small town as it existed earlier in this century. Despite Lewis's attempt to have us see through Carol's eyes, though, the overall effect of this kind of writing is disengagement—the inevitable consequence of his obsessive listing and cataloging. The emphasis throughout is visual, however, although it is Lewis who is conducting the tour, not Carol, and he accomplishes an admirable feat in daydreaming his small-town origins into

fictional existence. The deep emotional experience a writer undergoes in remembering things and scenes as they were and recreating them in vivid detail—the nostalgic vision—can be attributed to the feeling of personal alienation or isolation when one is subjected to the strangeness of a different, more remote environment. The result is a heightened awareness of and sensitivity to the gulf between past and present. It is an emotional reaction that pervades much of the Expatriate literature of the 1920–1930 era, and it is probably best exemplified in the writings of Thomas Wolfe, who gained this inspiration during his European sojourn. Paradoxically, yet in line with a basic contention of this book, many writers of this period were inherently fond of the way of life against which they appeared to be revolting, and nostalgic undercurrents surface on occasion to reveal these writers' repressed, ambivalent feelings about their origins.

Sinclair Lewis, whether in Europe or America, seems nostalgic for a homeland of an earlier time, fresh and primeval, free from hypocrisy, social pride, and commercial self-aggrandizement. The irony underlying Lewis's outlook is that we are now far enough away from him that his day appears far more engaging in a nostalgic sense than does our fast-paced present with its increased pressures, which have been generated by multiplying social, economic, and psychological complexities. At heart, Lewis's travels abroad were catalytic in reminding him of the inherent greatness and abundant potential of his native country, especially its unlimited opportunity for individual expression and development. Consequently, the things that Lewis attacked in American society were those things that actually gave rise to his creative expression. In fact, Mark Schorer, Lewis's biographer, has noted that his literary manner and attitude were really molded by the very things he criticized: "His trust in 'culture' was equaled by his trust in 'things' . . . In his novels, he loved what he deplored; in his life, he was happiest with the kind of people who might have been the models for his own caricatures."[8]

If the nostalgic impulse, for both writer and reader, is kindled by a yearning for the familiar, then the sameness of American life, the contentment born of the dullness of routine, and the crass commercialism of American business can be the very stuff of fictional nostalgia, simply because these are areas that represent a commonly recognized form of security in the polarities of American expe-

THE HOLLYWOOD MUSICAL: SINGING AND DANCING YOUR BLUES AWAY

In the Hollywood musical there was a lot of singing, dancing, and talking, but not much of a plot. In fact, the whole affair of a film musical was usually strung together by a series of dance and/or song routines in the Busby Berkeley manner of the 1930s. The result was a nostalgic showbill of tunes of the past like Rose of Washington Square (20th Fox, 1939) or a melange of current melodies like Louisiana Purchase (Paramount, 1941). The genre had its fine moments, however, that included the conscious fantasy of The Wizard of Oz (MGM, 1939) and the spectacular interpretations of Gene Kelly in superb productions like An American in Paris (MGM, 1951).

Follow THE YELLOW BRICK ROAD TO

M-G-M'S GREATEST ACHIEVEMENT!

...over two years in production... utilizing 9200 actors, 30 giant sound stages, 65 enormous sets and the brains and brawn of 6275 technicians representing 165 separate arts and crafts...glassblowers, color-mixers, flowermakers, powder and fire-handlers, animal trainers, magicians and others too numerous to mention. The musical score alone required a symphony orchestra of 120 pieces, and a chorus of 300 voices. The result—over half a million feet of Technicolor film—to translate the mystic Land of Oz into vivid, exciting screen entertainment!

SPARKLING with ear-tingling tunes that will make you want to dance in the aisles...music to make you whistle...lyrics to make you sing...laughter to make you happier than you have been in years...the story that is beloved by the young-in-heart of all ages has now been brought to the screens of the world, peopled with the brightest stars of stage and screen.

In gorgeous Technicolor, the WIZARD OF OZ represents a magnificent achievement by M-G-M,

who performed almost daily miracles during its production. They dared things that had never been done on the screen before...made a lion out of a man, made monkeys fly, trained trees to dance. made a tin man walk, a scarecrow talk...photographed the *inside* of the tornado that swept Dorothy away to a land of her imagining that was as excitingly real as life itself yet utterly unlike anything ever seen on earth...all to bring you 100 scintillating minutes of unparalleled entertainment.

Metro-Goldwyn-Mayer's Glorious Technicolor Triumph

The WIZARD OF OZ

with JUDY GARLAND (*as Dorothy*), FRANK MORGAN (*as the Wizard*), RAY BOLGER (*as the Scarecrow*), BERT LAHR (*as the Cowardly Lion*), JACK HALEY (*as the Tin Woodman*), BILLIE BURKE (*as the Good Witch*), MARGARET HAMILTON (*as the Bad Witch*), CHARLEY GRAPEWIN (*as Uncle Henry*) and the Munchkins • Screenplay by Noel Langley, Florence Ryerson and Edgar Allan Woolf • A VICTOR FLEMING Production • Produced by MERVYN LE ROY • Directed by VICTOR FLEMING

Hit Songs by Arlen & Harburg: "*Over the Rainbow*", "*If I Only Had a Brain*", "*We're Off to See the Wizard*", "*The Merry Old Land of Oz*", "*Ding Dong*", "*If I Were King of the Forest*"

rience—that kind of familiar identification which the nostalgia neurosis demands. Despite his critical tone, the basis for both Sinclair Lewis's art and for his nostalgic vision is contained in the following excerpt from *Main Street:*

> Nine-tenths of the American towns are so alike that it is the completest boredom to wander from one to another. Always, west of Pittsburg, and often, east of it, there is the same lumber yard, the same railroad station, the same Ford garage, the same creamery, the same box-like houses and two-story shops. The new, more conscious houses are alike in their very attempts at diversity: the same bungalows, the same square houses of stucco or tapestry brick. The shops show the same standardized nationally advertised wares; the newspapers of sections three thousand miles apart have the same "syndicated features"; the boy in Arkansas displays just such a flamboyant ready-made suit as is found on just such a boy in Delaware, both of them iterate the same slang phrases from the same sporting-pages, and if one of them is in college and the other is a barber, no one may surmise which is which.[9]

As Lewis reasserted in *Babbitt* (1922), his satirical portrait of the American businessman, life in a technological democracy has a strong basis in equalized or shared experience, and the "sameness" in American society that we recognize, for example, in a Norman Rockwell painting projects nostalgic feelings because of its depiction of ordinary people who relate to familiar physical objects and backgrounds. This is a visual preoccupation—the relationship of apparently insignificant physical details to character and environment—evident in the nostalgic vision of other American writers as well as Sinclair Lewis.

When we look at the fiction of F. Scott Fitzgerald, another midwesterner who frequently traveled abroad, we discover a pervasive fascination with physical details that enlarge personal experience, but Fitzgerald is more artistically selective than Lewis, choosing to describe only those salient and pertinent physical things that are integral to the mood or emotion he would like to convey. He thereby illuminates character and human relationships rather than focusing on physical objects as ends in themselves. However, like Lewis, his method projects a strong nostalgic sense of place. It is fitting that Fitzgerald became a screen writer over the course of his career, for even though he lacked the personal temperament for the job, he was creatively suited to the writing task which demanded recognizable character types who acted out

their roles against a glamorous background. Countless movies of the 1930s and 1940s, starring the specially created public images of the day, were set in some make-believe, exotic locale or even in a fairytale New York City and employed scriptwriters who doubtless found the inspiration for their subject matter in the popular appeal of a Scott Fitzgerald story.

Fitzgerald's beautiful people, whether in film or fiction, are characterized not only by their relationship with things, but by their desire for things. As Dexter Green, another Gatsby variation and the central character of the 1926 story "Winter Dreams," is described: "He wanted not association with glittering things and glittering people—he wanted the glittering things themselves."[10] However, the Fitzgerald hero's attempt to satisfy materialistic dreams while attempting to relate to people in a meaningful way prepares us for a condition of the nostalgia neurosis that is difficult to accept—the acquisition of things associated with direct personal experience may in later life trigger a response to a fond memory or experience, but these things are no substitute for the experience itself, nor do they guarantee that it can be relived. This is a lesson that the Fitzgerald hero must ignore or learn to live up to.

The lead character in a standard Fitgerald piece is archetypally Hollywood in his conception and, as such, must have influenced the characterization methods of many a contemporary writer who sought to emulate Fitzgerald's success. At first, this kind of hero plays the role of an outsider, as Dexter Green does upon his receipt of a weekend guest card to the Sherry Island Golf Club. From the veranda, he begins to absorb the atmosphere of this symbol of the "good life" by watching the

> . . . even overlap of the waters in the little wind, silver molasses under the harvest-moon. Then the moon held a finger to her lips and the lake became a clear pool, pale and quiet. Dexter put on his bathing-suit and swam out to the farthest raft, where he stretched dripping on the wet canvas of the springboard.
> There was a fish jumping and a star shining and the lights around the lake were gleaming. Over on a dark peninsula a piano was playing the songs of last summer and of summers before that—songs from "Chin-Chin" and "The Count of Luxemburg" and "The Chocolate Soldier"—and because the sound of a piano over a stretch of water had always seemed beautiful to Dexter he lay perfectly quiet and listened.
> The tune the piano was playing at that moment

had been gay and new five years before when Dexter was a sophomore at college. They had played it at a prom once when he could not afford the luxury of proms, and he had stood outside the gymnasium and listened. The sound of the tune precipitated in him a sort of ecstasy and it was with that ecstasy he viewed what happened to him now. It was a mood of intense appreciation, a sense that, for once, he was magnificently attune to life and that everything about him was radiating a brightness and a glamour he might never know again.[11]

The setting of this central moment, integral to the story's nostalgic mood and denouement, next invites the introduction of a heroine of the Zelda mold and a series of stormy courtship episodes which, unlike Hollywood and most magazine fiction of the day, never find reconciliation. Yet throughout it all, Dexter's golden moment of "intense appreciation" grows in recollection and is the key to analyzing his characterization. Thus by the close of "Winter Dreams," Dexter, now an older man, has become even more sensitive to the nostalgic distance between what once was seemingly so beautiful and is now no more. When a business associate inadvertently informs him that the girl he has been in love with all his life—the same girl he first met that long ago night on Sherry Island—is now married, Dexter reacts emotionally to the fact that now his

> . . . dream was gone. Something had been taken from him. In a sort of panic he pushed the palms of his hands into his eyes and tried to bring up a picture of the waters lapping on Sherry Island and the moonlit veranda, and gingham on the golf-links and the dry sun and the gold color of her neck's soft down. And her mouth damp to his kisses and her eyes plaintive with melancholy and her freshness like new fine linen in the morning. Why, these things were no longer in the world! They had existed and they existed no longer.
>
> For the first time in years the tears were streaming down his face. But they were for himself now. He did not care about mouth and eyes and moving hands. He wanted to care, and he could not care. For he had gone away and he could never go back any more. The gates were closed, the sun was gone down, and there was no beauty but the gray beauty of steel that withstands all time. Even the grief he could have borne was left behind in the country of illusion, of youth, of the richness of life, where his winter dreams had flourished.
>
> "Long ago," he said, "long ago, there was something in me, but now that thing is gone. Now that thing is gone, that thing is gone. I cannot cry. I cannot care. That thing will come back no more."[12]

The obligatory scene in a Fitzgerald story and in a thousand stories imitative of it is one in which a Dexter Green is overcome with nostalgic longing, finally realizing that the fleeting pleasures of life's finer, more sensual moments are always sacrificed to fate, circumstance, and the relentless demands of "Time's winged chariot," compelling the hero to look back on a past suddenly and pathetically vanished. V. S. Pritchett's observation concerning our nostalgic attachment to the past as it affects the tragedy of a lost future finds its fictionally dramatic equivalent in Fitzgerald. The nostalgia associated with an irrecoverable past heightened by a strong sense of the physical details or things associated with it, then, is the subject of Fitzgerald, and even though he had the talent and craftsmanship to create some of the more influential works in twentieth-century American literature, the period popularity of his subject matter, as well as the problems of his personal life, limited the bulk of his output to the mass-conscious standards of *The Saturday Evening Post,* a most revealing fact in itself about the image of the writer as popular hero. In a way, Fitzgerald is representative of Lionel Trilling's "neurotic" artist, for he was more possessed by his subject matter than he was in control of it. Only at rare moments did he exercise a sure mastery of his subject, and as a result we witness his commercial side perennially at war with the artist that produced *The Great Gatsby.* Fitzgerald's struggle to channel his talent in the right direction epitomized that of many another promising writer on the American literary scene. Perhaps his special feel for the nostalgic part of American experience helps explain his continued popularity in a commercial sense. We recognize the nostalgic relationship of the Fitzgerald hero with his past as not only that of Fitzgerald himself, but our own as well.

Although Scott Fitzgerald's fiction reveals the futility of our attempt to relive the past, Thomas Wolfe's approach to fictional experience exhibits an honest, all-out effort to recapture the feel of time and place through the intensity of his own sense of recall, especially when he finds himself in an environment contrasting with that of his Southern origins, an atmosphere like New York City or Europe, for example. Wolfe describes the inspiration for this kind of writing in his "The Story of a Novel" (1936):

> The quality of my memory is characterized, I believe, in a more than ordinary degree by the intensity of its sense impressions, its power to

Thomas Wolfe (1900–1938), more than any other American writer, contributed to the mythical image of the possessed writer who imposes will upon subject matter to make it uniquely his own. Wolfe also added to the legend of the writer who, in making the necessary sacrifice and commitment, can produce what has been characteristically referred to as the "Great American Novel." Here is Wolfe in a symbolic 1935 photograph, perusing a part of his "Great American Novel"—the mammoth manuscript that would eventually be published as Of Time and the River. PACK MEMORIAL PUBLIC LIBRARY, ASHEVILLE, N.C. REPRINTED BY PERMISSION.

evoke and bring back the odors, sounds, colors, shapes, and feel of things with concrete vividness. Now my memory was at work night and day, in a way that I could at first neither check nor control and that swarmed unbidden in a stream of blazing pageantry across my mind, with the million forms and substances of the life that I had left, which was my own, America.[13]

As self-revealing as he is throughout the body of his work, nowhere else is Wolfe any closer to the truth about himself and his method than here, for in his writing, sensory impressions inspired by a feeling of romantic alienation trigger dominant nostalgic moods that reveal him as a kind of American Marcel

Proust. In fact, Thomas Wolfe's subject matter is nostalgia in its most literal sense, and of all our writers he appears to be the one who is the most possessed by his subject matter. In a work like *Of Time and the River* (1935), for example, there are places in which his brand of lyrical nostalgia is so vividly intense and self-declamatory that story and character are sacrificed to it, and the reader may wonder if Wolfe has any story at all to relate, but rather only a mood to dramatize.

Significantly, Fitzgerald and Wolfe were among the first American writers to discover how to project a sense of fictional reality by correlating the sensory experiences of their characters with the physical and material reality of their environments, thus intensifying the nostalgic ingredients of character and place. The ultimate effect is to make the reader see or feel an experience through a vivid sense of fictional immediacy that must have been subconsciously inspired by both writers' sensitivity to the expanding communications technology of the time. In assessing American writers of the first half of the twentieth century, Arthur Mizener declares that certain of them "resembled each other in fundamental ways," one of which is the "conviction . . . that the meaningful link between consciousness and the external world is the association of objects and places with strong personal feelings. . . ."[14] Both Fitzgerald and Wolfe shared this conviction, although they expressed it differently. As heirs of the romantic imagination which is Wordsworthian in its attempt to relate to specific times and places, they were both aware in a Keatsian manner that only art could triumph over the inevitable passage of time. Thus each writer in his own way expresses his unique vision of and personal obsession for fixing the golden moment, for extracting the essence of what is good from the past. But, as we have seen in the case of Fitzgerald, the attempt to fix the beautiful moment in terms of human experience always results in frustration and futility, underscoring the Keatsian outlook that only in appreciation for the creative act or work of art itself can there be any real feeling of lasting satisfaction.

Wolfe, obsessed by the concept of time's relentless passage and the structural challenge of harnessing it and relating it to his artistic purpose, naively attempted to synthesize the whole of his personal experience in order to impose meaning on general American experience. It is this intent that is so markedly evident in a fictional work like *Of Time and the River,* in which the poetic function of the river is that of both a structural unit and symbol of immutable time in its ceaseless flow. The upshot of Wolfe's obsession for putting down on paper the whole fabric of American experience, at least as he saw and understood it, is the most self-dramatized expression of the nostalgia neurosis in American literature. In Wolfe it was generated by an intensely personal conflict between his understanding of a meaningful past and the shortcomings of the present. An obvious example of this frame of mind occurs in *Of Time and the River* when Eugene Gant, the novel's protagonist and Wolfe's fictional counterpart, becomes caught up in a fit of creative energy, sparked by a nostalgic longing for his origins, and writes "as only a madman could write":

Seated at a table in his cold, little room that overlooked the old cobbled court of the hotel, he wrote ceaselessly from dawn to dark, sometimes from darkness on to dawn again—hurling himself upon the bed to dream, in a state of comatose awareness, strange sleeping-wakeful visions, dreams mad and terrible as the blinding imagery that now swept constantly across his brain its blaze of fire.

The words were wrung out of him in a kind of bloody sweat, they poured out of his finger tips, spat out of his snarling throat like writhing snakes; he wrote them with his heart, his brain, his sweat, his guts; he wrote them with his blood, his spirit; they were wrenched out of the last secret source and substance of his life.

And in those words was packed the whole image of his bitter homelessness, his intolerable desire, his maddened longing for return. In those wild and broken phrases was packed the whole bitter burden of his famished, driven, over-laden spirit—all the longing of the wanderer, all the impossible and unutterable homesickness that the American, or any man on earth, can know.

They were all there—without coherence, scheme, or reason—flung down upon paper like figures blasted by the spirit's lightning stroke, and in them was the huge chronicle of the billion forms, the million names, the huge, single, and incomparable substance of America.[15]

A stronger sense of romantic isolation and nostalgic longing would be difficult to imagine, but we realize that, at heart, this kind of expression has its source of being in Wolfe's exceptional visual sensitivity to physical reality or, in his words, the "incomparable substance of America"—all the familiar but now alien scenes and images of his own past as they had been filtered and refined by an extremely vivid imagination. But let Wolfe himself, while reflecting on his time in Paris, describe to us what he means by his nostalgic visualization of "substance":

I would be sitting, for example, on the terrace of a cafe watching the flash and play of life before me on the Avenue de l'Opera and suddenly I would remember the iron railing that goes along the boardwalk at Atlantic City. I could see it instantly just the way it was, the heavy iron pipe; its raw, galvanized look; the way the joints were fitted together. It was all so vivid and concrete that I could feel my hand upon it and know the exact dimensions, its size and weight and shape. And suddenly I would realize that I had never seen any railing that looked like this in Europe. And this utterly familiar, common thing would suddenly be revealed to me with all the wonder with which we discover a thing which we have seen all our life and yet have never known before. Or again, it would be a bridge, the look of an old iron bridge across an American river, the sound the train makes as it goes across it; the spoke-and-hollow rumble of the ties below; the look of the muddy banks; the slow, thick, yellow wash of an American river; an old flat-bottomed boat half filled with water stogged in the muddy bank; or it would be, most lonely and haunting of all the sounds I know, the sound of a milk wagon as it entered an American street just at the first gray of the morning, the slow and lonely clopping of the hoof upon the street, the jink of bottles, the sudden rattle of a battered old milk can, the swift and hurried footsteps of the milkman, and again the jink of bottles, a low word spoken to his horse, and then the great, slow, clopping hoof receding into silence, and then quietness and a bird song rising in the street again. Or it would be a little wooden shed out in the country two miles from my home town where people waited for the street car, and I could see and feel again the dull and rusty color of the old green paint and see and feel all of the initials that had been carved out with jackknives on the planks and benches within the shed, and smell the warm and sultry smell so resinous and so thrilling, so filled with a strange and nameless excitement of an unknown joy, a coming prophecy, and hear the street car as it came to a stop, the moment of brooding, drowzing silence; a hot thrum and drowsy stitch at three o'clock; the smell of grass and hot sweet clover; and then the sudden sense of absence, loneliness and departure when the street car had gone and there was nothing but the hot and drowsy stitch at three o'clock again.

Or again, it would be an American street with all its jumble of a thousand ugly architectures. It would be Montague Street or Fulton Street in Brooklyn, or Eleventh Street in New York, or other streets where I had lived; and suddenly I would see the gaunt and savage webbing of the elevated structure along Fulton Street, and how the light swarmed through in dusty broken bars, and I could remember the old, familiar rusty color, that incomparable rusty color that gets into so many things here in America. And this also would be like something I had seen a million times and lived with all my life.

I would sit there, looking out upon the Avenue de l'Opera and my life would ache with the whole memory of it; the desire to see it again; somehow to find a word for it; a language that would tell its shape, its color, the way we have all known and felt and seen it.[16]

In contrast to Sinclair Lewis, the visual emphasis in Thomas Wolfe seems to draw its inspiration from Mark Twain in its poetic feeling for the ordinary, even to the extent that Wolfe can find beauty in the very ugliness that Lewis somewhat hypocritically despaired of. Apparently not sure of his personal relationship to the conditions around him, Wolfe, through his fictional alter egos, persistently searches out the familiar sights, scenes, and objects of his past as if grasping for some kind of reassurance that life does have order, pattern, and meaning. Although Southern in its cultural origins, his quest is really that of the nostalgiac, and for all his idealism and professed belief in the American Dream, Wolfe, of all our writers, strikes us as the least self-assured, reverberating with doubts, questions, and soul searching—the persistent characteristics of youth itself on the verge of discovering self and the world. In fact, to read Wolfe is a nostalgic experience, for he helps us to remember the emotions and self-awakening experiences of our own youth. In the writings of Thomas Wolfe, the nostalgia neurosis springs from the extreme sensitivity of his visual perception of the wide gulf between the precarious present and a lost youth.

Strange bedfellows are Wolfe, Fitzgerald, Hemingway, and Faulkner, yet according to the stimulating and perceptive analysis of novelist Wright Morris, all these writers have much in common since their mutual subject, ". . . however various the backgrounds, however contrasting the styles, pushed to its extremity, is nostalgia."[17] Perhaps it must be that our reputably serious writers are "serious" because of their recognition of and ability to dramatize and communicate the tragic and poignant implications of life's apparently insignificant but, in retrospect, more meaningful moments which are so quickly experienced, it seems, and then forever lost to time's relentless passage.

It can be demonstrated that American writers who engage in sport or demanding physical activity of an athletic nature are exceptionally sensitive to this condition, more so than those who relate to any other kind of physical experience, even the sexual, simply because sporting endeavor incites an all-enveloping sense of personal immediacy and of being alive. Obsessed by the sporting experience throughout his life, Ernest Hemingway appeared always to be searching out in his fiction the right fishing stream, the best woods for hunting—the "great, good place," as it were—to realize and intensify his sporting fantasies. Indeed, Hemingway's perennial quest metaphorically explains the meaning of his fiction. From the autobiographical portrayal of Nick Adams in the early short stories to that of Thomas Hudson in the posthumously published *Islands in the Stream* (1970), Hemingway, like Mark Twain, his literary ancestor, and Stephen Crane, a writer closer to him in time and manner, draws on the visual resources of a lifetime of demanding physical experience to project his personal philosophy of what it takes to be a real person in an absurd world. To dramatize this outlook, Hemingway developed his clean, spare, visually-oriented prose style, which delineated the appropriate objective correlative for emotional focus. The style was seemingly the result of a sculptor's or photographer's attention to the shape of physical objects, highlighted by their relationships to special places. It was a literary manner that would have such a far-reaching effect on twentieth-century writing styles that its impact is still being felt among both our popular as well as serious writers.

Almost any passage in Hemingway's fiction affords us an example of his visual preoccupation, but one of the most anthologized short works emphasizing his photographic manner is "Big Two-hearted River," a seemingly plotless series of vignettes that concentrate on a solitary young man's fishing experiences. Observe, for example, the time when Nick Adams comes out of the river after having lost what apparently would have been a big catch:

Nick climbed out onto the meadow and stood, water running down his trousers and out of his shoes, his shoes squlchy. He went over and sat on the logs. He did not want to rush his sensations any.

He wriggled his toes in the water, in his shoes, and got out a cigarette from his breast pocket. He lit it and tossed the match into the fast water below the logs. A tiny trout rose at the match, as

The writing inspiration of Ernest Hemingway (1898–1961) found its psychological roots in the archetypal figure of Huck Finn and the quest for the right fishing stream or source with its ultimate reward—the intense feeling of being alive through physical communion with nature. To catch the big fish was a dominant metaphor in both Hemingway's life and literature. Here it is expressed at age five, in his thirties, and even posthumously in the film of his novel, Islands in the Stream *(1977).*

it swung around in the fast current. Nick laughed. He would finish the cigarette.

He sat on the logs, smoking, drying in the sun, the sun warm on his back, the river shallow ahead entering the woods, curving into the woods, shallows, light glittering, big water-smooth rocks, cedars along the bank and white birches, the logs warm in the sun, smooth to sit on, without bark, gray to the touch; slowly the feeling of disappointment left him. It went away slowly, the feeling of disappointment that came sharply after the thrill that made his shoulders ache. It was all right now. His rod lying out on the logs, Nick tied a new hook on the leader, pulling the gut tight until it grimped into itself in a hard knot.[18]

Characteristically, the emphasis here is on physical sensation and the simple basic pleasures that accompany it. Thus every word in this passage, as Hemingway's prose always is when he is at his most visually precise, is carefully selected to create a mosaic of intense physical awareness of and sensitivity to the surrounding world, a pleasingly natural world, no matter how insignificant in detail, but one whose physical challenges serve to remind us of our uniqueness as individuals. Through Nick's episodic experiences the reader is presented a snapshot album of remembered emotion from Hemingway's own youth in the Michigan woods, and many of these "candid shots," like the one just quoted, appear to focus on special objects in their places, so that an epiphany-like relationship is set up between physical object and central character. The result is a heightened sense of character and place through a recognizable, nostalgic feeling of oneness with nature, the same emotion we first detect a sincere attempt to relate in Mark Twain, and one we keep running across throughout the fiction of Hemingway, as well as throughout the work of another critically acclaimed, though popularly misunderstood, writer—William Faulkner.

The mythic rituals of hunting and fishing have given more than one writer the opportunity to recapture meaningful moments from past experience, and Faulkner, a writer whose best work tran-

This artist's conception of "The Bear" from a collection of hunting stories by William Faulkner (1897–1962) suggests that Faulkner is in the literary tradition of those American writers concerned with the mythical interpretation of experience—Melville, Hawthorne, and Poe, for example. However, Faulkner's powers of verbal observation seem visually superior to any of his predecessors while exemplifying one of the major premises of this book: a fiction writer's dependence on the past can contribute to a more complex way of visualizing the present. COPYRIGHT RANDOM HOUSE, INC. REPRINTED BY PERMISSION.

BIG WOODS

BY WILLIAM FAULKNER

DECORATIONS BY Edward Shenton

RANDOM HOUSE · NEW YORK

scends the boundaries of his Southern heritage, is no exception to this fact.[19] His well-known long story, "The Bear," which first appeared in *The Saturday Evening Post* in 1942, is one of the best examples in our literature of the use of nostalgic experience to make a serious comment on human relationships. Faulkner's complex writing style, at the other extreme from the apparent simplicity of Hemingway's, is integral and functional to the underlying meaning of this story, which is structured around the moral ambiguities of the Southern past and the reinterpretation of these ambiguities in terms of the present. It is the metaphor of the hunt, however, that lends the story its visual impact of direction and focus.

As Hemingway does with Nick Adams, Faulkner recreates through Ike McCaslin the vividly remembered scenes of his youth—especially those derived from hunting—and for the Southern male who has taken part in the hunt during the hard crispness of late fall days in the deep South, "The Bear" can generate waves of nostalgic feeling. In the outdoor tradition of American writers before him, from James Fenimore Cooper on, Faulkner is at his best in describing natural scenes and outdoor experiences, especially those that have their origins in the memories of an earlier, more pastorally innocent time. In fact, the best written parts of "The Bear" are the revelatory scenes in the woods that are doubtless based on Faulkner's personal reminiscences of life in the hunting camps and that are revisualized through the experiences of young Ike McCaslin. A representative scene controlled by visual imagery is the dramatic moment when young Ike, alone in the wilderness, first glimpses the giant bear that the hunters refer to as Old Ben:

> It did not emerge, appear: it was just there, immobile, fixed in the green and windless noon's hot dappling, not as big as he had dreamed it but as big as he had expected, bigger, dimensionless against the dappled obscurity, looking at him. Then it moved. It crossed the glade without haste, walking for an instance into the sun's full glare and out of it, and stopped again and looked back at him across one shoulder. Then it was gone. It didn't walk into the woods. It faded, sank back into the wilderness without motion as he watched a fish, a huge old bass, sink back into the dark depths of its pool and vanish without even any movement of its fins.[20]

The total visual effect of this passage is cinematic in its spatial development, with central image at first fixed, then in motion, finally followed by a slow fadeout into another image from nature that helps not only to enhance the mysterious, mythic qualities of the bear, but also to establish a sense of nature's unity as opposed to the fragmentation of life divorced from the wilderness or a natural environment. The emotional synthesis of the striking image and nostalgic feeling for place is a trademark of Faulkner's technique and can be attributed to his reliance on a powerful memory as the basis for his narrative expression. Actually, though, "The Bear," with its shifts in the sequence of time suggesting the changeless ritual of the hunting camp over a stretch of years, comes across as more than just a spontaneous overflowing of the author's nostalgic feeling for his past. Appropriately for our purpose, the physical object or symbol around which the complex section IV of the story is built—the ledgers accounting for the slave holdings of Ike's grandfather—provides the catalyst for the grown Ike McCaslin to realize the difference between what was nostalgically appealing about his youth and the underlying significance of his present dilemma. Thus Ike's decision to renounce his heritage raises "The Bear" above the level of nostalgic identification and enhances the impact of the story's moral meaning. It also reveals Faulkner as an artist who is in sure control of his material. In contrast to the moonlight-and-magnolia school of Southern writers, which conditioned us to popular fiction in the tradition of *Gone with the Wind*, William Faulkner's nostalgic vision is tempered by his feel for a piney-woods, delta-dirt interpretation of his Mississippi past. The fact that he could adjust his standards to write movie scripts designed to appeal to popular taste is but another facet of his unique visual talent whose impact on our culture's way of seeing is still being evaluated.

But of all our so-called serious writers whose books contain both story quality and extraordinary visual imagery that readily transcribed to film, John Steinbeck generated a large popular following mainly because his work addresses the reader's most basic emotions—those feelings we all experience in everyday living and which, when tied to a particular time and place, have the power to elicit nostalgic identification.[21] His stories and novels also espouse an optimistic philosophy that stress the brotherhood of man as a redemptive force in the face of adversity and an apparently mechanistic universe. In the classically popular *The Grapes of Wrath*

The popularity of John Steinbeck (1902–1968) was achieved through his novels that were made into outstanding films capitalizing on his ability to dramatize the basic concerns of life, described on the cover of a 1955 paperback edition of East of Eden *as "... good and evil, lust and love, death and birth and life."*

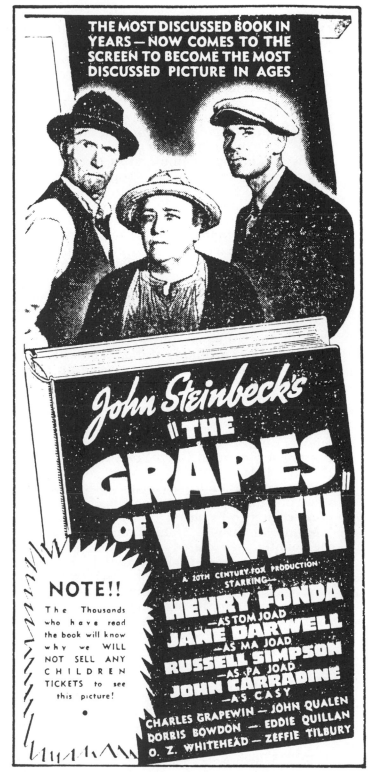

(1939), Steinbeck selects the sociological and economic plight of a family victimized by the Oklahoma dust bowl of the 1930s and then visualizes their trek west as symbolic of all people's simple humanity and stubborn persistence in confronting and overcoming forces supposedly greater than they. Although Steinbeck reveals an organic understanding of the physical reality surrounding his characters by describing things and their interrelationships to conjure up a feeling for time and place, his is ultimately the fascination of the biologist for a special kind of environment and its effect on human rela-

tions and development. This sensibility accounts for Steinbeck's period feel, which is probably nowhere better displayed than in the introduction to the roadside cafe scene in *The Grapes of Wrath*. This passage reflects an attention to visual stimuli and surface detail that combines both realism and nostalgic feeling:

Along 66 the hamburger stands—Al & Susy's Place—Carl's Lunch—Joe & Minnie—Will's Eats. Board-and-bat shacks. Two gasoline pumps in front, a screen door, a long bar, stools, and a foot rail. Near the door three slot machines, showing through glass the wealth of nickels three bars will bring. And beside them, the nickel phonograph with records piled up like pies, ready to swing out to the turntable and play dance music, "Ti-pi-ti-pi-tin," "Thanks for the Memory," Bing Crosby, Benny Goodman. At one end of the counter a covered case; candy cough drops, caffeine sulphate called Sleepless, No-Doze; candy, cigarettes, razor blades, aspirin, Bromo-Seltzer, Alka-Seltzer. The walls decorated with posters, bathing girls, blondes with big breasts and slender hips and waxen faces, in white bathing suits, and holding a bottle of Coca-Cola and smiling—see what you get with a Coca-Cola. Long bar, and salts, peppers, mustard pots, and paper napkins. Beer taps behind the counter, and in back the coffee urns, shiny and steaming, with glass gauges showing the coffee level. And pies in wire cages and oranges in pyramids of four. And little piles of Post Toasties, corn flakes, stacked up in designs.

The signs on cards, picked out with shining mica: Pies Like Mother Used to Make. Credit Makes Enemies. Let's Be Friends. Ladies May Smoke But Be Careful Where You Lay Your Butts. Eat Here and Keep Your Wife for a Pet. IITYWYBAD?

Down at one end the cooking plates, pots of stew, potatoes, pot roast, roast beef, gray roast pork waiting to be sliced.

Minnie or Susy or Mae, middle-aging behind the counter, hair curled and rouge and powder on a sweating face. Taking orders in a soft low voice, calling them to the cook with a screech like a peacock. Mopping the counter with circular strokes, polishing the big shiny coffee urns. The cook is Joe or Carl or Al, hot in a white coat and apron, beady sweat on white forehead, below the white cook's cap; moody, rarely speaking, looking up for a moment at each new entry. Wiping the griddle, slapping down the hamburger. He repeats Mae's orders gently, scrapes the griddle, wipes it down with burlap. Moody and silent. . . .[22]

Steinbeck makes use of the present tense—the tense of visual immediacy—to pull the reader into the actual feel of the scene; and after setting it, he proceeds to use it as a backdrop to set off the variety of human types who stop in off busy Highway 66— a few well-to-do but most of them truck drivers and Okies—all the wanderers of the road who make up the endless migration westward, and, by extension, the ongoing pageant of mankind and the petty obsessions and psychological problems that reveal

his human side. Steinbeck's literary method here— the use of the present tense and the singling out of seemingly insignificant physical details that contribute to the wholeness and meaningfulness of a scene —is still an effective technique in the hands of contemporary writers, most notably John Updike in his Rabbit Angstrom saga. In this kind of writing, the most precious detail functions poetically and can have momentous meaning when related to the totality in which it exists. Thus in the excerpt above, the description of trivia that contributes to the physical reality of the total scene is organically essential, and although the nostalgiac revels in it, it is both the background and the casual dialogue between the counter help and their customers—the ingredients of character and place—that alert the reader to the underlying social problems of the time and the fact that Steinbeck's real intent is to project a message. Written primarily as a tract for its time, *The Grapes of Wrath*, even though it still manages a strong dramatic effect, comes off today much like Sinclair Lewis's *Main Street*— as a sociologically valuable work, which, because of its fascination with the surface details of time and place, has a special nostalgic appeal.

There seems to be something of the journalist's sense of immediacy and reliance on physical details in all successful American writers of this century, and the same acute powers of visual perception that distinguish our major fiction writers also preoccupy those writers whose general appeal is to a wider popular audience. But as a rule our more popular writers are not interested in the function of physical things as philosophical and psychological symbols or metaphors or in how they might be used to comment on sociological phenomena (although some academicians have attempted to fit them into this mold). Instead, their method is primarily that of describing environment in so far as it can enhance or define the function and role of their major characters. Often, however, their description of the physical exists as an end in itself with no more purpose than to add to the overall atmosphere of the narrative. As a result, the literary method of many of our popularly received writers of the past is highly effective in capturing the nostalgic feel or essence of a particular time and place in our social history.

For example, if you were to peruse the fiction of the so-called "hardboiled" or "tough-guy" writers of the 1930s for its attention to visually-observed detail, the effect would be to conjure up a whole way of life that is now submerged under layers of newer lifestyles, especially with respect to personal mannerisms, period cliches, and other nuances of language, not to mention dress styles, even though an era's fashions can resurface periodically in one form or another as in the recent Fitzgerald revival. The fact remains that the literary styles of writers like Dashiell Hammett, Raymond Chandler, and James Cain carried such visual impact that many of their books were easily adaptable as popular films which today have tremendous nostalgic appeal. Some of these movies—*The Maltese Falcon* (WB, 1941), *The Big Sleep* (WB, 1946), and *The Postman Always Rings Twice* (MGM, 1946)—have become even more famous than their book versions and suggest the pervasive influence of film technique on their authors' approach to narrative expression. All three writers worked at one time or another for the film industry, and Hammett even tried his hand at writing the story line for a comic strip—*Secret Agent X-9*—which, with its narrative method of visualized action in panel sequence, is the closest visual equivalent to film that any other medium can produce. In the following visually inspired scene from Hammett's *The Maltese Falcon* (1930), the reader senses the ease of translating the action of the detective hero Sam Spade to the screen, despite Hammett's understated manner:

A telephone-bell rang in darkness. When it had rung three times bed-springs creaked, fingers fumbled on wood, something small and hard thudded on a carpeted floor, the springs creaked again, and a man's voice said:

"Hello. . . . Yes, speaking. . . . Dead? . . . Yes. . . . Fifteen minutes. Thanks."

A switch clicked and a white bowl hung on three gilded chains from the ceiling's center filled the room with light. Spade, barefooted in green and white checked pajamas, sat on the side of his bed. He scowled at the telephone on the table while his hands took from beside it a packet of brown papers and a sack of Bull Durham tobacco.

Cold steamy air blew in through two open windows, bringing with it half a dozen times a minute the Alcatraz foghorn's dull moaning. A tinny alarm-clock, insecurely mounted on a corner of Duke's *Celebrated Criminal Cases of America*—face down on the table—held its hands at five minutes past two.

Spade's thick fingers made a cigarette with deliberate care, sifting a measured quantity of tan flakes down into curved paper, spreading the flakes so that they lay equal at the ends with a slight depression in the middle, thumbs rolling the paper's inner edge down and up under the outer edge as forefingers pressed it over, thumbs and fingers sliding to the paper cylinder's ends to hold it even while tongue licked the flap, left forefinger and thumb pinching their end while right forefinger and thumb smoothed the damp seam, right forefinger and thumb twisting their end and lifting the other to Spade's mouth.

He picked up the pigskin and nickel lighter that had fallen to the floor, manipulated it, and with the cigarette burning in a corner of his mouth stood up. He took off his pajamas. The smooth thickness of his arms, legs, and body, the sag of his big rounded shoulders, made his body like a bear's. It was like a shaved bear's: his chest was hairless. His skin was childishly soft and pink.

He scratched the back of his neck and began to dress. He put on a thin white union-suit, grey socks, black garters, and dark brown shoes. When he had fastened his shoes he picked up the telephone, called Graystone 4500, and ordered a taxicab. He put on a green-striped white shirt, a soft white collar, a green necktie, the grey suit he had worn that day, a loose tweed overcoat, and a dark grey hat. The street-door-bell rang as he stuffed tobacco, keys, and money into his pockets.[23]

The writing style is sparse, of course, but the overall visual effect is such that no detail appears to have been left out in the attempt to convey to the reader a sense of reality. Even the seemingly insignificant act of rolling a cigarette is described in such meticulous manner that a novice should be able to "roll his own" from these directions. And even though this scene contains hardly any action in a physical sense, we learn a lot about the kind of man Sam Spade is through Hammett's description of his relationship to the physical things around him. In a word, this kind of writing represents a script writer's or film director's dream, and it inspired a host of imitators from Hammett's day to the present.

Even in a scene containing significantly more physical action, the descriptive details are controlled to the extent that a camera could faithfully record them, and yet the literary style of expression is spare and concise. Take, for example, the incident in which Joe Cairo pulls a gun on Spade:

Cairo coughed a little apologetic cough and smiled nervously with lips that had lost some of their redness. His dark eyes were humid and bashful and very earnest. "I intend to search your offices, Mr. Spade. I warn you that if you attempt to prevent me I shall certainly shoot you."

"Go ahead." Spade's voice was as empty of expression as his face.

"You will please stand," the man with the pistol

If Hemingway established the lifestyle of the writer as sportsman for the mass eye, then Raymond Chandler (1888–1959) was your picture of the "hardboiled" writer of fiction, seen here with the essential cigarette and grim visage that he fictionally transcribed as descriptive props for his characters. The Black Mask *logo represents the popular pulp magazine of the 1930s that pioneered Chandler's style of writing—a fresh, visually intense way of describing experience.*   PHOTO BY JOHN ENGSTEAD. REPRINTED BY PERMISSION.

instructed him at whose thick chest the pistol was aimed. "I shall have to make sure that you are not armed."

Spade stood up pushing his chair back with his calves as he straightened his legs.

Cairo went around behind him. He transferred the pistol from his right hand to his left. He lifted Spade's coattail and looked under it. Holding the pistol close to Spade's back, he put his right hand around Spade's side and patted his chest. The Levantine face was then no more than six inches below and behind Spade's right elbow.

Spade's elbow dropped as Spade spun to the right. Cairo's face jerked back not far enough: Spade's right heel on the patent-leathered toes anchored the smaller man in the elbow's path. The elbow struck him beneath the cheek-bone, staggering him so that he must have fallen had he not been held by Spade's foot on his foot. Spade's elbow went on past the astonished dark face and straightened when Spade's hand struck down at the pistol. Cairo let the pistol go the instant that Spade's fingers touched it. The pistol was small in Spade's hand. . . .[24]

Again the stage directions are implicit, and the reader or viewer, as the case may be, is drawn into the action, even feels himself a part of it. The formula for this kind of writing can be traced to the reportorial manner of Mark Twain, and it is simply that the appropriate image (here, the pistol) equated with the desired emotion will generate the necessary visual effect. These details of artifact and style blend to create nostalgic overtones that remind us of a specific time and place from the past, since the elliptical style of this kind of writing demands an involvement on the part of the reader to fill in any anticipated gaps in action and description, even though the overall effect is one of apparent completeness. Significantly, the visual effect of "hard-boiled" fiction parallels the effect of listening to radio dramatizations of the 1930s and '40s, which, of course, generated their own kind of audience identification and nostalgic appeal.

One of the most outstanding examples of the "tough-guy" school of writing is the opening chapter of *The Postman Always Rings Twice* (1934) wherein James Cain, in only two pages of action and description, introduces the reader to his novel's major dramatic ingredients: the central scene of action (the roadside restaurant); the main characters (Frank, the drifter; Nick, the restaurant owner; and Cora, his attractive but sexually frustrated wife); and the suggested basis for a plot (the illicit affair between Frank and Cora that precipitates the planned murder of Nick). This is writing that is, of course, movie-oriented—among the first of a kind of fiction designed to condition the reader to anticipate the film version of the book. The movie people, ever sensitive to our fantasy appetites, have always been quick to seize upon the sensational elements of our popular fiction to help sell their productions.

As masters of the movie-scenario type of fiction writing, the hard-boiled group has undergone both a print and film revival in recent years concurrent with the nostalgia boom. It is fairly easy to understand why this kind of fiction would have nostalgic appeal, for it is a brand of storytelling not only redolent of the times that produced it, it *is* those times. That the 1930s was a most trying time in our economic and social history appears to be no deterrent to building up a nostalgic feeling for what was popularly representative of the era. Surely Richard Armour's theory, which was mentioned earlier, about our special regard for the past, applies also to our emotional response to even a bleak period like the 1930s. For a person who lived through those times, recalling the exploits of pop culture heroes like Phillip Marlowe, Sam Spade, or Nick Charles represents an agreeable alternative to recalling the actual life of that period. Not only are these characters dream embodiments, as Gore Vidal suggested, they are existential heroes who make the most of an absurd and uncertain world by confronting their indifferent environments with a stoic effrontery that must have made their admirers feel much more secure about their own personal lives. It is a feeling akin to what many people must have experienced in retreating from the real world to watch their favorite movie stars perform in the film palaces of those times. Vicariously, characters like Sam Spade and the Continental Op took their fans on a fantasy ride that transcended all mortal fears, even death itself. This kind of writing may have provided a healthy prescription to relieve the sagging morale of those undergoing a period in our history seemingly stacked against them, but it also helped in the long run to perpetuate visually the myth of the past as being more attractive than the present.

Another kind of period fiction interrelated with that turned out by the hard-boiled school was appearing in the appropriately named "pulp" magazines. These publications faded as popular items in the early 1950s, but in their heyday of the 1930s and 1940s, they supplied many a fledgling writer with a medium for expression as well as a reading public with an outlet for its fantasy fulfillment.[25] We should be aware that, because of the profusion of

*The pulp magazine, so named because of the cheap, wood-flecked paper on which its stories were printed, faded from popularity in the 1950s, but enjoyed a long history as one of the more popular forms of mass entertainment. Here are two highly successful pulps whose covers portray favorite subject matter of their day—*Red Book *(1911), the romantic story and* Argosy All-Story Weekly *(1925), the Western.*

pulp titles produced during this era, this body of fiction has much more intrinsically to offer us as a conscious literary form than just nostalgic interest. That there were so many of them (every successful pulp spawned dozens of imitations) tells us something significant and meaningful about the times that produced them. Thus, to the sociologist and the historian, the pulp magazine is as much a measure and mirror of its day as the sexually oriented "men's" and "women's" magazines of the 1980s will undoubtedly be to future students of the trends and forces that help make our day what it is.[26] As the foreword to a recent anthology of pulp fiction expressed it, ". . . popular entertainment provides an accurate barometric record of emotional climate which reveals the anxiety of the masses."[27] This assessment has relevance to my contention that

today's anxieties have a way of evolving into tomorrow's nostalgia obsessions.

The nostalgia that works of pulp fiction elicit is traceable to their melodramatic emphasis on action as wish-fulfillment, projected in a highly visual fashion that, once experienced, makes a lasting impression. Readers remember The Shadow's sinister way of making his presence known to criminals, or Doc Savage's ability to summon forth his superhuman talents in dealing with any kind of adversary, or the science-fiction writer's manner of describing his hero's relationship to the hostile, strange environment of an alien planet, or even the compelling fascination for the supernatural that an H.P. Lovecraft story or a pulp like *Weird Tales* always seemed to generate. This kind of fiction was popular for a number of reasons. In a pulp story the main character does things that engage the reader's attention in a purely escapist sense—traveling to exotic places despite barriers of time and distance; solving complex murder cases; winning the big ball game in the final seconds; engaging in countless trysts with beautiful, sexually arousing women; rocketing through millions of miles of interplanetary space; fighting and overcoming any foe, whether human, animal, plant, or machine; and of course riding the Western plains to keep them clear of any wrongdoing. In short, the pulp hero does whatever the reader feels would be specially exciting or pleasurable to do if given the opportunity. And why not if merely reading about wish fulfillment can eliminate the element of personal danger?

A couple of excerpts from typical stories of the pulp era will help exemplify the visually compelling, although somewhat elementary, fictional technique of the pulp writer. In fact, for a writer to publish in the pulps he had to abide by a code of reader expectations or be rejected by an editor. Typical is the opening passage of "The Devil Must Pay" in which the author wastes little time in involving his reader in the difficult situation of his soldier-of-fortune hero:

> . . . A hot night in Marseilles with a south wind out of Africa drying the sweat on you instantly; parching your lips. I had jumped my ship, the *Exmarch,* and with fifty dollars in my pocket I had strolled down the Cannebiere and off toward the Joliette basin. I had heard that Marseilles was the most vicious city in the world. Young, hell-bent for adventure, I wanted to find out for myself. A fool? Certainly, but a man is only twenty-four once, and that is the time to stride the world with seven league boots and grin into the bright face of peril.
>
> The alleyways stank from the filth emptied from upper floors. The darkness was filled with flitting figures. A few *bistros* gave forth feeble light where whiskered men crouched over cheap wine and schemed their schemes to gain money and food.
>
> Girls there were who beckoned with bold provocative eyes. But I had heard of them; how they drugged a man, robbed him, threw him into the street. Lodging housekeepers cried, "Sleep here the night, sailor." But I had heard of them, too, how the closets in their establishments, where you hung your clothes, had turning panels so that no matter if you locked your door you awoke in the morning penniless. *Agents de police* patrolled in pairs and ignored the jeers and curses thrown at them. Yes, Marseilles is a tough port, a fetid place where live the maggots of the world. I finally began to feel uneasy and when two soldiers in the uniform of Foreign Legionnaires warned me to turn back, I did so.
>
> But I missed a turning and found myself in an alley scarcely the width of my shoulders, stone walls on each side. I hurried on, my breath sticking in my throat, my heart thudding. I never saw the two shadows who had crouched in the darkness of the wall on the right. . . .[28]

With the scene set, the expectant reader is now visually prepared as he would be in a grade-B movie to participate in an action-oriented tale dramatizing the hero's unique problems as opposed to the cares and concerns of the reader's workaday world. No pulp hero, it seemed, ever had to concern himself with the mundane problem of earning a living. The magic stuff of the pulps and of many a popular movie of the period would never allow their heroes to stoop so low.

Just as so many adventure stories opened by plunging the reader into the action, so the tale of horror, an extremely popular genre obviously inspired by the successful monster-vampire films of the 1930s, contained an obligatory scene in which the hero rescued the heroine from the devious designs of the physically grotesque henchman to the story's mad scientist. An example is this excerpt from a 1937 *Spicy Mystery,* a pulp reflecting the sexual overtones of the horror story:

> Within that chamber, the ape-like servant was forcing Anne Barnard toward a cot. The girl had recovered consciousness, and she was fighting with all her vain, useless strength. Gorill was bending her backward. . . .
>
> With a mighty, snarling oath, Travis Brant leaped into that foul place. In his iron-bound hands he grasped the spike which he had pulled from the wall. He raised it high—brought it plunging down into the liveried servant's skull. The iron spike split through bone as though it had been tissue paper; pierced Gorill's brain. The servant slumped lifelessly to the earthen floor, limp, dead.
>
> Travis Brant sprang at Anne Barnard, swept her into his arms. And that instant, a harsh voice floated through the labyrinth of caverns. Dr. Zenarro's voice. "Gorill—where are you? What have you done with that girl? Gorill—Gorill!"
>
> The voice was coming closer now. Travis Brant's face was white, grim, set. "Listen, Anne darling!" he whispered. "This is our only chance of overcoming that mad doctor. Are you willing?" And he whispered something into the girl's ear.
>
> She clung to him, pressed her body close to his own. "Y-yes!" she answered faintly.[29]

Perverse sex and romantic love suggested over the space of five short paragraphs, and the readers loved what they read and kept clamoring for more. Those four points of ellipsis closing the first paragraph hint at all manner of sordid behavior on Gorill's part and remind us that while the pulps were wrestling with the problem of explicit sex, writers like Erskine Caldwell and even William Faulkner in

The covers of pulp magazines were commercial masterpieces, visually inspired to sell their contents. During the peak years of the pulps' popularity, several hundred different publications could appear on a newstand over the course of a month. With such competition, it is little wonder then that a pulp cover strained for sensational effect. Here is a collection of popular pulp covers ranging from the 1930s to the '50s, the heart period of this fictional form.

Startling Stories   COPYRIGHT BETTER PUBLICATIONS, INC.

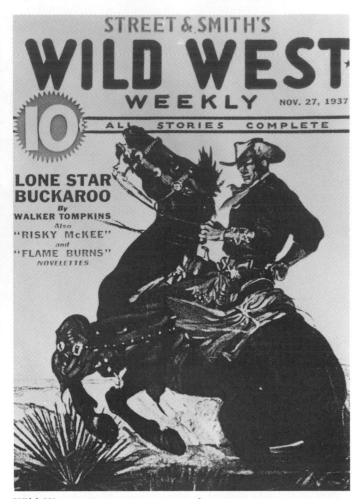

Wild West   COPYRIGHT STREET & SMITH, INC.

Marvel   COPYRIGHT RED CIRCLE PUBLICATIONS, INC.

Planet Stories   COPYRIGHT LOVE ROMANCES PUBLICATIONS, INC.

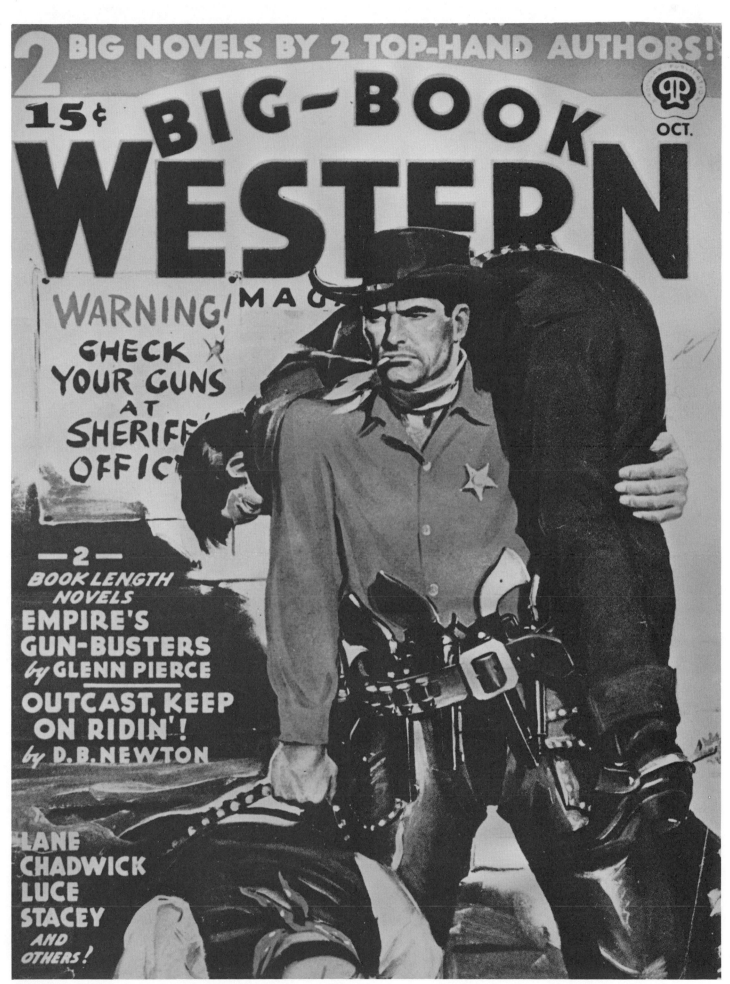

2 BIG NOVELS BY 2 TOP-HAND AUTHORS!

15¢ **BIG-BOOK WESTERN** MAG.

OCT.

WARNING! CHECK YOUR GUNS AT SHERIFF OFFICE

—2—
BOOK LENGTH
NOVELS
EMPIRE'S
GUN-BUSTERS
by GLENN PIERCE

OUTCAST, KEEP
ON RIDIN'!
by D. B. NEWTON

LANE
CHADWICK
LUCE
STACEY
AND
OTHERS!

Big-Book Western COPYRIGHT POPULAR PUBLICATIONS, INC.

Famous Fantastic Mysteries COPYRIGHT POPULAR PUBLICA-
TIONS, INC.

Operator 5 COPYRIGHT POPULAR PUBLICATIONS, INC.

Sanctuary (1931) were discovering what powers the English language possessed to connote the underground subject of sexual behavior. The language of visual stimulation they pioneered, in fact, is still being explored and expanded upon today, to the extent that much of this kind of writing, while bordering on or crossing over into the realm of pornography—to many the ultimate visual experience —thrives as fantasy and dream fulfillment in itself.

For each romantic field of endeavor or interest, there was a pulp magazine, and sometimes several, and their number inhibits my delving into a discussion here of even the major variations. Regardless of their infinite variety, all pulp magazines appeared to abide by a single formula for their brand of fiction. It was simply that *action* combined with a unique *environment* provided *escape* for the reader. Surely the pulp illustrators must have been mindful of these ingredients, and the magazines' covers, which attempted to advertise their contents in the most graphic, startling manner, are vivid testimony to this self-consciousness. In some cases, a reader might have to search the stories from end to end for the precise scene that matched the perilous situation or melodramatic effect of the cover; yet in many instances it was the visual impact of the cover art that stayed with the pulp fan long after the story was forgotten. In fact, a great deal of the nostalgia associated with one's remembrance of the pulps is generated by those glaringly lurid and, in some cases, nearly obscene covers, which, once glimpsed by a potential reader, seemed to imprint themselves permanently on the mind's eye. Thus, in looking back on this visual forerunner in fiction of both the action-oriented comic book and the sexually directed man's magazine, we experience a feeling that is akin to rediscovering something that appealed to us as children but that has since been lost. We may marvel at how anything so inherently naive and immature could have cast such a spell over us, yet the nostalgic tie persists, reminding us that yesterday's anxieties may not have been so bad after all.

Pulp fiction has a natural parallel in juvenile fiction, both in storytelling technique and in the kind of illustrations used to complement story. What we really remember about the books we were fond of as children is the visual projection and interpretation that some forgotten commercial artist produced to dress up the dust jackets for sales purposes and liven up the long stretch of printed pages in series like Tom Swift, Nancy Drew, Bomba the Jungle Boy, and Jerry Todd, to name only a few. This type of literature had a long history but, like the pulps, peaked for its audience in the 1920s and

READ THE TOM EDISON, Jr., STORIES IN THE NUGGET LIBRARY.

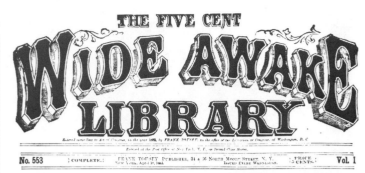

The Series Book
As one of the most famous of the series book characters, Tom Swift enjoyed a popularity based on the increasing fascination with gadgetry and marvelous inventions as the technology of the twentieth century progressed. Here are the title page and frontispiece of a 1917 edition. COPYRIGHT GROSSET & DUNLAP, INC. REPRINTED BY PERMISSION.

The Half-dime Weekly
The fantasy-inspired covers of the half-dime weekly reveal them as the visual predecessor of the comic book. Here are two of the more popular series read by thousands of juveniles toward the end of the last century.

TOM SWIFT IN THE
LAND OF WONDERS

OR

The Underground Search
for the Idol of Gold

BY

VICTOR APPLETON

AUTHOR OF "TOM SWIFT AND HIS MOTOR CYCLE," "TOM SWIFT
AND HIS BIG TUNNEL," "THE MOVING PICTURE BOYS
SERIES," "THE MOTION PICTURE CHUMS
SERIES," ETC.

ILLUSTRATED

NEW YORK
GROSSET AND DUNLAP
PUBLISHERS
Made in the United States of America

TOUCHDOWN!
BY HAROLD M. SHERMAN

Author of
"ONE MINUTE TO PLAY"

Other popular series were inspired by school boy athletics (Touch-down! by Harold M. Sherman) and mystery-crime detection (the Hardy Boys).

THE HARDY BOYS

THE SINISTER SIGN POST

*The Hardy series has been periodically updated to suit the tastes of new audiences, as these covers indicate—*The Sinister Signpost *(1936) and* The Secret Warning *(1966)* REPRINTED BY PERMISSION OF THE STRATEMEYER SYNDICATE.

THE HARDY BOYS

THE SECRET WARNING

FRANKLIN W. DIXON

W. DIXON

The Family Book
Margaret Sidney's Five Little Peppers and How They Grew
*(1904 edition) is typical of the book depending on the joys and
minor crises of family life to generate appeal.*

The Animal Story
*Animal characters have always been popular with children. The
visual appeal of the popular characters created by Walt Disney
and Dr. Seuss can be traced to the talents of artists like A.B. Frost
who illustrated the Uncle Remus stories of Joel Chandler Harris.
Here, an illustration from the story of Brer Rabbit and the Tar
Baby (1892).*

1930s. The illustrations in these books could, in their special way, be just as entertaining as those magnificent graphics for the classics drawn by the likes of Howard Pyle and N.C. Wyeth. When you have less to work with, the resources of the imagination must surely be put to the test, as many an artist assigned to illustrate a series book found out. Illustrators of fictional works that appeal to a mass audience, whether juvenile or adult, have apparently taken a cue from the writers of these books in that they too are inspired by a fact of American idealism —that we continually search for ways to delude ourselves into believing that life is more interesting, exciting, or attractive than it actually is. There is, for example, much more behind the commercial pitch of today's sensational paperback cover than meets the eye.

The nostalgic involvement begins in our childhood with the books that are presented us on birthdays, at Christmas, or on other special occasions. Once read, these books seem to provide us with not only a sense of time and place but an idealized interpretation of American experience that persists throughout our lives. However, in the boys and girls series books to which millions of youths have been exposed over the years, we sense an ambivalent attitude toward the American experience, and this attitude controls both purpose and theme. Although written for the tastes of a more innocent age, the incredibly naive stories of Horatio Alger, Jr., will serve here as an appropriate introduction to juvenile fiction because, at bottom, Alger's writing,

The Fantasy Classic
In America the all-time fantasy classic of childhood is undoubtedly
L. Frank Baum's The Wizard of Oz, *first published in 1900*
and since acquiring even more popularity through the 1939
MGM movie. In fact, illustrator W.A. Denslow's original inter-
pretations of the major characters have been visually replaced in
the minds of today's children by those of the movie version.
REPRINTED BY PERMISSION OF DOVER PUBLICATIONS, INC.

like most fiction for youth, reflects a sensitive awareness of the wide division between dream and fact in
American life. His puppetlike characters who get
ahead in life, despite what appears to be unbeatable
odds, are ironic and dramatic testimony to his perceptiveness.

If the religion of success had a ritual, then Alger
was its high priest, who sanctified and perpetuated
the myth for generations of boys (and who knows
how many girls?) from the latter half of the nineteenth century to well into the twentieth. A multitude of characters like Ragged Dick and Tattered
Tom, who overcame the hard facts of their existence to become economically independent, con-
verted thousands of readers to Alger's "religion," a
paradoxical synthesis of moral strictness and economic acquisitiveness. In illustration, observe the
following excerpt from the windup to *Silas Snobden's
Office Boy* (1890) in which the hero, Frank Manton,
is handsomely rewarded for his part in resolving a
kidnap case perpetrated by his deceitful and scheming stepfather. Frank's benefactor presents him
with an unsealed envelope which contains a cer-
tified check for $10,000:

> "Is this for me?" he asked in amazement.
> "Yes, for I know you will make good use of it."
> "How can I thank you, sir?" exclaimed Frank,
> in a burst of gratitude. "There will be no more
> poverty, no more hard work for my mother."
> "Yes, Frank, it is your duty to make things easy
> for her. She has been your best friend. But keep
> the money in your own hands. Remember that
> you have a stepfather who has no claim upon you,
> but who might give your mother trouble."
> "Thank you, sir. May I go home and tell mother
> of my good fortune?"
> "Certainly."
> "And would you keep and invest this money for
> me?"
> "I will do so, and allow you six per cent inter-
> est, payable monthly. I will also take you into my
> banking house at a salary, to begin on, of ten
> dollars a week. But it will be necessary for you to
> give up your place with the historian."
> ":He can easily get some one to fill it. I think I
> would rather become a banker than a historian."
> "There is probably more money in it," said Mr.
> Palmer with a smile.[30]

"I think I would rather become a banker than a
historian." Never did Alger express the obsessive
quest of his heroes more characteristically than in
Frank Manton's candid statement, which no doubt
inspired readers of whatever age to concur with Mr.
Palmer's rejoinder. Appropriately, the key to re-

solving personal problems in an Alger story is economic while the abstractions of integrity, honesty,
and hard work are really not so much admired as is
Alger's pleasant assumption that the good life is in
reach of everyone, provided, of course, that the
moral essentials are not totally ignored but rather
considered as worthy means to an end. The Alger
canon contains bountiful evidence of our national
mania for willful self-delusion brought on by an
idealism that refuses to accept things the way they
are.

The inspirational intent of an Alger book generates a nostalgic flavor that reminds a reader of his
youth and of simpler, more pleasant times, but another attribute that enhances the nostalgic appeal of
an Alger story is the author's ability to depict a way
of urban life that has literally vanished. In drawing
on the sights and scenes of nineteenth-century New
York City as the background for his fictional melo-
dramas of youth against the world, Alger exhibits an
intimate familiarity with the physical layout of his
day's "little old New York," using his knowledge of
the city's landmarks to enhance atmosphere in the
manner of those O. Henry short stories that were
set in the great metropolis. The lure of the city as
the mecca where personal dreams can be realized
has long been an overworked metaphor for American writers to express what they think is meaningful
or significant in our experience, but most of our
serious writers seem to paint the city or urbanized
experience for what it is—a powerful force coldly
indifferent to individual will and purpose. Despite
what comes across on the surface as an unbelievable
naivete about real human relationships, Alger's
contrived plots do reflect an understanding of the
city as a formidable entity, yet one that could be
tamed and subdued in order to realize personal
goals, provided the individual had the necessary
drive and desire to do so. In sum, the Alger hero is
really the visual prototype of the modern novel's
businessman-hero or anti-hero, as the case may be.
So in conceiving of the city as an adversary, Alger
was compelled to create characters who come on
stage as distortions, larger than their backgrounds,
simply because they had to be to cope with the
pitfalls around them. As fantasized and unrealistic
as they are, it is in this conception of Alger's stories

*Millions of boys were influenced and inspired by dozens of books
like this one by Horatio Alger, Jr., whose popularity extended from
the last half of the nineteenth century well on into the twentieth.
In preaching the author's brand of the Gospel of Success, these
books originated the visual prototype of the kind of character that
would evolve into Sinclair Lewis's* Babbitt *and the contemporary
businessman. High on Alger's list of admirable traits, "self-reliance" is undoubtedly the lesson depicted on this hardback cover,
published during the early years of this century.*

STRIVE and SUCCEED
By HORATIO ALGER JR.

that one finds much of their nostalgic vision and appeal. As we have seen, it is not the real but the fanciful and escapist that attract the nostalgiac.

The nostalgic reverberations of the success story specially created for a juvenile audience have also echoed in a type of fiction devoted to glamorizing sports experience. Since their origin, organized athletics, especially of the prep school and college variety, have offered youthful readers a time-tested method to realize personal identity in a world that seems structured to deny them this end. Thus the experience of reading about the daring exploits and spectacular achievements of the fictionalized sports heroes of Ralph Henry Barbour, William Heyliger, Harold M. Sherman, and Everett T. Tomlinson, who turned out books with titles like *For the Honor of the School, One Minute to Play, Goal to Go!* and *Winning His W,* has contributed not only to a unique nostalgic identification for men who were boys during the twenties, thirties, and forties, but also to a system of awards and a code of behavior that could only be realized through participation in organized sports. From the 1950s on, sports stories written expressly for juveniles began to be more concerned with the psychological problems of their major characters, rather than the climactic episode dealing with how the big game was won for old Siwash. Nevertheless, these more recent stories are not so different that they haven't begun to develop a nostalgic following all their own, as, for example, the Chip Hilton series by former coach Clair Bee.

Yet of all the superheroic characters spawned by fiction dealing with American sports, the archetypal figure to whom all others owe allegiance is Frank Merriwell, created in the 1890s by Gilbert Patten, an extremely prolific writer who entertained serious literary goals, so always signed the Merriwell stories as Burt L. Standish. Ironically, Patten's reputation rests with his creation of the Merriwell character. In fact, it would be impossible to measure the visual impact of the Merriwell image on our collective understanding of American team sports as they have evolved over the years. As a composite character who excels not only on the playing field but in all his interpersonal dealings as well, Frank Merriwell is the personification of the super athlete literally daydreamed into being, and the neurotic inspiration responsible for Frank's creation no doubt accounts for his one-sided personality. Patten, in his autobiography, reveals an important clue to understanding both his creative vision and the nature of the writer as nostalgiac:

I was the liar in the family, but some of my falsehoods did not seem like lies to me. Many were born of daydreams that seemed quite as real as natural happenings. Bidden or not, such dreams came to me often in reverie which let me escape into a magic land of fanciful excitement and adventure.[31]

The world of Frank Merriwell, as it was presented in the seemingly endless nickel-and-dime novel series of his day, was both the product of Patten's fanciful thinking, which expressed itself in hundreds of stories over a span of some thirty years, and of his understanding of how young males of his day wanted to interpret the world, or rather have it interpreted for them. The psychological effect of these stories on the thousands upon thousands of boys who read them would, of course, be impossible to determine, but one thing is certain, that the snugly plotted, secure world of a Frank Merriwell is the very stuff of nostalgia. Even so, these stories, like the pulps, offer us more than just nostalgic interest, for they can tell us, however awkwardly, a great deal about our basic hopes and fears as a people, as well as point out the underlying psychological temper of an earlier, more innocent time, a way of looking at experience that may be nostalgic but that is no longer tolerable by current standards of taste.

The polarity of innocence and experience in American culture, like the clash between past and present, contributes immeasurably to the psychic tension responsible for the nostalgia obsession or neurosis in American literary expression. All our important fiction writers reveal an inherent awareness of this condition, and we have seen how critically acclaimed writers like Mark Twain and Ernest Hemingway effect a precarious balance between innocence and experience. But those writers whose appeal is to large segments of a mass audience, as, for example, Gilbert Patten's was, exhibit an obvious predilection for dramatizing the state of innocence itself. For such a writer the return to this state through our daydreaming inclinations can be most nearly approached through recreating them as written experience, however unreal it might be. In other words, if the writer can compel the reader to liter-

The fictional archetype of all American super-jocks is Frank Merriwell, a larger-than-life character created toward the end of the last century by Gilbert Patten, who wrote under the pen name of Burt L. Standish. Frank's spectacular exploits were carried in weekly tabloids like this one which eventually became known as Tip Top Weekly. *Its covers are the visual prototype of the super-hero comic book that came into being in the late 1930s.* CULVER PICTURES.

Tip Top Library

Issued Weekly—By Subscription $2.50 per year. Entered as Second Class Matter at the N. Y. Post Office by STREET & SMITH.

| April 25, 1896. | Vol. 1, No. 2. | Price Five Cents |

Frank Merriwell's Foe
OR
Plebe Life in Barracks
BY Burt L. Standish

FRANK SAW INZA GAZING AT HIM APPEALINGLY, HER FACE ASHEN WITH TERROR.

ally *see* the experience of wish fulfillment or fantasy and create an opportunity to relive a familiar part of his life, the reader may realize through nostalgic identification what, in a sense, is a kind of psychological rebirth.

Because of their peculiar, apparently intuitive understanding of this situation, many of our technically weak and philosophically shallow novelists became best-selling authors. If Gilbert Patten and a host of others wrote in response to what they thought were the fantasy wishes of the youth of their day, then writers like Francis Marion Crawford, Harold Bell Wright, Alice Hegan Rice, and Gene Stratton Porter were doing the same thing for a predominantly adult audience toward the end of the last century and on into the first quarter of this century. Even now a reading of their once tremendously popular output reveals their basic subject matter as wish fulfillment—the appeal of exotic experience in the case of Crawford, or, in the works of the other writers just mentioned, the attraction of simpler times when innocence seemed to play a more meaningful part in human relationships. The overwhelming popularity of these authors in their day attests to their perceptive ability to both recognize and visualize, in the true manner of the best-selling novelist, the kind of material the masses demanded for their reading pleasure or inspiration. Harold Bell Wright, for example, had a way of fathoming and staging what was popularly recognized as a meaningful religious experience. This is still an appealing subject area in the annals of American best-sellers, with novelists as disparate as Lloyd C. Douglas and Flannery O'Connor reinterpreting this kind of experience for successive generations. Gene Stratton Porter relied for her popular appeal primarily on dramatizing the common experience of family life and evoking an identification with nature. Virtually unknown today, novels like Wright's *The Shepherd of the Hills* (1907) and Porter's *The Girl of the Limberlost* (1909) had receptions that helped rank both authors significantly high on the all-time best-selling list. In fact, during the heyday of their writing success both Wright and Porter occasionally found themselves on the best-seller lists simultaneously, a fact that probably tells us more about the tenor and real concerns of the time than most scholarly historical explication. Surely a historian or sociologist could do much worse than to consult the novels of these two amazingly successful writers to comprehend a feel for time and place or assess how the masses of people felt and thought about the basic emotional issues and problems of their day.

There were other eminently successful writers of this era who appealed to large segments of the population for different reasons. Rising to popularity roughly during the same time as Wright and Porter, Zane Grey discovered how to use the visual characteristics of the American West, indeed of the whole outdoors, as meaningful subject matter, and he attracted one of the largest followings of all time. Grey's popularity, in contrast to that of most of his contemporaries, is still in evidence today, as any paperback book section in most stores will attest. Since their first publication over half a century ago, the novels of Zane Grey have sold in the millions, placing him among the most widely read writers of all time. Grey's success lay in his treatment of the Western story, one of the most popular fiction and film genres of all time, and even though this form

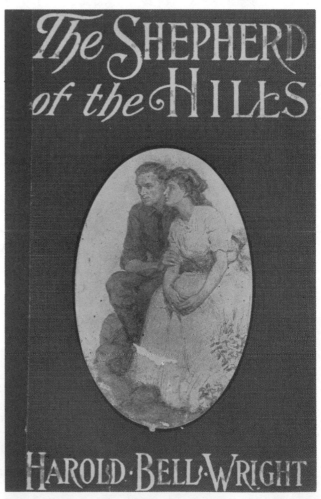

Here is the cover of a 1907 edition of The Shepherd of the Hills, *published by A. L. Burt, and one of a series of novels that made Harold Bell Wright one of the most popular writers of all time. The secret of his mass appeal lay in his ability to dramatize scenes of emotionally charged religious significance, a special talent that can still help sell a book.*

has attracted a large number of talented writers, only a few have been as popularly acclaimed as Zane Grey.[32] How then do we account for his special success story? On the surface it appears a product of the frustrated creative urge of an intensely ambitious individual who, before he found himself as a writer, attempted such disparate careers as professional baseball and dentistry with little personal satisfaction. Even after experiencing a series of rejections by publishers, Grey wrote in his spare time and subsidized the publication of his first novel, so dedicated and intense was his desire to become an accepted writer of fiction.

Actually, Zane Grey is an outstanding example of the popular writer as nostalgiac, and the key to understanding his tremendous success lies in recognizing that he himself, without the benefit of a press agent, dreamed his writing career into being—dreaming and then evolving into that unique image of the internationally known author he intuitively knew he could become. Once he overcame his initial awkward attempts at writing fiction and learned to control his daydreaming powers, it was only a matter of time until he transformed his innate talent into written expression that even by today's standards of realism still retain a certain dramatic power and excitement. The reason for his achievement is that Grey is a fictional daydreamer whose power of physical description aids considerably in enriching the vividness of his narration and conveying a sense of time and place. Despite any faltering in characterization or weakening of plot in a Grey story, there is always a consistency and naturalness in describing vegetation and environment as well as a spontaneous, though appropriate, feel for the background of his stories. Following is an example of his organic use of natural description near the close of *The U.P. Trail* (1918) when Slingerland, the old trapper, returns to his "beloved hills" after the great railroad has been completed:

> Slingerland hated the railroad, and he could not see as Neale did, or any of the engineers or builders. This old trapper had the vision of the Indian—that far-seeing eye cleared by distance and silence, and the force of the great, lonely hills. Progress was great, but nature undespoiled was greater. . . .
> He made his first camp on a stream watering a valley twenty miles from the railroad. There were Indian tracks on the trails. But he had nothing to fear from Indians. That night, though all was starry and silent around him as he lay, he still held the insupportable feeling.

Next day he penetrated deeper into the foothills, and soon he had gained the fastnesses of the mountains. No longer did he meet trails except those of deer and wildcat and bear. And so day after day he drove the burros, climbing and descending the rocky ways, until he had penetrated to the very heart of the great wild range.

In all his roaming over untrodden lands he had never come into such a wild place. No foot, not even an Indian's, had ever desecrated this green valley with its clear, singing stream, its herds of tame deer, its curious beaver, its pine-covered slopes, its looming, gray, protective peaks. And at last he was satisfied to halt there—to build his cabin and his corral.

Discontent and longing, and then hate, passed into oblivion. These useless passions could not long survive in such an environment. By and by the old trapper's only link with the past was memory of a stalwart youth, and of a girl with violet eyes, and of their sad and wonderful romance, in which he had played a happy part.

The rosy dawn, the days of sun and cloud, the still, windy nights, the solemn stars, the moon-blanched valley with its grazing herds, the beautiful wild mourn of the hunting wolf and the whistle of the stag, and always and ever the murmur of the stream—in these, and in the solitude and loneliness of their haunts, he found his goal, his serenity, the truth and best of remaining life for him.[33]

There is something of James Fenimore Cooper in this passage, and even though Grey's description of natural scenery here is somewhat restrained, it is played up just enough to highlight his philosophical intent at this point in the story—the contrast between the railroad as a symbol of encroaching civilization with its changing, corrupting customs and the eternal, immutable cycle of nature as represented by Slingerland's retreat. Thus Grey's attempt to visualize for his readers the proper feel of a particular locale, regardless of whatever message he might be trying to express, lends a high degree of authenticity to his storytelling technique. In fact, Zane Grey was one of the few writers of romanticized subject matter who chose to visit, explore, or even live where his stories were supposed to have taken place, and it is relevant to my purpose here that his rise to success as a popular writer can be directly related to the travels that nostalgically inspired the descriptive attributes of his works, whether they were set in the American West or in the exotic South Pacific where he sailed on extended fishing ventures. Only a person who had viewed a similar scene could have written the passage from *The Arizona Clan* (1958) in which the central character, Mercer, rides his horse to the summit of a hill and then looks around:

Rolling hills of green, like colossal waves of a slanted sea, rose to meet a black and red and gray mountain front, bold and wild, running from east to west as far as he could see, gashed by many canyons, with a magnificent broad belt of rock gold in the sun, that zigzagged under the level, timber-fringed rim. This undoubtedly was what the lad Tom had called Rock Rim. Mercer reveled in the sight. How wonderful to a plainsman, whose eyes had grown seared with the monotony of the endless sun-blasted prairie! The air was still and hot. He heard the dreamy hum of falling water, and that seemed the only thing needed to make this wilderness scene perfect.

Then Mercer shifted his gaze and looked down more to his right than directly behind. And he was struck with amazement. He appeared to be high enough to look down upon a region of winding rounded ridges, like silver-backed, green-spotted snakes, between which yawned forest-choked gorges from which cliffs of bronze and crags of gray stood out. These ridges were miles long and they sloped down into a dark blue rent in the wildest cut-up bit of earth Mercer had ever looked upon. Beyond the bold, far wall of that canyon stood up a hummocky sea of domes and peaks, shaggy and black, remote and apparently inaccessible.[34]

The visual effect, as in many of the panoramic scenes that Zane Grey described, is like that created by the sweep of a movie camera with all local detail contributing to the wholeness of the scene. It is a technique that endeared his writing to the movie

The power of Zane Grey's wide popularity lay in his unique ability to visualize in his fiction the American's elemental concern for taming his environment—the "Wild West," as it was affectionately known to legions of fans. For this reason, dozens of his stories have been readily transcribed to the screen, from the silent era, when Tom Mix starred in numerous Zane Grey features, to Western Union, *a popular Western of the 1940s.*

people, but it is by no means Grey's finest cinematic characteristic.

With his great ear, or eye for titles, many of which have a sound of epic grandeur about them—*The Last of the Plainsmen* (1908), *Riders of the Purple Sage* (1912), *The Light of Western Stars* (1915), and *The Thundering Herd* (1925)—Grey wrote novels that were controlled and directed by a visualized line of action which made them naturals for adaptation to the screen. Of course, many of them were made into some of the most popular movies of their day. Both the beauty and violence of nature as well as the achievement and cruelty of man were the subjects of Zane Grey, and film studios from the twenties to the forties were quick to recognize the visually dramatic appeal of such material. Perhaps the key to comprehending the tremendous vitality and popularity of the Western film is contained in its unique capability to visualize for us the basic dramatic elements of American experience—the conflicts between good and evil and between man and nature played out in a naturally beautiful but apparently indifferent environment, a dramatic situation that found popularly accepted visual expression in a writer like Zane Grey.

A paradoxical composite of the man of action and daydreamer, Grey was a spiritual brother of Jack London and Ernest Hemingway in his lifelong quest for the adventure to be found in hunting and fishing, but he was uniquely himself in his ability to retreat wholly into the depths of his imagination and literally daydream his fictional world into being. Whereas London and Hemingway can transcribe physical experience for its own sake, almost as though it were a necessary stimulant for the nervous system, Grey appears to undergo a kind of personal conflict between his basic desire to experience life directly and an inner fear that what has made this kind of life possible is rapidly disappearing. Well over fifty Western novels by Grey overwhelmingly attest to both his obsessive nostalgia for and underlying desire to recreate a way of life that is no more. The final passages in *The U.P. Trail,* in which the Sioux chief expresses his feeling about the white man's coming new order, unquestionably represent the voice of Zane Grey:

> The chief was old and wise, taught by sage and star and mountain and wind and the loneliness of the prairie-land. He recognized a superior race, but not a nobler one. White men would glut the treasures of water and earth. The Indian had been born to hunt his meat, to repel his red foes, to watch the clouds and serve his goods. But these white men would come like a great flight of grasshoppers to cover the length and breadth of the prairie-land. The buffalo would roll away, like a dust-cloud, in the distance, and never return. No meat for the Indian—no grass for his mustang—no place for his home. The Sioux must fight till he died or be driven back into waste places where grief and hardship would end him.
>
> Red and dusky, the sun was setting beyond the desert. The old chief swept aloft his arm, and then in his acceptance of the inevitable bitterness he stood in magnificent austerity, somber as death, seeing in this railroad train creeping, fading into the ruddy sunset, a symbol of the destiny of the Indian—vanishing—vanishing—vanishing—[35]

Despite Zane Grey's achievement as a fictional dreamer, the champion daydreamer in all American fiction would undoubtedly have to be Edgar Rice Burroughs, whose fantastically conceived adventures of lost jungle kingdoms and warring civilizations on alien planets and at the center of the earth appear to have influenced and inspired more spinoffs in the various media than the creative output of any other writer. Burroughs' creations were not only successful as fiction (like Zane Grey he is still selling prolifically); they were also successfully and appealingly transcribed into film, comic strips, and radio and television—in short, into all the major media forms of twentieth-century popular culture. For this achievement, Burroughs qualifies, for the purposes of my analysis, as the most representative fiction writer, and his success story in becoming one of the world's most popular writers at a relatively late age has special meaning for my examination of the visual impact of popular fiction on our nostalgic fantasies. In fact, we now realize that Burroughs, more than any other American fiction writer, projected through both his life and his writings a fantasy world that complements both his nostalgic vision and that of his audience.

Despite a series of failures at military career options and business ventures before turning to his writing career, Edgar Rice Burroughs doggedly pursued a life style that personifies the American quest for material success and that simultaneously expresses our need to retreat into the pleasant confines of our private fantasy worlds, regardless of whether we are successful. His most popular character, Tarzan, the natural man with an aristocratic background, epitomizes the Thoreauvian tension in the American makeup, which compels us to function as an integral part of our natural environment

at the same time that we wish to master and subdue it. This pervasive and persistent paradox of American experience found full expression in the life and creative instincts of Edgar Rice Burroughs. Like a character out of a Horatio Alger story himself in his dream and pursuit of material success, Burroughs worked perfunctorily at a variety of jobs, many in the business world, but, unlike an Alger hero, succeeded at none of them.[36] Burroughs said that it was the circumstances of having to provide for a family that goaded him into writing for the pulps, a medium which he felt published inferior stories he could easily outdo. But it now seems reasonable to assume that his real-world failures paradoxically supplied the catalyst for Burroughs to turn to the inner world of imaginative fantasy that had been fermenting within his being for some thirty-five years. In the long run, it was the private daydreams of the nostalgiac that allowed him to realize material success in the tradition of the best-selling novelist. He finally discovered how he could parlay his energies for creating fantasy into the kind of fictional entertainment the public demanded.

In his stimulating survey of the literary achievement of Burroughs, Richard Lupoff notes that "from the very beginning of Burroughs' first work we see a blurring of reality and fantasy, of truth and dream," a revealing comment that not only emphasizes what we have just observed about Burroughs' inner self, but also highlights my basic premise concerning popular fiction as the product of nostalgic fantasizing.[37] The "blurring" effect in Burroughs' fiction results from the conflict between his nostalgic vision and the demands of society or civilization, an antithesis reiterated throughout his writings. In one of his better novels, *Tarzan the Untamed* (1920), for example, Burroughs writes:

> Civilization meant to Tarzan of the Apes a curtailment of freedom in all its aspects—freedom of action, freedom of thought, freedom of love, freedom of hate. Clothes he abhorred—uncomfortable, hideous, confining things that reminded him somehow of bonds securing him to the life he had seen the poor creatures of London and Paris living. Clothes were the emblems of that hypocrisy for which civilization stood—a pretense that the wearers were ashamed of what the clothes covered, of the human form made in the semblance of God. . . .
> In civilization Tarzan had found greed and selfishness and cruelty far beyond that which he

had known in his familiar, savage jungle, and though civilization had given him his mate and several friends whom he loved and admired, he never had come to accept it as you and I who have known little or nothing else; so it was with a sense of relief that he now definitely abandoned it and all that it stood for, and went forth into the jungle once again stripped to his loin cloth and weapons.[38]

Later in the same novel, at a point when Tarzan has just made a kill, we are reminded of the high seriousness of life in the fantasized jungle in contrast to the artificial routine of civilized existence:

> Tarzan then descended from the tree, dispatched those that were not already dead and proceeded to skin the carcasses. As he worked, rapidly and with great skill, he neither hummed nor whistled as does the average man of civilization. It was in numerous little ways such as these that he differed from other men, due, probably, to his early jungle training. The beasts of the jungle that he had been reared among were playful to maturity and seldom thereafter. His fellow-apes, especially the bulls, became fierce and surly as they grew older. Life was a serious matter during lean seasons—one had to fight to secure one's share of food then and the habit once formed became lifelong. Hunting for food was the life labor of the jungle bred, and a life labor is a thing not to be approached with levity nor prosecuted lightly. So all work found Tarzan serious, though he still retained what the other beasts lost as they grew older—a sense of humor, which he gave play to when the mood suited him. It was a grim humor and sometimes ghastly; but it satisfied Tarzan.[39]

In this "blurring of fantasy and reality," there is an underlying irony in that many modern writers have used the imagery of the jungle to satirize life in a so-called civilized society, but throughout the Burroughs canon there lurks a realization of and sensitivity to the direful and devious underside of the "real world," and all it stands for in contrast to a world like Pellucidar in *Tarzan at the Earth's Core* (1929), which is

> . . . a timeless world which must necessarily be free from those pests who are constantly calling our attention to "the busy little bee" and to the fact that "time is money." While time may be "the soul of this world" and the "essence of contracts," in the beatific existence of Pellucidar it is nothing and less than nothing.[40]

Actually, Burroughs is realist enough to recognize

The work of Edgar Rice Burroughs has lent itself naturally to interpretation by the various media forms of our culture. The character of Tarzan is the most popular example, but The Land That Time Forgot, *a novel first published in 1918, has recently appeared as a first-run movie, on television, and as a comic book. It appears that the fantasy content of Burroughs' stories openly invites reinterpretation by our popular culture.*

and comprehend the ugliness, deceit, and falseness of most human relationships, and his stories are filled with characters caught up in dramatic situations that represent these feelings. In *Tarzan of the Apes* (1914), Burroughs dared to create a fictional climate in which a human could have meaningful communications and intimate, positive interrelationships with animals! If there is a message concerning the human condition anywhere in Burroughs, surely it is here.[41]

The major defect of Burroughs' fiction, as it is in most popular writing, is weak characterization, which in itself can be construed as a comment on his basic understanding of man's relationship to man. It is through his unique ability to visualize exotic settings for the telling of an exciting, fast-paced story that Edgar Rice Burroughs wins his readers. So reputable a writer of our day as Gore Vidal has admitted to a respect for the Burroughs canon and for the visual impact of his action-oriented stories by referring to him as "the master of American daydreamers." Vidal recognizes, too, that the daydreaming syndrome may be more pervasive in our society than we realize:

> Until recently I assumed that most people were like myself: daydreaming ceases when the real world becomes interesting and reasonably manageable. Now I am not so certain. Pondering the life and success of Burroughs leads one to believe that a good many people find their lives so unsatisfactory that they go right on year after year telling themselves stories in which they are able to dominate their environment in a way that is not possible in this over-organized society.[42]

In this age of the diminished self, then, daydreaming may be more addictive than we realize for both successful writer and transported reader. It will doubtless continue to be so as long as what is human in all of us persists in searching out an identity that transcends the crassness of the workaday, self-enclosing world around us.

In assessing the critical worth of Edgar Rice Burroughs, we are immediately aware that in dealing with a writer who seems to be not so much concerned with the philosophical problems and larger questions of human existence, we must evaluate his body of work purely on the basis of its popular reception and acceptance. Of American writers who have attained major critical ranking, Edgar Allan Poe best lends himself to comparison with Burroughs in that his work is also inspired by a symbolic

retreat from reality and distinguished by a penchant for creating his own private worlds in poetry and fiction. Israfel, Ulalume, and the House of Usher have their counterparts in the realm of Burroughs' imagination—John Carter's Martian landscape, Pellucidar, the Land that Time Forgot, as well as Tarzan's Africa, a place never actually visited by Burroughs but nevertheless one of his most vividly imagined settings. In Poe there is no such thing as geography that corresponds to actual places, and what there is in Burroughs is utilized to expand the horizons of his fanciful imagination. Both Poe and Burroughs represent that side of the American psyche which cannot compromise with the fact that "time is money."

Of all our fiction writers who visualize a fancifully unique escape from reality, Burroughs best epitomizes the neurotic makeup of the popular writer's nostalgic vision brought on by a conflict between fantasy and reality and his intuitive understanding of the difference between the two. In this sense Burroughs is writing for all of us who have developed nostalgic affinities with our fantasy experiences over the years. In the person who enjoys again a Burroughs book he has read in his youth, we see the nostalgic vision operative in its purest form. The stories of Edgar Rice Burroughs happily allow us to flee the world of "the busy little bee," return

unfettered to the charm and innocence of a lost Eden, and, responding to the needs of our diminished selves, confront and engage in some of our most satisfying adventure fantasies. Like Poe, Burroughs speaks mainly to the fantasy side of our psyches that identifies with both the daydream and the nightmare, and Burroughs' popularity, like Poe's, should transmit itself indefinitely, recruiting even more adherents to the fictional mode of the nostalgic vision.

If the daydream-fantasy in fiction is chiefly responsible for inspiring the nostalgic vision among writers and inciting nostalgic affection among readers who look back on these writers and their work, what is there about recent fictional output of a popular nature that might give us some insight into the place of the nostalgic vision in today's fiction? Writing nearly twenty years ago, novelist Philip Roth informed us

> . . . that the American writer in the middle of the 20th century has his hands full in trying to understand, and then describe, and then make *credible* much of the American reality. It stupifies, it sickens, it infuriates, and finally it it is even a kind of embarrassment to one's own meager imagination.[43]

If such a statement was applicable to the 1960s, what might we say of the 1980s, a time when the gamut of sensational experience appears to have been thoroughly described, even exhausted in some areas? Assuming that there may be limitations on the human imagination, what is left, we ask, that we haven't read about or been exposed to within the province of fiction? Here Roth's comment poses an insightful lead to assessing the present state of the nostalgic vision. If societal circumstance has truly diminished the self in its frustrating quest for personal identity, Roth intimates that it has at the same time given us cause for an all-enveloping fear of what the future may hold due to a common awareness of the tragedies, horrors, and catastrophes that assault us daily through the mass media. These occurrences have become so pronounced that we may

Before Edgar Rice Burroughs, Edgar Allan Poe established a body of fictional fantasy to fire the visual imaginations of artists down through the years. Like Burroughs, Poe's influence has expressed itself in a variety of media forms, particularly the movies. This illustration for "The Black Cat" is by Harry Clarke in an edition of Poe's tales published in the 1920s.

have begun to wonder if the real world does not operate according to a fantasy formula of its own. Accordingly, living in a world that appears to be growing more absurd every day has compelled many writers to retreat from it and take us into the private fantasy worlds of their characters for some semblance of meaning, if such can be realized through alcohol, drugs, sex, occultism, or some other intensely personal indulgence. Since making the remarks just quoted, Roth himself appears to have subscribed to this outlook by producing fictional works like *Portnoy's Complaint* (1969), in which psychoanalysis reveals the masturbatory confessions of a very confused Jewish male trying to make it sexually and socially in contemporary society, and *The Breast* (1972), a short piece in which sexual metaphor is used to express a variety of psychological preoccupations and obsessions.

Today most writers would tend to agree that because contemporary life comes across as something out of our wildest fantasies, using it as a direct source for fictional material can be a considerable boon to helping the daydream process along. Thus, many writers who started out drawing on traditional subject matter have begun to construct narrative forms based on actual happenings. Truman Capote —possessed of a talent that at first seemed destined only to create sophisticated tales about socially eccentric people and their peculiar problems—surprised everyone, including the critics, by producing what he termed a "non-fiction novel," *In Cold Blood* (1966), a brutally frank piece of writing that describes the events surrounding one of the more sensational mass murders of our time, the pursuit and capture of the culprits, and their eventual execution. Similarly, William Styron deglamorized the historical romance by attempting to revisualize the harsh circumstances in the life of a Virginia slave in *The Confessions of Nat Turner* (1970). This book was a forerunner of a work like *Roots* (1976), which, because of its narrative technique of mixing fact and fiction, led author Alex Haley to coin the word "faction" to describe his method. Along these same lines, Gore Vidal in *Burr* (1973) and *1876* (1976) drew directly upon historical fact to create fictional works that probably reveal more about the tenor of these novels' times than actual historical explication does. American fiction began to undergo a kind of revolution in the 1960s in the discovery that reality itself was indeed stranger, and in many cases more fantastic, than fiction. Even writers dependent on the traditional mode and format of the novel—Norman Mailer, James Jones, Bernard Malamud, John Updike, and others too numerous to mention—could locate fascinating material in seamy, scatological, and taboo subject areas like sexual promiscuity, drug addiction, sadistic violence, as well as a variety of assorted perversions and aberrations.

The mood still prevails, although our jaded senses are no longer as likely to be startled or shocked as they used to. While today's brand of fictional narrative exhibits its fascination with the abomination, the writer who seeks the big payoff by incorporating it into his fiction must still be able to react to changes in public mood and discern the appropriate visual approach to produce a work that is both unique and popular. Consequently, the visual approach of much contemporary fiction is emphasized to the extent that a number of authors, with an obvious eye toward eventual sales to either the movies or television, apparently have nothing more to offer than sensationalism itself, and their works are written so that they can be easily transcribed into screen or TV plays. Occasionally, though, the process may work the other way around. It is ironic and yet characteristic of our time that a writer like Irwin Shaw could publish a novel called *Rich Man, Poor Man* (1970) and hardly make a splash with it; then, after the book was dramatized as a highly successful television series, Shaw saw it become a best-seller overnight. Even so, many of our popular novels are not necessarily written with just a reading audience in mind, but rather are designed to appeal to a viewing audience. The ABC network's "Novel for Television" and NBC "Bestseller" series bear out this trend.

Significantly, too, the recent best-selling novels that have been made into films appear to achieve more popularity (or notoriety) as films, surpassing even the tremendous success of their book versions. This situation is primarily a result of the commercial ballyhoo attendant on the books' sensational visual features. *The Exorcist, Jaws, The Omen,* and *Black Sunday* were all books that readily translated to the screen because their fictional origins were visualized or constructed in a filmic sense, rather than in the traditional mode of the novel with its lengthy descriptive narrative allowing for gradual character development over a passage of years. Today, whole novels are written around the passing of a few days or hours, a situation which not only reveals to us the pervasive influence of film and television on the writer but also tells us something about the quality of life itself. To counteract the frustrations that novelists may encounter in dramatizing life's most significant moments, many of them have resorted to visualizing a big event in their characters' otherwise ordinary lives so that they may be brought into sharper focus by a catastrophe, disaster, or horrific ordeal. Again, the fact that numerous contemporary writers depend on the calamitous experience for fictional material can reveal to us a great deal about the daydream habits and increasing appetite for vicarious thrills of present-day reading audiences.

Undoubtedly, the changes in choice of and attitude toward subject matter that marked the literary revolution of the 1960s have brought about a general agreement between writer and reader in the 1980s as to what is visually desirable and satisfying in fiction. This agreement serves to substantiate a basic contention of this chapter—that the writer is a mirror of the popular tastes and moods of his audience and that these tastes and moods may live on in a writer's work to reexpress themselves as nostalgic reminders of another time and another place. Although the writer of popular fiction now enjoys considerable freedom of expression, his success and popularity as a writer is still dependent upon how well he can daydream into being whatever image of life a fickle public may crave to satisfy its fantasy urges. In spite of the visual influence of the mass media, the writer's only limitation in the creative process will continue to be the breadth and depth of his own imagination. As a consequence, all those paperbacks we see on the market will keep coming at us in an endless deluge, the result of the individual writer's effort to produce the ultimate visual experience. Representative of the anxieties, preoccupations, and obsessions of our day, the fiction of sensation will itself evolve into a nostalgic reminder of the present, proving once again that each age looks ahead by looking back and that popular fiction can readily reflect the nature and extent of an era's fantasy involvement.

There are other characteristic examples of this outlook, but the work of a uniquely popular writer, Kurt Vonnegut, can help epitomize here what I have reiterated throughout this chapter about the writer as daydreamer and nostalgiac. That there is something of the nostalgia neurosis affecting the outlook of Vonnegut is attested to by the fact that the body of his work also echoes V. S. Pritchett's comment about American nostalgia, quoted earlier in this chapter. In fact, many of Vonnegut's fantasy situations appear to be predicated on the contrast between what we may have "lost in the past" and the "tragedy of a lost future." In a novel like *Slaughter-House Five* (1969), for example, the interrupted time sequences that cut back and forth between the so-called real world and that of science fiction express this intent by contrasting the worlds of fantasy and reality· to let the reader decide which has more meaning for the human predicament. In the tradition of the writer as a daydreamer who exhibits a distinct distaste for the real world, Vonnegut has fashioned a fictional attitude that condemns the world as absurd and meaningless; thus, according to Vonnegut, the writer's obligation to his reader is to dramatize or visualize the lies or fantasies that have supplanted a true sense of reality. With Kurt Vonnegut, then, the daydreaming compulsion of the fiction writer takes on a unique perspective in that his peculiar vision compels the reader to identify directly with the writer's daydreams to realize meaning through fantasy. While only time will reveal the extent of nostalgic vision that Vonnegut's work will generate, we may safely assume, on the basis of evidence presented in this chapter, that the reader's personal involvement with this kind of fiction will eventually inspire nostalgic affection for it.

Notes

1. Gore Vidal, "Tarzan Revisited," *Esquire* 80 (October 1973), 486.

2. William O. Aydelotte, "The Detective Story as a Historical Source," *The Yale Review* 39 (Autumn 1949), 76–95.

3. V. S. Pritchett, "Cruelty in *The Adventures of Huckleberry Finn*," *New Statesman and Nation* 22 (August 1941), 113.

4. Mark Twain, *The Adventures of Huckleberry Finn* (New York: Grosset & Dunlap, 1918), pp. 163–4.

5. Mark Twain, *Autobiography* (New York: Harper & Brothers, 1924), I: p. 110.

6. Lionel Trilling, *The Liberal Imagination* (Garden City: Doubleday & Co., 1957), p. 42.

7. Sinclair Lewis, *Main Street* (New York: New American Library, 1961), p. 38.

8. Mark Schorer, *Sinclair Lewis: An American Life* (New York: McGraw-Hill, 1961), p. 812. Lewis's peculiarly American faith in "things" explains why in 1940 he wrote the foreword to a history of American manners and morals as illustrated by the Sears, Roebuck catalog. Curiously enough, the book was nostalgically titled *The Good Old Days*.

9. Sinclair Lewis, *op. cit.*, pp. 260–61.

10. F. Scott Fitzgerald, "Winter Dreams" in *Short Story Masterpieces*, eds. Robert Penn Warren and Albert Erskine (New York: Dell, 1954), p. 187.

11. *Ibid.*, pp. 189–90.

12. *Ibid.*, pp. 206–7.

13. Thomas Wolfe, "The Story of a Novel" in *The Thomas Wolfe Reader*, ed. C. Hugh Holman (New York: Charles Scribner's Sons, 1962), p. 25.

14. Arthur Mizener, *Scott Fitzgerald and His World* (London: Thames & Hudson, 1972), p. 109.

15. Thomas Wolfe, *Of Time and the River* in *op. cit.*, pp. 421–22.

16. Wolfe, *op. cit.*, pp. 25–6.

17. Wright Morris, *The Territory Ahead* (New York: Atheneum, 1963), p. 157.

18. Ernest Hemingway, "Big Two-hearted River" in *The Short Stories of Ernest Hemingway* (New York: Charles Scribner's Sons, 1953), p. 227.

19. My *The Sporting Myth and the American Experience* (Lewisburg, Pa.: Bucknell University Press, 1975) demonstrates how both Faulkner and Hemingway relied on their knowledge and understanding of the sporting rituals of hunting and fishing to expand the meaning of their fiction.

20. William Faulkner, "The Bear" from *Go Down, Moses* (New York: Modern Library), 1942, p. 209.

21. On film, Hemingway and Faulkner are rarely convincing. On the other hand, Steinbeck's fiction inspired numerous films that were well received—*Tortilla Flat, Of Mice and Men, The Grapes of Wrath,* and *East of Eden,* to name several. Even his long story, "The Red Pony," has been made into an outstanding television production.

22. John Steinbéck, *The Grapes of Wrath* (New York: Modern Library, 1939), pp. 208–9.

23. Dashiell Hammett, *The Maltese Falcon* in *The Novels of Dashiell Hammett* (New York: Alfred A. Knopf, 1965), pp. 300–1.

24. *Ibid.*, pp. 323–24.

25. In addition to Hammett and Chandler, some other well-known writers who trained by writing for the pulps were Ray Bradbury, Max Brand, Edgar Rice Burroughs, McKinley Kantor, Sinclair Lewis, Luke Short, Philip Wylie, and Erle Stanley Gardner.

26. Respecting this observation, note the emergence of the so-called "Tijuana 8-page bible" as a nostalgic item of collectible interest. In fact, one organization offering reprints of these crudely drawn booklets depicting well-known comic-strip characters of the twenties and thirties performing as sexual athletes, bills itself as Nostalgic Publications. It appears, then, that what may be generally taboo in one era may be acceptable in another because of nostalgic or sociological interest. Incidentally, the pulps themselves were a popular source of advertising for these little booklets as "the kind men like," a fact which in itself tells us something about the repressed sexual attitudes of the time.

27. Tony Goodstone, foreword, *The Pulps*, (New York: Chelsea House, 1970).

28. Frederick C. Painton, "The Devil Must Pay," *ibid.*, pp. 17–23.

29. Robert Leslie Bellem, "Labyrinth of Monsters," Goodstone, *op. cit.*, pp. 151–9.

30. Horatio Alger, Jr., *Silas Snobden's Office Boy* (New York: Popular Library, 1973), pp. 237–38.

31. Gilbert Patten, *Frank Merriwell's "Father"* (Norman, Okla.: University of Oklahoma Press, 1964), p. 14.

32. The current record holder for total copies of Western novels in print is Louis L'Amour, a writer whose name is not too well known except among his legion of fans.

33. Zane Grey, *The U. P. Trail* (New York: Pocket Books, 1968), pp. 311–12.

34. Zane Grey, *The Arizona Clan* (New York: Pocket Books, 1974), p. 18.

35. Grey, *The U. P. Trail*, p. 313.

36. Irwin Porges, in his thoroughly researched biography of Burroughs, has pointed out that Burroughs performed efficiently and commendably in his position with the Sears, Roebuck Company in Chicago. But the fact that he chose to quit of his own accord attests that within his own mind, he still considered himself a failure in a material sense.

37. Richard A. Lupoff, *Edgar Rice Burroughs: Master of Adventure* (New York: Ace Books, 1968), p. 41.

38. Edgar Rice Burroughs, *Tarzan the Untamed* (New York: Grosset & Dunlap, 1920) pp. 11–13.

39. *Ibid.,* pp. 55–56.

40. Edgar Rice Burroughs, *Tarzan at the Earth's Core* (New York: Ace Books, 1929), p. 6.

41. Camille Cazedessus, Jr., one of the more knowledgeable students of Burroughsiana, has written, with some justification, that *Tarzan of the Apes* is the "classic novel of the twentieth century, transcending all ideology, nationality, and geography—truly a story for all mankind. . . ." See "Lords of the Jungle" in Don Thompson and Dick Lupoff's *The Comic-Book Book* (New Rochelle: Arlington House, 1973).

42. Vidal, *op. cit.,* p. 281.

43. Philip Roth, "Writing American Fiction," *Commentary* 31 (March 1961), 223–233.

2

The Nostalgic Vision in Comic-Strip Art

No popular art, whatever the medium, is so pervasive
and persistent in American society as the comics.
—Russell Nye,
The Unembarrassed Muse

It is not by chance that photography, films and comics developed simultaneously, producing billions of
images for consumption by millions of people annually. They are new sources of information breaking
the centuries-old privileged position of written text.
Further, they are a democratizing force.
—David Pascal,
"The Art of the Comic Strip"

Since the beginning of this century, the evolution of
the American comic strip into the familiar form of
visual expression that we know today has paralleled
developments in media technology and fictional
narrative techniques, and, for the purposes of this
book, it is convenient to see the comic strip as a
bridge between popular fiction and film. As the
comic strip evolved, it assimilated storytelling techniques pioneered by popular fiction, such as the
historical novel, the dime novel, and the pulps; by
radio soap opera; and by the character series in
movies, particularly the form known as the serial.
There is, in fact, an interrelationship between the
various forms of fiction, film, and comics that points
to a mutual influence of one medium on the other
during this century. Of the three forms of creative
communication, the movies, because of the vivid
sense of dramatic immediacy they convey, have
been predominant since the 1920s, but the one
thing that all three forms have in common is an
obsession to relate visually to an audience by focusing primarily on character and place, a motive which
accounts in large part for these forms' exceptional
ability to project nostalgic feeling and mood for
those who have experienced them. The crossovers
among popular art forms over the years are ample
testimony to their interdependence in satisfying the
fantasy hungers of the American people: fiction into
comic strips (Edgar Rice Burroughs' *Tarzan,* Philip
Nowlan's *Buck Rogers,* Earl Derr Biggers' *Charlie*

Chan, and Zane Grey's *King of the Royal Mounted,* to name only a few outstanding examples); the transposition of characters from the comics onto the screen, as we shall see in the next section; and the countless works of fiction that have been made into films (and in some cases, film into fiction), not to mention the recent trend in fictional works written directly for television.

The modern comic-strip form which contributed immeasurably to this interdependence had its inception at a time when conditions were most favorable to the proliferation of the medium. The advancement in printing technology around the turn of the century made it possible to duplicate more than just print and black-and-white illustrations; newspapers finally had the capability to reproduce pen-and-ink drawings in color. Even though daily comic strips made their appearance in black and white, the comics and color came to be thought of as inseparable. This attitude came about primarily because the big city newspapers ran Sunday comic sections in color, and for a number of years in this century, particularly after the system of syndicated distribution came into being, these color sections exerted a tremendous influence on the mass eye.

Technological knowhow, though, is only part of the story behind the comic strip's rise to popularity. American competitive zeal must be given a lion's share of the credit for the innovative use of color in newspaper art. The big city dailies, especially those in New York, perennially in cutthroat competition with each other to increase their circulations, devised highly original ways to make use of this new selling point. An important development in both newspaper sales and the reception of the comic strip was the assignment by warring papers of special artists to produce a picturized narrative series that in time came to be recognized by various names, the most popular being the "funnies" or "comics." The artists may have had strange, foreign-sounding names like Outcault, Opper, Swinnerton, or Dirks, but it was soon obvious to satisfied readers that these fellows knew their stuff: they turned out the kind of humor most Americans could appreciate. Actually, the popular acceptance of the newspaper comic strip represented another step toward creating a more passive role on the part of an audience since stories told through pictures made it even easier for an audience conditioned to reading fiction to comprehend a storyteller's viewpoint and method. Consequently, the appeal of following the exploits of a favorite comic-strip character was in-

stantaneous, and even though the comics were originated to help sell newspapers, they developed in time their own reason for being and became as much a part of a newspaper's makeup as the editorial or sports page. Even today, when the individual space allotted comics has been considerably lessened, they still lend any newspaper a certain amount of sales appeal.

For my purpose here, the fact that a particular series title appeared daily and/or on Sunday over a long stretch of time identifies the comics as the most visually inspired of all our media. Because of this attribute, the comics offer a wonderfully subtle mirror of the times that produced them. Indeed, for anyone who wants to comprehend the peculiar feel and sense of a specific time and place earlier in this century, the comics, with their diurnal recording of the whims, foibles, fads, and vicissitudes of everyday living, exist as one of our richest sources for research. Here on these now musty and yellowing pages, many of them a part of newspapers that have long since ceased publishing, are the unique personal expressions, fantasies, and fancies of thousands of our forgotten yesterdays—both verbalized and visualized as the artist himself perceived life's unexpected situations and predicaments. These daily records are vivid testimony to the visual impact and nostalgic influence of the comic strip or the whole area of American popular culture known as comic art. Take, for example, a strip like *Bringing Up Father,* which the late George McManus began as long ago as 1913. It spans nearly seven decades of American manners and morals, and for the millions of readers who have followed the misadventures of Maggie and Jiggs at some time during that long period (the McManus version ended in 1954), there is a common meeting place, a point of recognition that no other medium can provide. Because of this fact and the great number of people who literally grew up with certain comic strips like *Little Orphan Annie, Dick Tracy,* and *Li'l Abner,* a kind of nostalgic recognition or bond has been established, an emotional feeling generated by the comics' visual hold on a reader because of their special way of rendering character and place. Russell Nye describes this emotion as "a common experience through childhood, maturity, and old age, intertwined with memories of sorrow and happiness, courtship, marriage, parenthood, war, and peace."[1] It would be difficult to come up with a more perceptively expressed rationale for the contagion of the nostalgia neurosis in any medium of our popular culture. As

HAPPY HOOLIGAN

As the Friend of the Duke of Chumley He Enters the Best English Society.

Copyrighted, 1914, by the Star Company. Great Britain Rights Reserved.

Many of the early comic strips found humor in the misadventures of a social outcast character like Richard Outcault's The Yellow Kid *or Frederick Opper's* Happy Hooligan. *Like their fictional counterpart, Huckleberry Finn, such characters appear to maintain their sense of self-dignity throughout any experience, as this* Happy Hooligan *page reveals.* COPYRIGHT 1914 BY THE STAR COMPANY.

Other strips exhibited a kind of humor inspired by the social fads of their times and as such exist as a nostalgic mirror of the times that produced them. Freddy the Sheik was undoubtedly a spinoff of the Valentino movie image of the 1920s. COPYRIGHT 1925 BY KING FEATURES SYNDICATE, INC.

cultural image, the visual stimulus of a well-known character in the comics has the unique power to transport us back to special parts of our lives we may have long since forgotten. The fact, too, that we have all been a part of the same readership at one time or another binds us all in a democratizing shock of recognition when we peruse the comics that have achieved a high level of popularity in our society. An interesting irony of comic-strip art, expressed in the *Penguin Book of Comics,* is that even though the comics may be considered as ephemera, they "more honestly represent their time than the work which is deliberately created to last, and which will perhaps be scorned by succeeding generations —like Victorian genre paintings, for example."[2]

The comic strip, then, is among our most reliable sources for characterizing the subtle flavor as well as the popular manners of our century's earlier days, and for the nostalgiac, as well as the social or cultural historian, there is wealth aplenty here. And no longer do we have to ply the dusty files of the newspaper morgue to find out what the popular strips were like. Although it is prohibitively costly for publishers to reproduce the original look of a full-page *Flash Gordon* or *Moon Mullins,* there have been numerous facsimile and reprint editions of representative comics published over the past several years by reputable firms. For example: *The Collected Works of Buck Rogers* (Chelsea House), *Great Comics of the New York Daily News and the Chicago Tribune* (Crown), *The Celebrated Cases of Dick Tracy* (Chelsea House), *Arf! The Life and Hard Times of Little Orphan Annie* (Arlington House), *Krazy Kat* (Madi-

son Square Press), and recently the best of them all, *The Smithsonian Collection of Newspaper Comics* (Abrams). These are just a few of the hardback coffee-table volumes that have appeared in the wake of the recent nostalgia upsurge, not to mention a spate of publications that feature comic-book characters like Superman, Batman, Captain Marvel and Wonder Woman. Thus far the best quality of color reproduction to convey the basic look and feel of the period that depended on the newspaper comic strip for mass entertainment has been produced by Chelsea House in its *The Sunday Funnies: 1896–1950,* a boxed set of "exact replicas of the Sunday comic pages" of those years.[3]

Much of the nostalgic appeal of the comics lies in the fact that, aside from the adventure strips that began to proliferate in the 1930s, they are largely about ordinary people in an identifiable time and place, engaging in their everyday tasks or leisure moments, that are usually interrupted in the last panel by a joke or comic situation perpetrated at the expense of a featured character. Bud Fisher's *Mutt and Jeff,* one of the longest running strips in the history of comics, capitalized on a vaudevillian relationship between its lead characters, but it is one of the best examples of the kind of humor that abounded in comic strips of this vintage. The visual inspiration of the Mutt and Jeff routine is derived from the stand-up comic/straight-man roles popular with vaudeville audiences in the late nineteenth and early twentieth centuries, before movies ever really caught on as a popular force. It is, in fact, the kind of routine that we can still witness in night clubs and on television. The punch lines themselves are derived from the pure slapstick not only of the vaudeville stage, but also of the minstrel shows of an even earlier era, and the routines evolved through the silent film period when, significantly, they took on more visual impact. Just as a Laurel and Hardy team would make their mark in the clas-

The slapstick kings of the early comic strip were Mutt and Jeff, here shown in a typical strip from 1917. The visual influence on this strip and many others was not so much the movies, just then making itself felt as a popular medium of expression, as it was vaudeville, a mode of entertainment that had wide influence on turn-of-the-century popular taste. COPYRIGHT 1917 BY BUD FISHER.

sic film comedies of the 1920s, so Mutt and Jeff established themselves as the comedy kings of the early comic strip, and it is not too difficult to realize why. Theirs is a broad, farcical humor born of earthy, democratizing elements. It was characteristically slapstick and cornball in its eagerness to come across, but it was recognized and appreciated not only by the man in the street, but by the company executive as well, and herein is the key to fathoming the strip's nostalgic appeal. Even though Fisher's drawing style imperceptibly changed over the years, the basic appearance and humor of *Mutt and Jeff* itself never did, and for this reason the strip exists as a timeless island within a sea of change since its first appearance in 1908.[4] Even a cursory look at its brand of innocent humor can still evoke a warm feeling for the visual delight this paragon of comedy teams produced for generations of "funny paper" fans.

Whether depicting a situation in the *Mutt and Jeff* tradition of the gag strip or recounting a story in the fashion of the 1930s adventure strip, the comics, like their fiction and film counterparts, have depended primarily and foremost on the drama or melodrama and comic aspects of human relationships. Exemplars of these dramatic ends range from the masterfully drawn *Prince Valiant* and *Steve Canyon* at one pole to the sketchily expressed, topically inspired strips like *B.C.* and *The Wizard of Id* at the other, but the innate talent of their creators to originate and then visualize the appropriate narrative technique to express character and place is present in not only these, but in any successful comic strip. At bottom, a comic strip's success or failure depends on the artist's ability to utilize technique to enhance his subject matter, a manner of drawing style that can be compared to a writer's voice or attitude toward subject matter.[5] As most twentieth-century fiction writers have developed styles that equate with or symbolically reflect their subject areas, so our cartoonists have originated drawing styles designed to aid the reader in comprehending the totality of a particular strip's dramatic, melodramatic, or comic purpose. In so doing, many of our artists have discovered or invented graphics styles that, because of their impact and influence on both later artists' and the public's interpretation of visual reality, could form the basis for a serious study of the evolution and influence of comic-art techniques in this century. Since the use of color has been an integral part of these techniques, we must not overlook its function in their development, for,

as was pointed out earlier, it was the advent of color that initially attracted the eye of many readers to the sun-splashed pages of the Sunday newspaper comics. In a psychological sense, color has the power to enhance even the most mediocre of entertainment forms, as present-day television programming will bear out.

In the beginning there were strips like *The Katzenjammer Kids* and *Happy Hooligan* with their cinematic use of panel sequences to convey a sense of continuing action in the manner of movies of the silent era. Visually, this was the most revolutionary technical device in the entire comics art field and one that is still being utilized today by cartoonists like Gary Trudeau *(Doonesbury)* when he projects a static scene over a series of panels as the backdrop to foreground action or conversation. Then came George Herriman's ingenious handling of open-ended panel sequences in *Krazy Kat,* which allowed an artist more freedom of movement and expression in the cinematic sense, a breakthrough that contributed to the fluid style of such masters of the adventure strip as Roy Crane *(Wash Tubbs* and *Captain Easy)* and Milton Caniff *(Terry and the Pirates* and *Steve Canyon).* Today the most imaginative exploration of the use of paneling and layout for narrative effect is still going on in the comic book, a protean form forever adapting itself to the demands of the times, and for this reason it is probably the most exemplary comic-art form to express the nostalgic vision.

From this discussion it should be fairly obvious that the technical development of the comic strip owes a great deal to the technique of the movie camera as it evolved over the course of this century, but conversely it may be observed that certain technical aspects of the film are indebted to the art of the comic strip.[6] No less a film director than Federico Fellini has expressed, in the foreword to Jim Steranko's *History of the Comics* (vol. I), that he was greatly influenced by the comics he read in his youth, that at times in his films he seeks "to find the color and verve of 'Flash Gordon' and his world. . . ."[7] His comment is indicative of an intuitive and sympathetic understanding between the film director and the comic-strip artist as to the nature and mission of their respective roles in discovering the visual approach that most enhances character and place. Undoubtedly, the influence of both film director and comic-strip artist on the popular grasp of the grammar of visual language has been tremendous.

THE MAN IN THE BROWN DERBY

By H. T. Webster
Trade Mark, 1929, Reg. U. S. Pat. Of.

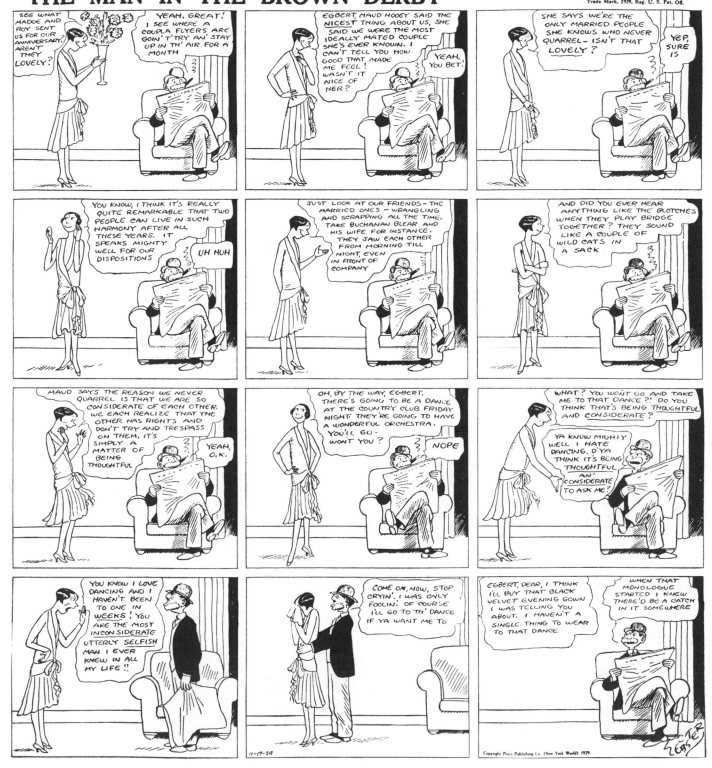

In this sequence from H.T. Webster's The Man in the Brown Derby, *a popular strip of the 1920s, practically all the action is drawn from the same viewpoint, as though a stationary camera has been trained on the scene. The most primitive of film techniques —treating subject matter as though it were on a stage—is an approach still being utilized effectively in strips like* Doonesbury.

Hairbreadth Harry

A Crashing Movie of Freckles and Disturbed Privacy.

By C. W. Kahles
Copyright, 1922, by
The McClure Newspaper Syndicate.

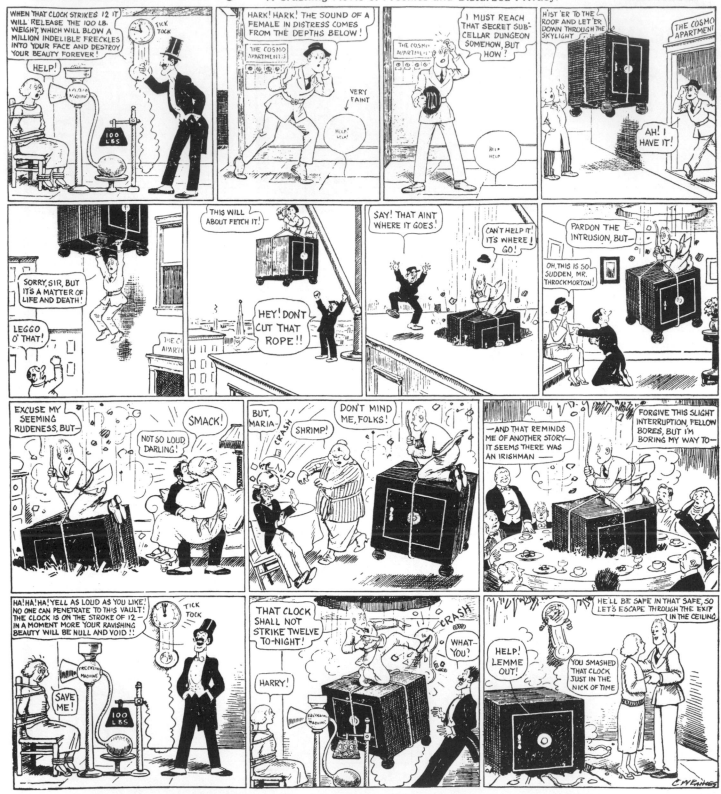

In this Hairbreadth Harry *page of the 1920s, the action is continuous and ongoing, the most cinematic of techniques. Artist C.W. Kahles even admits his debt to the movies in the sub-title at the top of the page.* COPYRIGHT 1923 BY THE MCCLURE SYNDICATE.

As a popular form of entertainment the movies came into their own during the 1920s, and Ed Wheelan's Minute Movies was a strip that revealed this influence both in title and in the technique of carrying on a featured story from day to day in serial fashion. These two samples exemplify Wheelan's manner of handling both classic and contemporary subject matter as the movies do. COPYRIGHT BY THE GEORGE MATTHEWS ADAMS SERVICE, INC.

By the 1930s, the movies' manner of visualizing violent action had been subtly integrated into the adventure strip. This 1938 sequence from Terry and the Pirates provides graphic evidence of Milton Caniff's ability to control and project his story through cinematic movement. Action is the central focus from the first panel to the last. COPYRIGHT 1938 BY THE CHICAGO TRIBUNE—N.Y. NEWS SYNDICATE, INC. REPRINTED BY PERMISSION.

TERRY AND THE PIRATES   - - *Super Cargo* - -   - **By MILTON CANIFF**

TERRY AND THE PIRATES   *Little Brawl on a Pleasure Boat*   - **By MILTON CANIFF**

It is a difficult task to single out the most technically and stylistically influential of the comic-strip artists who have impressed upon us their peculiar vision of the world or "non-world," as the case may be. The number and variety of significant talents in this area over the years have been considerable. We are reminded right off of the surrealistic, yet superbly crafted and colored *Little Nemo in Slumberland* of Winsor McCay; the tableau-like illustrations of Harold Foster's *Prince Valiant;* Burne Hogarth's action-inspired *Tarzan;* Alex Raymond's *Flash Gordon,* whose highly stylized panels echo the magazine illustrator's manner; the razor-honed penmanship of George McManus that lends so much to the period look of *Bringing Up Father* and its panorama of urban backgrounds inhabited by an assortment of eccentric, though recognizably human, characters; Ches-

In 1979, Buck Rogers, *one of the first adventure comic strips, dating back fifty years, was revived in the Glen A. Larson production of* Buck Rogers in the 25th Century. *"Buster" Crabbe had played in an earlier serial version in 1939.*

If the movies influenced the development of the comics, it may also be said that the comics had a degree of influence on the movies, particularly in their selection of popular subject matter. Blondie, Chic Young's appealing comic strip about middle-class family life, was a successful movie series for over ten years. This 1938 ad publicizes the beginning of the series.

Alex Raymond's expertly drawn Flash Gordon *received faithful translation in three serials (1936–40) with Larry "Buster" Crabbe (left) as Flash and Charles Middleton (right) as the Emperor Ming, one of the alltime movie villains.*

ter Gould's austere, two-dimensional interpretation of the Depression-era world of *Dick Tracy,* which emphasizes the violent mood of this strip; the somber, menacing atmosphere of Harold Gray's *Little Orphan Annie,* with its distinctive portrayal of looming, hulking figures who functionally frame the action of the title character; and, of course, the strips in the tradition of George Herriman's strange cat— *Pogo* and *Peanuts*—which in their unique way represent the perfect marriage of style and subject matter in comic art, inspiring a legion of imitators. The list of technical and stylistic triumphs is endless, but the outstanding examples just named serve to remind us that the visual impact of comic art in our century is really immeasurable and that it is the comic strip's

visual signature or sense of style as symbol that feeds our nostalgic hunger to see things the way they were. The *Peanuts* characters, for example, are now recognized by the general public in a way that is comparable to the identification attached to Mickey Mouse and other Disney characters by an earlier generation. The comic-strip world of these characters presents us with a language of visual stimulation that is at once specific, symbolic, and universal, characteristics that in a fantasy and nostalgic sense both enclose and expand the real world.

To single out those comic-strip creations, then, that have had the most impact on our visual sense is admittedly a practically impossible task, but for my purpose, I have broken down what I deem to be the most visually influential comic strips created since 1900 into four categories: pure fantasy,

TWO MASTERS OF SUBSTANCE AND FORM IN THE COMIC STRIP

In the attempt to find an appropriate graphics mode to project fantasy and still comment on the human condition, George Herriman's Krazy Kat was a continuous experiment with language, draftsmanship, and layout. As such, many have thought of it as the crowning achievement of what a comic strip should do visually —the forerunner of strips like Pogo and Peanuts. COPYRIGHT 1942 BY KING FEATURES SYNDICATE, INC. REPRINTED BY PERMISSION.

At the other pole, but with no less a motive than Herriman, was Harold Foster and his realistically portrayed Prince Valiant. Foster's work, which was marked by balance, symmetry, and a meticulous attention to detail, helped contribute an air of respectability to the comic-strip form. Like Herriman, Foster demonstrated what a superior talent could accomplish within the so-called limited confines of the comic-strip medium. COPYRIGHT 1948 BY KING FEATURES SYNDICATE, INC. REPRINTED BY PERMISSION.

Prince Valiant IN THE DAYS OF KING ARTHUR
BY HAROLD R FOSTER

Synopsis: CEDRIC, LAST OF THE MAD TOURIENS, IS DEAD; SLAIN BY HIS OWN DESPERATE SERFS. PRINCE VALIANT LEANS WEARILY UPON HIS SWORD, PANTING, HIS TERRIBLE ORDEAL OVER. THEN HE BECOMES AWARE OF AN EVEN GREATER DANGER! THE FEAR ON THE FACES OF THE SOLDIERS SLOWLY GIVES WAY TO A MORE DANGEROUS MOOD:— FREEDOM! FOR THE FIRST TIME IN THEIR DRAB LIVES THEY ARE FREE OF THEIR HORRIBLE MASTERS!

AND VAL WELL KNOWS THAT FREEDOM IS ONLY FOR THOSE WHO EARN IT; WHEN IT COMES SUDDENLY TO A SLAVE PEOPLE IT IS TOO INTOXICATING AND ENDS IN CHAOS!

"ATTENTION!" HE BARKS. "I HOLD THIS CASTLE IN KING ARTHUR'S NAME! YOU WILL TAKE ORDERS FROM ME UNTIL THE KING APPOINTS AN ADMINISTRATOR. RETURN TO YOUR DUTIES!"

THE SOLDIERS HESITATE. IN THEIR EYES GLOWS THE LUST FOR AN ORGY OF DESTRUCTION. BEFORE THE COMMANDING FIGURE OF THIS RESOLUTE YOUNG KNIGHT THE OLD HABIT OF OBEDIENCE RETURNS. THEY OBEY.

OSK IS RELEASED AND COMES TO HELP VAL CARE FOR HIS WOUNDS.

ALTHOUGH HE HAS FULFILLED A QUEST IN THE SERVICE OF HIS KING, VAL FEELS NO SATISFACTION. DECEIT, BETRAYAL, SHREWDNESS AND FALSEHOOD HAVE BEEN THE WEAPONS HE HAS USED, AND IN THIS GRIMY CASTLE, AMONG THE BRUTALLY DOWNTRODDEN SERFS, HIS HEART IS SICK WITHIN HIM.

NEXT WEEK — *The Dungeons.*

HAL FOSTER

human interest, adventure, and humor.[8] For convenience sake, I shall discuss only one or a few of the most prominent examples of each category and try to broaden our understanding of their influence on our visual understanding, as well as of their contribution to the nostalgic vision in popular culture. The omission of certain popular strips will perhaps be glaringly evident, but surely no one will deny the extent of influence of those selected for discussion.

High atop the prolific output of American comic-strip art and certainly most appropriate for our consideration of this visual art form as pure fantasy is *Little Nemo in Slumberland,* a Sunday page that must have exerted considerable influence on the imagination of anyone who saw it since its beginning in 1905. Winsor McCay, a prime example of the cartoonist as nostalgiac, has himself expressed that he was never so happy as when he was drawing *Nemo,* and obviously the creative act of producing a weekly strip of such imaginative magnitude over a period of years must have provided as much escape for him as it did for his readers. As an obsessive labor of love, *Little Nemo* reflects McCay's neurotic attachment to the dream adventures of his title character throughout the strip's entire body of work, the first period ending in 1911 and the second occurring during a three-year period of the 1920s.[9] Looking back over the *Little Nemo* pages today is like uncovering a lost treasure chest of nostalgic fantasy from a forgotten era. Undoubtedly McCay's technical skill in the use of visual innovations to project his special sense of character and place accounts primarily for our feeling of awe in viewing his work.

First, we observe a theatrical quality throughout the narrative design of *Nemo* that reveals McCay's sensitive ability to coordinate spectacular stage settings. Perhaps the time in his youth he spent turning out publicity posters for a traveling circus had much to do with developing his unique vision of fantasy as a staged spectacular, or perhaps his later period performing as a chalk-talk artist on the vaudeville circuit enhanced his visual fascination for the stage as a focal point for illustrated action. We know that the poster style of the day leaned heavily on the theatrical influence of Art Nouveau technique, and the strip's visualization of Nemo's escapades is apparently derived from this manner of heavily outlined characters portrayed against a baroque background that vividly attests to McCay's uncanny powers of dramatic observation. Regardless of influence, his *Nemo* pages exist as stage settings in themselves and fairly stun the senses with their lavish displays of panoramic scenes that would have done justice to any D.W. Griffith film of the time.

This leads us to a second important visual characteristic of *Little Nemo:* an acute attention to physical detail that, for a comic strip, is simply astounding in its overall visual impact. The detail does not detract from, but actually enhances the fantasy aspects of the page, even more than we could expect. When we observe the pages that depict natural backgrounds or a particular style of architecture, McCay's draftsmanship and alignment of perspective stand out above anything else. Like the fiction writer of nostalgic tendencies, McCay is a stickler for the precise appearance of things, particularly man-made objects and structures. Rather than resort to the impressionistic manner of most fantasists, McCay emphasizes the physical detail of his backgrounds in order to dramatize or contrast graphically the foreground experiences of Nemo and his companions. The total effect of this technique, which rarely ever lags, is to impress a vivid sense of character and place.

Another visual highlight of the art of Winsor McCay, not only in *Little Nemo* but throughout the whole body of his work, is the cinematic movement of action within a designated sequence of frames. This method probably had the greatest influence on later artists of all his techniques because of the way he experimented with different size frames and their organic relationship to each other in a single episode. Because of their movie-camera attention to the development of action, many of the Nemo pages seem to look ahead to the wild chase sequences of 1920s movies, particularly the comedies produced by Hal Roach and Mack Sennett. That McCay was aware of the visual effects to be attained by film is attested by his pioneer work in the animated cartoon field as well as his technical approach in certain sequences of his *Dream of the Rarebit Fiend,* which preceded *Little Nemo* as a popular newspaper comic strip and was later made into a film. Because of the great commercial success of cartoon animators like Walt Disney and Max Fleischer, most people were never aware that there was a precedent set for them, but Winsor McCay was creating animated cartoons as early as 1909, and his Gertie the Dinosaur predated Disney's Mickey Mouse creation by some fifteen years.[10] There are those who feel that the influence of Winsor McCay on the development of film technique has been more considerable than is generally known, and John Fell, in an attempt to set the record straight, devotes an entire chapter ("Mr.

This 1906 sequence from Winsor McCay's brilliant Little Nemo in Slumberland *demonstrates the artist's flair for the theatrical. His main characters perform front-stage center amid a consistently resplendent setting offset by architectural detail and perspective.*

An obvious but interesting example of Winsor McCay's experimentation with cinematic technique is this 1906 rendition of Dream of the Rarebit Fiend, *another of the artist's strips reflecting his obsession with dreams and their effects—this one based on the nightmarish results of eating a welsh rarebit.* COPYRIGHT 1906 BY THE NEW YORK HERALD CO.

Griffith, Meet Winsor McCay") in his *Film and the Narrative Tradition* (1974) to the possible influence of McCay's graphics technique on early movie pioneers like D.W. Griffith.

In contrast to the intent of other comic strips of the time, there seems to be no deliberate attempt in a *Nemo* piece to create a conscious humorous effect, and what little there is comes off in a highly restrained manner. Perhaps the reason for this is that dreams are not funny anyway. The main thing that intrigues and fascinates us about a *Nemo* adventure is its creator's flights of dream-like fantasy, which exist, it seems, as ends in themselves although transcribed in a medium that many have felt to be too narrow and restricted for such uninhibited expression. McCay, at his best, proved that the comic-strip form in the hands of a superior imagination offers unlimited opportunities for the visual expression of character and place. The anticlimactic and inevitable awakening of Nemo in each page's final, almost too abrupt, panel, actually had an essential function in that it served to heighten and sharpen the fantasy experience of Nemo's dream world by exposing the reader to a brief glimpse of the so-called real world —the sudden but often relieved awakening from either an entrancing dream or terrifying nightmare, an experience common to us all at one time or another. In a way, our fondest nostalgic wishes give rise to those dream fantasies that underlie our inmost desires and feelings, but in another sense, the dreams we encounter in our sleep may represent what the future has in store for us—the basic fear of the nostalgiac. Perhaps there are Freudian parallels in the work of McCay that would invite comparison with the theories of the great Viennese pioneer and explorer of the inner world of the dream; Freud's ideas, incidentally, were just becoming widespread during the early popularity of *Little Nemo.* Maurice Horn, a perceptive student of the comic art form, has observed that McCay's delving into dream fantasy in strips like *Rarebit Fiend, Nemo,* and a number of others was an attempt on his part to "exorcize his own demons."[11] If this is true, we should acknowledge that McCay reciprocally exorcized a great many of his readers' demons as well, for McCay's art poses little difficulty in identifying with the basic human conflict which is at the heart of the nostalgia neurosis. While he so lovingly and skillfully created his beautiful fantasy world of dreams, McCay also revealed the dark side of that world with its paradoxes, contradictions, and the fears and doubts embedded in our subconscious. As the comic-strip fantasist who was to have a special influence on later graphics style, Winsor McCay fits comfortably the basic mold of the fiction writer as nostalgiac because of his peculiar attention to the details of character and place. It is highly fitting that a collection of his work in Hyperion Press's Classic American Comic Strip series is symbolically entitled *Winsor McCay's Dream Days,* for surely his dreams were and still are our own.

A fact of American comic art history, perhaps due to the democratizing effect of a mass readership, and one that stands out in stark contrast to the high aesthetic standards of Winsor McCay, is that some of our most popular comic strips were those that were most poorly drawn. Sidney Smith's *The Gumps* is a case in point. Although the art work on many another long-running strip improved as the artists sharpened their styles over the years, Smith's awkward manner never did.[12] He had one important thing going for him, however. He could relate to character and place by telling a story that the public took to heart, and because of this talent, Sidney Smith became our first million-dollar cartoonist, the comic art field's equivalent of a best-selling novelist. When Gus Edson took over the strip on Smith's accidental death in 1935, the fans of *The Gumps* had grown so accustomed and conditioned to the strip's inferior drawing style that Edson had to concentrate at first on capturing its characteristic look and feel so that the reader would be unaware of any interruption in continuity.

The major ingredient in this kind of strip is the story line or sense of continuity, and *The Gumps* is at the very beginning of what might be referred to as the "soap opera" or human interest tradition of comic art, wherein aesthetic standards are sacrificed to the hard fact that life does not adhere to form, but moves day by day in a relentless pattern of the unexpected. What better media form, then, than the comic strip to develop and demonstrate this concept in action? There were a number and variety of strips of the human interest mold, but the one that did a better job of it than any other was *Little Orphan Annie.*

When we compare Harold Gray's draftsmanship with that of other artists of the genre, Gray was poles apart from a comic-strip artist like Winsor McCay, even though we might say his manner was a distinct improvement over that of Sidney Smith.[13] Yet in his own inimitable way, Gray fashioned a dream world out of the absurd world he saw around him—a world that bordered on nightmare and one from which the central character, unlike Nemo, never woke. Both crude and unique, the art of *Little Orphan Annie* has its own atmosphere no less than does the technically brilliant *Little Nemo.* Whereas the world of Little Nemo appears to be perpetually in motion, as befits the chaotic and irrational happenings of a dream, the action of Annie's world exists, it seems, in a state of suspended animation, a product of Gray's instinct for the didactic, captured by periodic lulls in the action so that we might hear one of Annie's commentaries on the significance of her present entanglements and by extension what might be happening, good or bad, to the country in both a political and sociological sense.

Despite Annie's penchant for soliloquizing, a great deal is always happening in this strip, and its story line keeps moving slowly but resolutely toward some climactic moment when Annie's foes once again get their comeuppance. If the drawing technique of Harold Gray projects itself in a stiff, static manner, this is justified in that such an approach is integral to his intent of creating the appropriate atmosphere and mood for the action of his kind of story—the nightmarish aura that envelops us with the helpless feeling of not being able to escape from a fearful predicament, no matter what we do. Time after time, Annie becomes entrapped in situations that would have done in the bravest and most intrepid of souls. Yet, mostly through her own resourcefulness, she manages to extricate herself from difficulty, reflect and wander for a while, only to confront other problems of equal or more ponderous proportions down the road. Such, in a nutshell, was Gray's formula, promulgating his peculiar view of what life is really all about. Thus the special mood he fostered for Annie's picaresque adventures is purposely designed to underscore the vagaries and inconsistencies of a perpetually threatening and imperfect world, which finds its visual focus in Gray's apocalyptic vision of our country's problems as stemming from our growing neglect of traditional values.

In the guise of a conservative, Harold Gray as comic-strip artist epitomizes my definition of the popular artist as nostalgiac. Like many of his literary counterparts, he harbored a fear of what the future portended because of what he felt were the unsettling, disorienting conditions of the present. He asserted through the character of Annie that these conditions were brought on by most people's rejection of the old verities. As a kind of popular novelist of the comic-strip medium, Gray derived his inspiration from the eighteenth-century sentimental novel and the later fiction of Charles Dickens, and for forty-five years, he drew Annie into situations centering on his feelings that the old-fashioned values and virtues were best for the country. The pity was, he felt, that they were slowly but inexorably being ground down by a phony, creeping liberalism.

Even though Gray generally told the same story over and over to hammer home his points, the seven-month Jack Boot story of 1936 stands out as a classic of its kind and can be cited as an example of Harold Gray, storyteller, at his best. After a hard time on the road, Annie is taken in by a kindly shoe repairman named Jack Boot (Gray was never subtle in his choice of names for his characters). A loner who has nothing to do with the rest of the townspeople, Boot supplies room and board while Annie, in her uniquely resourceful way, keeps house, cooks, and attends school. All goes fairly well until Annie discovers the plight of a poor family with whom she has struck up an acquaintance. It seems their farm is about to be foreclosed because a $400 debt on the mortgage is overdue. She mentions their predicament to Boot who, unknown to Annie and the family, withdraws money from his bank ac-

count to pay off the debt. Later Annie finds out who the mysterious benefactor is and is even more convinced of the old man's basic goodness. When a rival shoe-repair shop opens up with all the latest equipment, she assists Boot and the cause of private enterprise in successfully competing with the new shop, despite several devious plots against Boot by the new shop's owner. The story takes a sudden twist when we discover, upon the arrival of two strangers on the scene, that old Boot has a questionable past. One of the newcomers is an independent wanderer named Fred Free, and the other a wealthy socialite, Huntingdon Halk. But Free provides the key to unraveling the mystery of Boot's past, for he recognizes the old shoemaker, who has since changed his name, as the person who had been wrongly convicted of murder over thirty years ago. Halk, the real murderer, has arrived to see that Boot goes back to jail from which he escaped after serving a year of his sentence. But Free, having worked as a boy for the murder victim, uncovers evidence that proves Halk to be the real murderer, and Boot is cleared. Such are the basic ingredients of one of Gray's most complex plots, but throughout his telling of the story, he stresses his favorite theme: individual integrity based on traditional values will overcome adversity and stealth. Ironically, Annie, who has been in and out of the action all along the way, is nowhere around by the tale's happy conclusion. Looking ahead, as he always had to in order to keep reader interest from flagging, Gray had eased her out of the picture to set the stage for another adventure of the human-interest type.[14]

In the thousands upon thousands of drawings produced by Gray from 1923 to 1968, Annie, accompanied by her dog Sandy and occasionally by her father protector, Daddy Warbucks, confronts a seemingly endless round of difficulties that arise primarily from the social problems and political is-

The social and political philosophy of Harold Gray is melodramatically visualized in this 1932 Little Orphan Annie *strip: because individualistic enterprise is the rockbed of the American economy and way of life, then the individual should express himself toward this end, even if it means resorting to violence to effect one's natural rights.* COPYRIGHT 1932 BY THE CHICAGO TRIBUNE–N.Y. NEWS SYNDICATE, INC. REPRINTED BY PERMISSION.

sues of this central period of the twentieth century. As a rule, Annie resolves her own problems, as well as those of the unfortunates with whom she comes in contact, through, what Gray obviously felt to be the greatest of American traits—self-reliance and resourcefulness. The dramatic interest of the *Annie* strip, then, is maintained by the title character's ability to come back at whatever society might throw her way. Some of the most absorbing incidents of the Jack Boot episode, for example, have to do with the conformist attitudes and thinking of the towns-people, and Annie's reaction to these visualized metaphors for mass behavior as Gray understood it. Thus the image of Annie and her dog taking on whatever a decadent society or the enemies of the American way had in store for them is stamped indelibly on the American popular mind, so much so that Annie's significance rises above the projection of character and place and approaches mythical stature. The image of an orphaned child confronting the congregate evil forces of the world obviously appealed to the individualistic nature of the American spirit. The movies had capitalized on this fact of fantasy by creating roles for little girl stars like Mary Pickford and later Shirley Temple, but Harold Gray appears to have first recognized the impact that a negative-type character—a homeless waif—could have on an audience if she were made up of the positive characteristics the American people revered.

Such was the genius of Gray whose portrait of Little Orphan Annie still radiates a strong nostalgic attraction.[15] In addition to her star qualities, Annie happens to be a faithful mirror of the times that produced her adventures. In contrast to Nemo and his fantasy-world experiences, over which he had little control other than to awaken, Annie is motivated by the underlying mood and spirit of her times to do something about her situation, no matter how complicated her plight. Whether in the clutches of the insidious Tong gang, outwitting the wiles of the stereotyped mortgage holder of the many homes in which she lived, fleeing the guns of 1930s gangsters, or even single-handedly taking on the Nazis of World War II, Annie stood out superbly against a background of controlled staging which complemented her being as uniquely and genuinely as Nemo's fantastic environment did his own.

In further contrast to the art of Winsor McCay, the technical achievement of Harold Gray is all the more remarkable for what he set out to do and eventually got done in the space of the conventional square-panel format of the daily strip and the Sunday page. Within this limitation, Gray designed a world of austere blacks and ambiguous greys, highlighted at a critical or meaningful moment by just enough light to limn the significant action of a panel. The dominant black accorded the malevolent figures who seemed always in pursuit of Annie lent them a hulking, menacing appearance that emphasized their formidability while playing up her vulnerability. And despite what appears to be a dearth of physical action in *Annie,* Gray artfully chooses to wait until the time is ripe for the action to create the proper dramatic effect.

Gray was certainly not averse to portraying violence when his story called for it, if only because the conditions of a world that Annie never made allowed for such. The nostalgic vision that one encounters in the work of Harold Gray is rooted in his conservatism, as it is with most purveyors of American popular culture, but Gray's is a defiant attitude that refuses to give in to the hard fact that the times must change as the attitudes of people change. Thus, he was able to justify the use of violence if the fate of an older, more tested and honorable system hung in the balance. His outlook is akin to that of the contemporary "hawk" who would champion the cause of war to preserve, not only the American way of life, but the honor of the system against those who would besmirch it. One naturally wonders how Harold Gray would have portrayed his tough, resilient little girl's reactions to the problems and issues of the sexually oriented and violence-ridden 1980s. No doubt Annie's performance would still echo both the rhetoric of her creator and the melodramatic rendition of character and place.

Is there, after all, a nostalgia of violence, a yearning for visualized physical brutality that can remind us of what now seem to be more meaningful and sensitive times? Among comic strips of the human-interest variety, *Dick Tracy* may qualify as an example of this kind of nostalgia. Spawned by an era of organized crime, *Dick Tracy* is permeated by a violent atmosphere specifically designed to dramatize the quality of the hero's exploits. Remove the violence and what we have left is just another routine police case. Through the creation of stories and villains that seemed right out of the theater of the absurd, Chester Gould involved his heroic detective in cases that were anything but run-of-the-mill. Even though audience reaction to the violence engendered by Tracy's countless confrontations has been tempered over the years by a variety of factors, of which the latest are television police dramas and hard-core movies, there are violent scenes in *Dick Tracy* which still retain their forcefulness, reflecting an interaction of mood and theme in the media forms of comic strip, film, and the "bloody pulps."[16] The result is to evoke memories of what character and place or the times were like that produced these stories of crime and violence. Looking back over the *Tracy* strips of the thirties and forties is a visual experience somewhat comparable to that of viewing an old Warner Brothers gangster movie in which James Cagney, George Raft, or Humphrey Bogart react in defiance of the law as heroes in their own right. In this light, it is probably correct to assume that *Tracy* fans would be more nostalgically moved by recalling certain characters from Gould's gallery of villains—Pruneface, 88 Keyes, Flattop, and Shaky, for example—than Tracy and his law-abiding companions themselves. In this sense, then, there may be a nostalgia of violence—a recognition of some forgotten emotional experience from our distant past through reexperiencing a graphically visualized portrayal of man's inhumanity to man.

Because the unique drawing style of Chester Gould is peculiarly suitable to his subject, it in itself has a unique power to generate a nostalgic attachment to the times which produced it, particularly the period of approximately 1935 to 1945 when Gould's manner seemed to be at its most characteristic. The stark, blunt style of his graphics—almost one dimensional in its total effect—is the visual

equivalent of Dashiell Hammett and the Black Mask school of pulp writers, which reached its zenith during the beginning years of *Dick Tracy*. What Dashiell Hammett and Raymond Chandler were visualizing through words, Chester Gould was projecting in graphics. If the language of crime detection and physical brutality could be effectively and intensely conveyed by tightly constructed, terse prose, then, as Gould's drawings express, certain scenes depicting this kind of action could be visualized more convincingly by rendering a gloom-ridden, mechanically utilitarian world, conceived in great areas of blacks, reds, and yellows—violent colors that complement the strip's central action, tone, and mood.[17] This is the *Tracy* of the 1930s through about the mid-1940s, a daily slice of a somber, existentialist world for an ever-expanding readership conditioned to expect the worst for Tracy in his latest case. After this period, the strip, apparently trying to keep pace with the rapidly changing social and technological climate, seemed to degenerate into a cartoon-like parody of its former self, sacrificing its characteristic pulp-fiction atmosphere for a never-never land of increasingly ridiculous characterizations, fantastic inventions, and even the incongruous feature of space travel. Dick Tracy himself, subject to all the new dress and hair styles of the changing times, seems bewildered by it all, an apparent victim of the nostalgiac's fear of the future.

But the *Tracy* that made the most visual impact was that of the years mentioned above, that period when Chester Gould combined his storytelling talent with his ability to create criminal characters who became urgent topics of daily discussion among the strip's growing legion of fans. Like Harold Gray, Gould could weave moods of suspense that would last for days, a highly effective storytelling technique made popular by the radio serial and soap opera of that day. Who, having followed this strip

THE PERILS OF DICK TRACY—In this strip from the heart period of Dick Tracy, *the violence has taken place off-stage, but artist Chester Gould was not averse to depicting brutality and violence in a myriad of forms. As if to emphasize the single-minded mission of his hero, Gould subjected Tracy and his associates to a veritable chamber-of-horror predicaments over the years.* COPYRIGHT 1936 BY THE CHICAGO TRIBUNE–N.Y. NEWS SYNDICATE, INC. REPRINTED BY PERMISSION.

DICK TRACY—Jim Trailer Comes Back

from day to day, can forget Tracy entrapped by the Blank in a decompression chamber for two weeks in 1937, or Tracy on the trail of the murderous midget Jerome Trohs (he traveled on the back of a St. Bernard) and his monstrous female companion, Mamma, in 1940, or Tracy smoking the Mole out of his underground lair in 1941? These are just a few of the unique story situations that come to mind from the classic *Tracy* period in which the detective and his cohorts—earlier, Pat Patton and later, Sam Catchem—were subjected to an endless round of torture trials masterminded by super criminals with names that matched their nefarious deeds.[18] Many of the characters from this gallery of grotesqúes dominated the strip's action and wove a kind of satanic hold over Gould's reading public. Functioning as a modern morality play, *Dick Tracy* always allowed its villains to hold the upper hand over a period of time for dramatic effect, only to be done in by the law in the end and to point out Gould's moral that a life of crime is futile.

For a comic strip, it all made for exciting, suspenseful drama, a visual fixation that still pursues us in the deluge of crime dramas that television seems to grind out endlessly. But the attitude toward criminal types pervading those Warner Brothers movies of the thirties and forties and the *Dick Tracy* comic strip of the same era has evolved to the point today that the role of the criminal has become increasingly glamorous and attractive, so that our fantasy tastes demand a detective-type molded in the image of a Baretta of the television series of that name. It is a telling fact about today's society that at times it is difficult to discern whose side Baretta is on. Even though Chester Gould as comic-strip artist helped establish the visual image of the police detective as modern society's heroic figure, imitated not only in the comics but in other media as well, the image has graduated into a highly sophisticated but hardly recognizable version of its former self. Our changing visual attitudes toward the law enforcement agent of the Dick Tracy type symbolize our society's ambivalent attitude toward the function of its law enforcement agencies and correctional institutions. As a result, the nostalgia of *Dick Tracy* reveals more about ourselves today than we are perhaps willing to admit.

To single out one comic strip that best typifies the *adventure* category of strips originating in the 1930s (really visualized novels depicting a series of suspenseful stories over a long period of time) would be an extremely difficult task. There were too many

good ones to choose from—*Tarzan, Wash Tubbs, Terry and the Pirates, Flash Gordon,* and *Scorchy Smith,* to name a few standouts; and they were all superbly drawn, too, in marked contrast to the naive, stylized manner of Harold Gray and Chester Gould. An important reason for the improved graphics of the adventure strip is that, by its very nature, it allowed for experimentation of technique in order to incite and hold reader interest. Although both Gray and Gould's work exemplifies how superior storytelling ability can overcome any weakness in draftsmanship, it was the adventure strip that showed to what extent character and place could develop when extraordinary storytelling and drawing abilities were harmoniously wed.

The heyday of the adventure strip, the 1930s, is what Ron Goulart, in his entertaining book on the subject, refers to as the "adventurous decade" and what Maurice Horn has designated as a time of "American dreaming," both appropriate enough phrases which capture the spirit of the times. Certainly the Depression years were responsible for stimulating a variety of fantasy sources among the forms of popular expression, as we have seen in the case of the pulps and "hard-boiled" fiction. But undoubtedly the most popular source of fantasizing for most people was film, and both Goulart and Horn are quick to point out the influence of the movies on the styles and techniques of the adventure-strip artist. Whereas the conventional mode of comic-strip action had been presented in a relatively static manner, the adventure strip was compounded of action in motion, a kind of fluid development best demonstrated by the framing sequence in a strip of film. Another direct movie influence shows up in the adventure-strip artist's intent of functioning in the role of movie director by utilizing techniques that not only focused attention on their characters, but emphasized the concept of motion by merging a sense of place with a fast-paced narrative.

A master of this kind of cinematic drawing style, which was to influence a host of later artists, was Milton Caniff in both his *Terry and the Pirates* and *Steve Canyon.*[19] Conditioned by the impressionistic style of Noel Sickles *(Scorchy Smith)* with whom he had worked in the mid-thirties, Caniff had progressed, by the late thirties, from a cartoon-like manner in *Dickie Dare,* his first big strip, to a graphics technique whose visual effect was predominantly cinematic in its projection. An important point to remember about Caniff's development as a newspa-

Because of its realistic graphics and compelling narrative with a contemporary backdrop, Milton Caniff's Terry and the Pirates *was one of the most technically influential and widely read comic strips of all time. The main cast of characters, many of whom are depicted here, came across to fans as featured players in a continuing drama.* COPYRIGHT BY THE CHICAGO TRIBUNE—N.Y. NEWS SYNDICATE, INC.

per cartoonist is that at one time in his youth he had harbored an ambition to become an actor and that whatever experience he had on the stage could have affected his unique approach to visualizing his characters' adventures. Like the fantasized work of Winsor McCay before him, Caniff's output, although highly realistic by contrast, exhibits his flair for staging the highly charged dramatic moment. Thus, as a powerful force in the comic-art medium for nearly half a century, Milton Caniff continues to impress readers through his ever popular *Steve Canyon,* a visual model of what the comic strip can achieve in the areas of both graphic effect and narrative continuity. But for those who avidly followed it, his *Terry* will be nostalgically remembered not only for its visual impact, but for its contribution to the war effort and its boost to morale during the dark days of World War II. The war that Milton Caniff visualized for us was probably the comic strip's last heroic interpretation of so consequential an event and as such wields a strong nostalgic influence on our imaginations.

But the adventure strip that carries more nostalgic import than any other, I feel, in spite of its technical weaknesses as comic-strip art, is *Buck Rogers in the 25th Century.* This strip was the first of its kind to fantasize or imaginatively consider what it could be like to live in the future—five hundred years in the future, to be precise. My choice of *Buck Rogers* in this category has application to the premise of this book, too; for the strip's inspiration appears to be a natural outgrowth of the psychological condition that I refer to throughout this book as the nostalgia neurosis, an uncertain relationship with traditional values and conventional lifestyles brought on by a fear of what the future might hold in store for us. The feeling or sense of conflict between the pastoral innocence of the past and a future-shock comprehension of what might lie ahead of us is really the basis for the theme which controls the visual development of *Buck Rogers* as a comic strip.

The *Buck Rogers* story line originates its version of character and place with the title character's entrapment in a mine shaft in 1929, the year the strip begins. But instead of dying, Buck falls prey to toxic gases that keep him in a state of suspended animation until he awakens 500 years into the future and finds himself not any older physically, but in a world transformed from the world he once knew. After following the strip's origin story over its first several weeks, we are led to realize that even though the world of the future may be markedly different from the present in terms of modes of travel, scientific advancement, and a variety of gadgetry, the perennial and persistent fears and failures of the human condition still abound. At this point in time, the United States has been overrun by the oriental menace it had always feared; crime and its attendant evils have expanded into an interplanetary operation; and the ingrained interpersonal defects of mankind—greed, envy, pettiness, and prejudicial hatred—unfortunately still run rampant. In effect, the future world that *Buck Rogers* depicts is indeed an unenviable one, and even though the strip is pervaded by the fantasy appeal of other-world escape, co-authors Phil Nowlan and Dick Calkins appear to have tempered their visualization of the future with all the psychological uncertainties and underlying fears that permeated their own times, indeed our own times as well. The fact that the strip anachronistically projects contemporary realities, inventions, and artifacts five hundred years into the future helps reinforce its characteristic attitude—no utopian life lies ahead. Instead, a *Buck Rogers* future serves to underscore the posture that with increased technological advancement and development comes an ever-increasing and complex multiplication of human problems. It is a prophecy that we have all come to know and to live with as a fact of existence in today's fast-moving world.

Not many people are aware of the pulp-magazine origins of *Buck Rogers,* Philip Nowlan's "Armageddon—2419," which appeared in a 1928 *Amazing Stories* and proved to be so popular a story that it demanded visual interpretation. Hence the comic-strip version. The movies were also highly instrumental in contributing to the Buck Rogers mystique with the release in 1939 of the Universal serial starring Buster Crabbe who had already made a name for himself as Flash Gordon.[20] It was the novelty of the *Buck Rogers* concept in its day and time that undoubtedly helped promote and sell it, and many of us who grew up within this comic strip's range of influence can comprehend it as having taught us a whole new way of looking at the world. For kids of my generation in particular, one of the more popular Christmas presents was a Buck Rogers "suit," complete with ray gun and space helmet. Attired in this outfit, you had a first-class ticket to the future as well as a unique fantasy identity, provided, of course, that you were the only one on the block with such an outfit. It was all very satisfying to our fantasy-starved psyches in the late 1930s, a world caught between the waning years of the great Depression and the approach of another world war, the aftermath of which was to be a world forever changed in many ways but especially in regard to the American people's innocent outlook. The highly talented science-fiction writer, Ray Bradbury, who confesses to being a "visual person"

long before Marshall McLuhan's dissection of mass media and their effects on us, attributes part of the reason for his visual awakening to the innocent part of his boyhood which developed a deep affection for *Buck Rogers.* To Bradbury the strip's adventures represented "dreams peeling off the bedroom wall into three dimensions that moved, recreated themselves, and became yet further dreams."[21] Beneath the surface of the innocent dream, however, lay the cold, hard fact, and taken for what it symbolically stands for, *Buck Rogers in the 25th Century* is the comic-strip epitome of the nostalgia neurosis because of its basic premise—the future is abhorrent and at best may be realized as a time when dream could transform itself into nightmare.

Despite the tremendous popularity of the adventure strip, the majority of comic-strip artists, during what came to be recognized as the golden age of comic art, were inspired to produce work in the humor category. This was the case even with many strips which contained a running narrative that bordered on the adventure type, for example, *Barney Google, Popeye,* and *Li'l Abner.* However, few artists in this group achieved the ranks of greatness, in the sense of being both popularly admired for their creations and envied by their peers for their technical achievements. One who did attain superior ranking in both these areas was George McManus, creator of one of the longest running and most popular humor strips of all time, *Bringing Up Father.* But before McManus found himself with his saga of Maggie and Jiggs, he was a tireless experimenter who tried his hand at a variety of strips in an attempt to discover what the public craved in the way of comic-strip entertainment.[22] Like a best-selling novelist, McManus set out to assess the popular tastes of his day and to respond to them. *Bringing Up Father* proved his assessment a valid one, particularly in its handling of character and place.

A painstaking draftsman whose impeccable sense of the fine pen line would keep improving over the years to become his trademark, McManus possessed the technical knowhow and skill to have rivaled the wizardry of Winsor McCay in the realm of pure fantasy, but McManus's intent in drawing was socially and satirically inspired.[23] Greatly influenced by the dress styles and social fads of the passing scene, he seemed theatrically obsessed to stage all these things in an endless comedy of manners that drew its inspiration from the comic tradition in drama of the war between the sexes. In the case of Maggie and Jiggs, the war between the sexes is brought into sharp focus because of the conflict in attitudes among the newly rich that these characters represent. This conflict is probably best symbolized in McManus's manner of drawing women of high fashion who seem to function as fashion models rather than characters while always portraying his males in the traditional cartoon style of the humorous comic strip. This obvious inconsistency in his work reveals McManus's understanding of women as instinctive social creatures and men as naturally democratic in behavior. It also affords us an important clue to understanding the art of George McManus: the serious artist in him appears to be at odds with his cartoonist side, an antithesis which accounts for the uniqueness of his odd drawing style —a kind of baroque sensibility fomented by the strip's persistent contrasting of symmetrical form with the distorted or exaggerated. Because of such a clash, we are witness to visual stimuli that have the power to trigger direct nostalgic identification for those who can relate to his feel for character and place.

The earliest McManus is unadulterated "bigfoot" drawing manner, but with the advent of an increasing social consciousness in the twenties and thirties, the style of *Bringing Up Father* began to take on an art-deco appearance and flavor, specifically with respect to the strip's architectural decor and background arrangements. Because of McManus's sensitivity and attention to physical detail in his work, we are heir to a wealth of visual evidence that reveals to us the way we were. The evolving, yet distinctive, graphics of *Bringing Up Father,* from its beginnings in 1913 to McManus's death in 1954 vividly captures the endless variety of this century's fads, temporal tastes, and social manners, becoming a nostalgiac's delight in harking back to those often overlooked things that have subtly changed us and made us into what we are today. Strips like *Gasoline Alley* and *Blondie* also have this quality, essentially because these strips' creators allowed their characters to react to changing manners and mores by aging and changing along with the times, but we should realize that by the time Frank King and Chic Young had mastered their special techniques, George McManus had preceded them by a number of years in developing effective graphic techniques for recording the daily foibles and follies of family life's minor crises.[24] Maggie and Jiggs are his lasting visual monuments to this achievement.

Actually, there is something archetypal about the Maggie-Jiggs matchup, for in their clash we are witness to a classic conflict embedded in the American consciousness—whether to seek happiness in the acquisition of material wealth, represented by Maggie's insistent social climbing, or to flee social demands and restrictions so as to realize individual freedom and self-fulfillment, symbolized by Jiggs's perennial attempts to seek out his boozing and card-playing companions at Dinty Moore's. Even if Maggie were more personally appealing in her eternal put downs of her apparently shiftless but more personable and well-meaning spouse, we would identify more with his cause than hers for deeper, more psychological reasons. In fact, we have a propensity to side with Jiggs for much the same reason we do with Huckleberry Finn, that prototype of American self-actualization. Thus part of the nostalgic effect that *Bringing Up Father* has on its readers

These two comic-book covers featuring comic-strip reprints of Buck Rogers in the 25th Century *may reflect changes in drawing style from the early '40s (right) to the mid-'50s (below), but the interior stories always projected the same message: the future will bring not only technological advancement but a variety of problems that will jeopardize the human right to individual freedom.* REPRINTED BY PERMISSION OF ROBERT C. DILLE, CARMEL, CA.

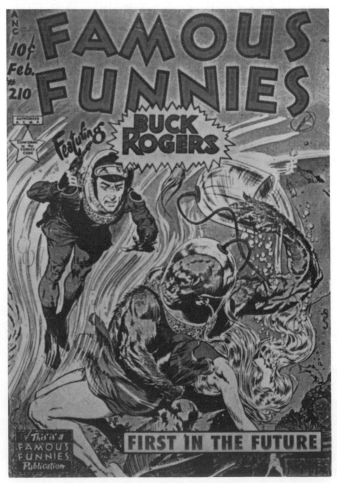

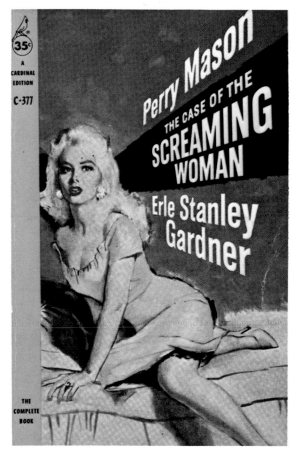

This paperback cover for one of the most popular examples of fictional escapism in recent years is obviously designed for the reader bothered by the feeling of a "diminished self," Gore Vidal's term for the failure of self-actualization in our day. The gothic novel, whose history dates back to the eighteenth century, is particularly suitable for a contemporary readership because of its focus on the melodramatic situation of a helpless protagonist pitted against what appears to be the supernatural forces of an alien environment. The problems encountered by the heroine as she attempts to cope with these forces stand as a metaphor for the fears and uncertainties of modern life and set up a direct identity between this character and the reader.   COPYRIGHT © 1974 BY SANDRA ABBOTT. COVER ART COPYRIGHT © 1974 BY AVON BOOKS. REPRINTED BY PERMISSION OF AVON BOOKS.

Edgar Allan Poe invented the most popular fictional genre of all time in the detective story, a form which contains insights into the daydreaming process. In fact, the image of Poe is a legend in itself, first introduced to us in our schools and later re-encountered in the various forms of our popular culture and their interpretations of the Poe heritage, especially the visual prototype of the detective hero. By the time of the attorney-detective characterization of Erle Stanley Gardner (here, 1960), visual intimations of sex are being utilized to sell the series.

PERRY MASON COVER COPYRIGHT 1960 BY SIMON & SCHUSTER, INC. REPRINTED BY PERMISSION.

The pulp magazine lives on in the reprints of Odyssey Publications, Inc. of Greenwood, Ma. These covers of some of their recent reprint publications reflect the range of interests that these popular magazines catered to during the highpoint of their popularity—the 1930s. REPRINTED BY PERMISSION OF ODYSSEY PUBLICATIONS, INC.

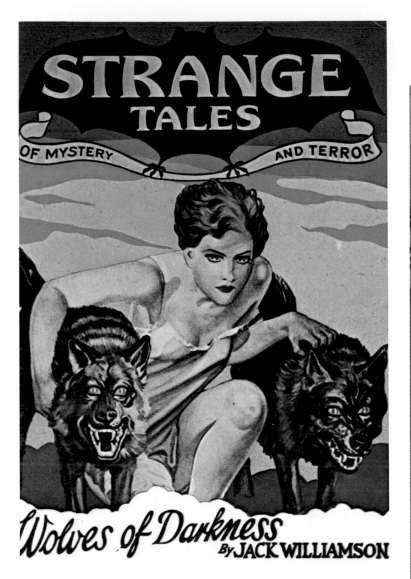

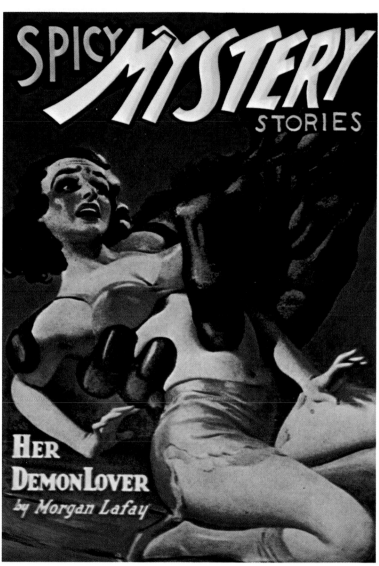

Nostalgically, the comic-book heroes of the 1940s live on in publications like this one whose cover attempts to capture the flavor and spirit of the typical comic book of that day. Note that the lineup of heroes featured here never achieved the long-lived popularity of characters like Superman and Batman, pointing out the intense competition that has always existed in this medium. REPRINTED BY PERMISSION OF SUPERLITH, INC. © 1977.

While women's fashions and architectural backgrounds were the major visual concerns of George McManus over a forty-year period in Bringing Up Father, *his most popular story situations were based on Jiggs's perennial maneuvering to get away from Maggie's societal restrictions and join the boys at Dinty's for a little game. This 1954 page, one of McManus's last, reveals Jiggs as our comic-strip counterpart of Mark Twain's Huck Finn.* COPYRIGHT 1954 BY KING FEATURES SYNDICATE, INC. REPRINTED BY PERMISSION.

trasts the accepted culture of the passing social scene with the traditions and customs of the past, and this contrast establishes *Bringing Up Father* as a leading example of the nostalgia neurosis that haunts our popular culture, expressed in this case through the democratizing medium of the newspaper comic strip.

over the years is the reassurance that one's personal code and dreams can win out over the gross and insensitive world in which we find ourselves. The daily recurrence of this theme in the homes of thousands of families over a forty-year period must have helped the American people, however subtly, to a better understanding of their materialistic goals as they related to their personal ideals. The focus of George McManus's nostalgic vision, as it is dramatized in the Maggie-Jiggs clash, continually con-

Since their inauspicious debut in the 1930s, comic books have been published in the billions of copies for audiences of countless millions. It would be fair to say that most children who have grown up since the comic book's introduction to our popular culture have come under its pervasive spell at one time or another, and not until the arrival of television, with its capability for instant transmission of comic-book inspired material on Saturday mornings and increasingly during prime time, was there a sharp decline in comic book sales. Today the comic book continues to manifest itself, although in different forms from its prototype of the 1930s, almost as though it were searching out the most effective way to satisfy the fantasy wishes of its audience.

Although its influence on the youth of today has been tempered by television, at the height of its popularity in the early 1940s the comic book was a unique visual phenomenon, which expressed itself, in most cases, in one standard format: a magazine of sixty-four pages in color, that primarily celebrated the exploits of superheroic characters. These magazines, moreover, featured action-packed, vividly colored covers that the ten-year-old eye found hard to resist. There were reprints of newspaper comics and the offering of original character types, but it was the superhero who dominated the pages of the early comic book. Although adults read them, many in secret, it was the ten-year-old smuggling his collection of contraband comics past

Want to buy a rare comic book? Then you'd better be prepared to put up some cash. Depending on condition and significance, certain comic books have been valued at even higher prices than the one advertised here recently in The Buyer's Guide for Comic Fandom. *This issue of* Action Comics *contains the first* Superman *story.* COURTESY ALAN LIGHT, PUBLISHER THE BUYER'S GUIDE FOR COMIC FANDOM © 1977.

the watchful eyes of his parents who grew up to exhibit a strong nostalgic affection for these much maligned story books that spoke to the visualized fantasies of childhood and, in a number of cases, adulthood as well. Indeed, many of those now grown ten-year-olds have created an international collectors' cult that, in spite of its decided emphasis on the soaring commercial value of a pop-culture product, reveals at heart an almost neurotic desire to recapture or keep alive the innocent part of their lives that these ephemera represent. Accordingly, the period between 1935 and 1945 has both a strong nostalgic and commercial appeal to the collector, and it is a common occurrence for dealers at comic-art conventions today to demand several thousand dollars for a first edition bought in 1939 for the newsstand price of ten cents. Ironically, the transitory characteristics of the comic book—its cheap construction and fragility—are among the main reasons for its present value on the market.[25] Once read, a comic book's usual fate was to be either tossed out with the trash, burned, or donated to the paper drives of World War II. Parents' and educators' low opinion of comic books, which also helped in thinning out the number of golden age editions available today, served mainly to encourage kids to engage in a kind of underground black market trading system among themselves (two *Spy Smasher*s for one *Captain Marvel* or a combination of funny animal comics for a *Batman* and so on) and to develop business acumen in a way that was not otherwise available to them except through paper routes and yard work.[26] The result is that there are innumerable grown-up "boys and girls" around today who count among their fondest nostalgic memories that part of their young lives devoted to collecting comic books and following the adventures of their favorite comic-book heroes. To these devotees the character-place obsession of the nostalgia neurosis has no greater source than the comic book.

In spite of its pervasive popularity and its unquestionable visual influence on generations of children, the comic book has been slow to be recognized as a sociological force worthy of serious attention and scrutiny. The reason for this is easy enough to understand. The comic book has always been looked upon by most pundits as a kind of bastard child, an inferior offshoot of a much purer form—the newspaper comic strip or even the pulp magazine, which many consider to be its fictional prototype. Coulton Waugh, in his pioneer history of the comic strip in

1940s. Here are excerpts from a 1940 Daredevil story and a 1941 Hangman story. REPRINTED BY PERMISSION OF SUPERLITH, INC., PUBLISHERS OF THE MAGNIFICENT SUPER-HEROES OF COMICS' GOLDEN AGE. © 1977.

America, *The Comics* (1947), somewhat begrudgingly allots a chapter (the last one in the book, by the way) to the novelty of the comic book's popularity, labeling the medium "ugly." A newspaper cartoonist himself, Waugh no doubt found it difficult to praise this upstart form, but the poor graphics displayed in many of the early comic books justify his opinion that most of these books, as products of assembly-line methods, appear to have been drawn by someone with hardly more talent or skill than that of a school child.

In feeding on the fantasies of its audience, the comic book has proven to be a tough, resilient form which has been quick to adapt to every problem it has met over the years. Much of the credit must be given to the imaginative and highly skilled artists the medium has attracted over the years, individuals like Louis Fine, Jack Kirby, Reed Crandall, Jerry Robinson, Alex Toth, Frank Frazetta, and Jim Steranko. These are just a few of the artists who have contributed to the comic book's visibility as a popular art form and whom mature comic book fans tout as among the finest graphic artists of all time, including the classic newspaper cartoonists. In contrast to the conservative policies of the newspaper strip, the freedom of expression that the comic-book medium provided the budding artist contributed to the vast improvement in graphics style evident in comic books since their inception. With cults springing up today around a number of popular comic-book artists and fans collecting both comic books with their work and their original art, the comic book as a sociological fact and visual art form has begun to be acknowledged in recent years.

Since Waugh's book in 1947, a variety of histories and specialized studies have appeared, and from the vantage point of over forty years since its initial appearance, the comic book has become recognized as a highly influential form in the development of our visual history.[27] Like the Alger books, the Frank Merriwell stories, or even the pulps, it would be futile to attempt to measure the extent and true significance of the comic book's visual influence on the generations of youths exposed to it, particularly those who grew up when the form was at the height of its popularity in the 1940s. Nevertheless, Russell Nye reveals the nostalgia neurosis condition inherent in this medium when he says that the comic book "reflected what millions hoped and feared, what they wanted and rejected, and what they thought about things that mattered to them."[28] Such an observation concurs with mine that the comic book is a visual extension of our private fantasies, our dream worlds, affecting us at a most impressionable period in our lives and making a lasting visual impression through its special power to spawn unique characters of the heroic mold and to depict exotic locales that feed our dream fantasies.

Even though the superhero was to evolve into the Spider-Man of today, a type that admits to the psychological doubts and uncertainties of our age, he, like his predecessors, still answers to Nye's assessment. Spider-Man is as much, and probably more, a symptom of the fears of our time as Captain America was of the fears of the war years, the heart of his popularity when we needed positive heroes to combat the many fears—some real, some imaginary—that threatened us from all sides. It was all very comforting to know there were champion crusaders like Captain Marvel, Spy Smasher, Superman, Wonder Woman, as well as Captain America on our side in taking on whatever the Axis powers had to throw our way. Perhaps *Supersnipe,* one of the era's most amusing and satirically revealing comic book series, best visualizes what it was like to grow up under the powerful and pervasive influence of the comic book. Billed as the "Boy with the Most Comic Books in America," Koppy McFad was a ten-year-old obsessed with the image of the costumed superhero, who devised himself a costume of mask, cape, and red flannels to "fight" crime and espionage. Each cover in the series depicted Koppy dreaming of himself as a heavily muscled superhero engaged in some heroic act like capturing Hitler or catching a falling bomb before it exploded. As gentle satire, the whole thing perfectly caught the fixation that a child might have with the comic-book heroes of that day. The model for that ten-year-old—and his face is legion—must have grown up still looking back on occasion and wishing, as the times became more uncertain, for the powers that his idols could so readily draw upon.

To recall the exploits of most popular superheroes as well as those of the proliferation of inferior spinoffs that they inspired is to realize that these mythlike creations actually existed as visual symbols of the innate American attitude that would never admit defeat. Even the Spider-Man of our own day resolutely forges ahead in spite of his inner doubts and concerns that would suggest a defeatist attitude. As we withdraw into the wars of the inner self, our comic-book heroes, as fantasy extensions of our selves, appear to reflect a similar retreat. Thus the comic book persists as both a psychological and sociological expression of the times that produce it, substantiating my interpretation of the medium as

BOSTON UNIVERSITY
Presents as part of the program
"COURSES OF CONTINUING EDUCATION"
The first greater Boston university
course on the comic book

The Comic Book:
An Historical Perspective

Beginning with an analysis of the European roots, the course will follow the influences that resulted in the growth of the comic book in America, continuing up to the present and including cultural ramifications during World War II, Korea, the McCarthy era and Vietnam.

Text materials used will include the Steranko History of Comics, Vols. I and II, Golden-age reprint comics, and extensive use of slides, films and guest speakers.

The course will consist of six two-hour classes during which the following will be discussed:

Classes I and II*- - - A general history of the comic book in America with emphasis on the different publishing houses and their best selling staples. Special emphasis on the Superman mythology.

Class III - - - World War II and the comics. A Study of the sociological impact of the Super-hero comic book; its use as an effective propaganda tool.

Class IV - - - Disney in comics, the Carl Barks story. The history of the Barks duck family.

Class V - - - The McCarthy era's effect on comics; a study of the "horror" trend and the impact of Dr. Frederick Wertham's 'Seduction of the Innocent'.

Class VI - - - The Marvel Age. From 1962 to the present. Fantastic Four, Spiderman, et al.

*Gary Grossman will assist on the Superman Mythology and other guest speakers will assist throughout the course.

Course taught by Don Phelps
**organizer of the Sunday Funnies
and Co-chairman of New England
Comic Arts Convention**

**Classes held Wednesdays 6:30 to 8:30 pm,
May 24 thru July 2.**

Course Registration Fee $60.

This course advertisement inviting formal study of the comic book is proof of its increasing acceptance in recent years as a cultural form worthy of serious scrutiny and analysis. COURTESY OF ALAN LIGHT, PUBLISHER THE BUYER'S GUIDE FOR COMIC FANDOM © 1977.

Today and every day in the comics SPIDER-MAN!

Look for Spider-Man in today's comics, Spider-Man—the most popular comic book character in the world and now a Daily News celebrity. Truly a wonder-working hero. for every man, woman and child.

Don't miss each exciting episode in the intriguing life of the world's most famous web spinner.

Watch him fight the worst criminals around, wrestle with his love life and worry about old Aunt May.

DAILY NEWS
NEW YORK'S PICTURE NEWSPAPER

Today...you really need it!

The superheroes of the comic book are created in response to both the outer and inner concerns of their times. In the 1940s, Captain America's self-declared war against the Axis powers relieved readers' anxieties about the War itself. On the other hand, a satirical character like Supersnipe played on the inner fantasies of comic-book fans who daydreamed of themselves as superheroes. Today the anti-heroic type like Spider-Man reflects the doubts and uncertainties of the individual in contemporary life.

thriving on the nostalgia neurosis of our popular culture. The comic book, because of its obsession with the exploration and dramatization of fantasy, is capable of plumbing the depths of both our psychic wish fulfillments and dreads as no other medium can, with the possible exception of the movies.[29]

If the artwork of the early comic book appears primitive and crude, it is only because the expression of any cultural form in its infancy would be so judged by a more sophisticated age. Regardless, the work of recent talent has more than made up for this earlier deficiency through highly experimental attempts to probe new realms of fantasy, creating other worlds and digging into the inner psyches of unique characters to visualize the psychological and sociological problems of our day. An example of this intent is the boldly experimental work of Jack Katz and James Steranko in what they refer to as the "visual novel," an accomplishment that backs up my contention that today's media forms are in a state of constant flux in seeking out ways to satisfy our fantasy desires. Both Katz and Steranko would be among the first to acknowledge that the fantasy quest has always been foremost in the comic-book artist's mind and that they and their peers owe a tremendous debt to the pioneers of the field. Because there have been so many who have been ascribed some influence of sorts in this highly competitive medium, my discussion here is limited to two artists who, because of their expansive imaginations and superior technical skills, have had a widespread impact on both the development of comic-book graphics and the nostalgia craze: Jack Cole and Will Eisner.[30]

Created by a graphics genius who is in the same company with Winsor McCay as one of the supreme fantasists in comic-art illustrating, *Plastic Man* is at once a symbol of the age that produced him and of the inner urge of the modern individual to transcend the confinement of self. Furthermore, creator Jack Cole, like many of our popular mythmakers, lived a life which exemplifies the psychological split

in our personal makeups responsible for the nostalgia neurosis—the urge to reject the exigencies of the present for the solace of fantasy or the meaningfulness of the past. Cole's boyhood was average enough up to a point: he had a tendency to daydream and become preoccupied in an other-worldly sense, habits he learned to satisfy through his drawing talent. He thus began a lifelong retreat from the world he saw around him, and even after he had become a successful cartoonist, turning out, between 1939 and 1945, some of the better drawn and more imaginative characters of the comic-book medium, he continued to live in the world of his comic-book creations. An important clue to understanding Cole's complex personality is contained in the following excerpt from one of his early *Silver Streak* stories in which he directly addresses the reader:

> Could Silver Streak ever be real? To me he is real! Yes, as real as the ideals you and I dream of. His purpose in life is to help others—to help those in need. Silver Streak does his best to make the world an ideal place to live in—a world in which you and I will have the things we most desire.
>
> And he is out to get those forces that stand in the way of his ideals. He fights hard!! He is strong because he is right—he is fast because he needs speed to conquer his enemies! Silver Streak is my hero and I hope he is your hero too, for he does the things you and I would do if we had his powers![31]

The idealistic roots of Cole the dreamer-fantasist were forever surfacing, sometimes suggesting a darker side to the man but in no way giving us an idea why this talented, congenial person, a forty-three-year-old at the pinnacle of success in his profession, would suddenly and inexplicably commit suicide. Perhaps the mind of Cole, like most creatively humorous types, could not accept his real-life achievements as matching up to what a world of fantasy had to offer. Consequently, his material success served primarily to underscore the imperfections of the human condition. Although we can never be sure of the dark thoughts that drove a man of Jack Cole's talents and accomplishments to turn a gun on himself, we are able to judge the man for the quality and achievement of his work as well as its impact on our visual sensibility.

The creation of Plastic Man in 1941 gave Jack Cole's fantastic imagination ample opportunity to visually express itself. This 1940 cover layout demonstrates Cole's unique ability to transcend the limitations of a form to express an idea. COPYRIGHT 1940 YOUR GUIDE PUBLICATIONS, INC.

Plastic Man is not only one of the most imaginatively drawn creations of comic-book art, but also a character who is a fitting visual symbol of his time. Like Koppy McFad alias Supersnipe and Cole himself, most of us have fantasized what it would be like to possess superhuman powers and how we would use them if we had them. Usually it is the power of invisibility, flight, or superior strength that controls our daydreaming of what it might be like to break out of the shell of our humdrum lives and lead a more romantic existence. In this popular daydream lies the rationale for characters like The Shadow and Superman who really exist as fantasized embodiments of our dream selves. But Jack Cole seems to have turned the tables on the whole superhero tradition with a character like Plastic Man who is designed to function on the level of a dream within a dream. Although we may admire Plastic Man his fantastic ability to stretch, shrink, and reshape himself into any material form he desires, we do not necessarily envy him this unique talent, simply because there is something freakish and unnatural about it.

Actually, everything about Plastic Man as a superhero was markedly different from the type that dominated the comic books of his day. In the first place, Cole introduced his character as having a criminal background. The original Plastic Man story, which appeared in the first issue of *Police Comics* for August 1941, tells how a petty crook named Eel O'Brian who, having been shot during his gang's robbery of a chemical works, is exposed to a powerful acid which he later discovers gives him the power to stretch and change his bodily form at will. Luckily for society, though, O'Brian decides to use his amazing powers to work with the police as Plastic Man. The inevitable sidekick, Woozy Winks, soon joins him, but Cole depicts him as somewhat atypical from the usual partner in that Woozy is also a person of shady background as well as a bumbling clown with a marked propensity for getting into all kinds of trouble. Without Woozy around, in fact, it soon became apparent that Plastic Man would have been hard pressed to locate any criminal activity at all.

Plastic Man was also unlike other superheroes in always wearing his red and yellow body suit with a goggle mask and not worrying about a dual identity in the least. Actually, with his special power to change his appearance when and as he desired, a secret identity or alter ego for Plastic Man would have been ludicrous. Thus a great deal of his popularity and appeal can be attributed to the refreshing, straightforward role that Cole assigned him. The exploits of most superheroes, with the exception of Captain Marvel, were presented with a seriousness that had the unintended effect of exaggerating an already absurd and melodramatic situation.[32] But in visualizing the zany adventures of Plastic Man, Jack Cole appeared to be having as much fun as his readers in attempting to make the most of a topsy-turvy world. The visual surprises and delights in *Plastic Man* are endless. A gangster might sit in an innocent looking chair only to have its arms become those of Plastic Man who encircles him while he writhes helplessly, or Plas, as he was affectionately known, might stretch his legs so that an onrushing car would zoom harmlessly between his ridiculously elongated limbs. Actually, there was no shape or disguise too challenging for Plastic Man to undertake. Sometimes the reader would be a good way through a story before recognizing one of the characters as Plas in disguise.

In Plastic Man, Jack Cole created an appropriate symbol to satirize and poke fun at the absurdities of our materialistic age. Plastic Man's abilities to transform the material world as we know it show us both the limitless challenges to reshaping the world as well as its unpredicability, but all this was done in a way that was visually appealing to the reader. Only an idealist like Cole could have pulled this trick off as skillfully and successfully as he did. The desire to make over or change things as they presently exist is the idealist's way of trying to make the world a better place for us all. Unfortunately, it is only in daydreams and fantasy that the frustrated idealist may hope to realize his ends. Thus through the graphic standards of *Plastic Man,* which, in its day, were way above the usual norm for the comic-book medium, a veritable three-ring circus of visual effects conditioned a generation of children (and adults) to view the world as fantasy in a uniquely materialistic sense. Jack Cole's wonderfully wacky vision of the world helped prepare us to live with the absurdities of an increasingly incomprehensible age. At the same time, his *Plastic Man* was the visual vehicle for expressing the full range of his imaginative powers, creating a unique vision of character and place, which in turn echoes the period's fantasies and the obsessions that inspired them.

Like Jack Cole, Will Eisner, who arrived on the scene as a comic-book illustrator in the mid-thirties, is a graphics specialist of exceptional talent. His career has spanned the development of the comic book in all its manifestations. What's more, Eisner's one major creation, *The Spirit,* has probably influenced more comic book artists with respect to style and technique than any other character. A highly innovative technician in his use of layout and narrative development, Eisner was in the vanguard of those artists who sought to transcend the conventional constraints of the comic-book page by working out new methods for paneling, lettering, and story expression. He contributed, in short, to all the visual elements responsible for expanding the capabilities of the comic-book form and helped give the form an organic unity. His influence can be observed in the controversial E.C. horror comics of the 1950s, the shock-oriented underground "comix" which surfaced in the 1960s, and the visually experimental forms that keep cropping up today.

The work Eisner turned out during the heart of his *Spirit* period clearly shows why his impact has been so great. Always interested in the unified effect of the fictional short story as practiced by masters like Edgar Allan Poe, Eisner experimented with his seven-page *Spirit* stories in translating the short-story form into the ultimate visual mode of expression. In introducing the comic-book format to the Sunday newspaper during the 1940s, he worked with the dedication of a poet in turning out self-contained gems of visualized narrative art in each *Spirit* story. These stories can be shown to function as yet another expression of the nostalgic vision in popular culture in that they reflect a past caught by their creator's exceptional attention to the detail that contributes to the meaningful expression of character and place.

In conception The Spirit character is in the best tradition of pulp heroes like Doc Savage and The Shadow, particularly respecting his unique origin. We are told in the initial story, first published as a newspaper supplement in 1940, that Denny Colt assumed the identity of The Spirit after coming in contact with a strange chemical that put him in a state of suspended animation. (In superhero origin stories, it seems that exposure to a "strange chemical" was a tried and tested method for getting a character off and running.) Declared legally dead, Denny Colt came back as The Spirit, a crime-fighter with a difference: he set up an underground apartment in the cemetery where he was supposedly buried and used it as a base of operations. Also, in contrast to the costumed heroes of the era, The Spirit went about attired in a blue dress suit and tie,

topped by a fedora worn in the manner of the time's fashion. His only attempt at disguise was a blue domino mask with gloves to match. The Spirit was unique, too, in that he was the first heroic character to have a black sidekick, a short, worldly-wise fellow with the ironic name of Ebony White and a forceful personality that markedly contrasted with the stereotyped black characters of that day.

A long line of villains was dreamed up by Eisner, with names that would have given even Dick Tracy pause, but it was the endless bevy of women in his life, both as adversaries and as potential lovers, that gave The Spirit his biggest headaches. This sexually intriguing side of The Spirit qualified him as one of our first "underground" characters with an adult appeal that places him in the James Bond–like mold of recent popular fiction and movie heroes. Eisner was also sensitive to the wide range of tastes of his Sunday audience and added the role of Commissioner Dolan's daughter, Ellen, to lend his feature the certain amount of marriage interest that might attract women readers. This situation afforded Eisner the opportunity to build into his stories some entertaining comic twists and thereby contribute significantly to the remarkably human side of *The Spirit,* certainly one of the reasons for the renewed nostalgic interest in this superb comic-art achievement, which had ceased to be a regular feature by 1952 after appearing for twelve years in the comic-book section of some of this country's leading newspapers.[33]

But it is in the strikingly original execution of a character like The Spirit that we are witness to the visual genius of Will Eisner as a graphics innovator and his peculiar nostalgic vision. Thinking of himself as a "visual writer," a link between fiction and the movies, he relied on many of the cinematic techniques that were popular in the 1930s and 1940s to create certain effects that gave his pages their special look.[34] In translating what would have been pulp-magazine fiction into the visual form of the comic-book page, Eisner expresses the feeling of most graphics people who have grown up in this century by admitting his debt to the movies: "I grew up on the movies, that's what I lived with," he has said. "The movies always influenced me."[35] Thus in his absorption of their visual influence, Eisner was able to evolve a filmlike technique of telling a story that allowed him to compress all the abundant action of his tales—and there was plenty of violent action, even by today's standards—into just seven pages. The result was an exquisitely unified story

Will Eisner is probably the most innovative artist to work in the comic-book medium. His inimitable talent is on display here in three technical areas of concentration from one of the most original of all comic-art creations, The Spirit. COPYRIGHT 1974 BY WILL EISNER. REPRINTED BY PERMISSION.

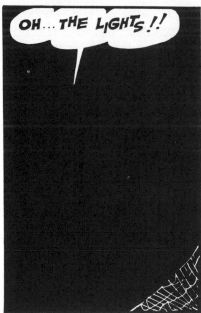

The projection of mood and atmosphere through angle shots, shadows, and even sound effect

The thematic "splash" page, of which no two were ever alike

The expression of violent action in a cinematic manner

effect that fairly leapt off the page at the reader.

He accomplished all this simply by making the most of traditional long shots that dissolved into sudden closeups and shots that were specially angled or foreshortened, all viewpoints permeated with an atmospheric blending of light to emphasize character and environment. Even Eisner's trademark, the originally conceived and masterfully drawn splash pages that set the story's theme were right out of the movies' title and credit lead-ins, but his talent was rich enough to actually keep improving on this method so that many of his title pages are awe-inspiring, particularly those that set the mood for a story of urban background. A New York City boy himself, Eisner was very "place" conscious and seemed to be at his best in pitting The Spirit against whatever the underworld of the city had to offer, and in a story of this stripe, the city's somber, almost overwhelming presence takes on the organic function of a key character, with an integral role in the narrative development.

Within such a function we find the basic nostalgic appeal of Will Eisner's art: in the tradition of the great visually inspired newspaper cartoonists who came before him, Eisner shows an obsessive attention to detail that blends in with and enhances the period atmosphere of his stories. In a nutshell, his work reveals the nostalgiac's preoccupation with familiar objects and scenes visualized as they are or were. Thus the heritage of Eisner's fantasy world is an awareness of his work as a bridge between the visual fiction of the pulp magazine, the comic strip and comic book, and the movies (and, by extension, television). His comic-art masterpiece, *The Spirit,* suggests that the visual revelation of a sense of character and place is interrelated with the development of all areas of popular culture and their nostalgic vision. For further understanding of this interrelationship, we now need to look at the medium which has had the greatest impact on our nostalgic vision in this century—the movies.

Notes

1. Russell Nye, *The Unembarrassed Muse: The Popular Arts in America* (New York: Dial Press, 1970), p. 236.

2. George Perry and Alan Aldridge, *The Penguin Book of Comics* (London: Penguin Press, 1971), p. 16.

3. Note that a leading comics reprint publishing house identifies itself as "Nostalgia Press." Yet there must be something more than nostalgic appeal behind Chelsea House's mammoth *World Encyclopedia of Comics* (1976) and Hyperion Press's Classic American Comic Strip series, which will be published on a continuing basis, the pilot series comprising twenty-two volumes! The Hyperion venture is a commendable one in that its stated mission is to draw attention to a long neglected area of popular American culture.

4. Actually, highly skilled assistants like Billy Liverpool and Al Smith helped perpetuate the public's comprehension of the Mutt and Jeff image over the years.

5. Rube Goldberg is the classic example of the comic-strip artist with mediocre drawing ability who became popularly known through a style or "voice" that beautifully transcribed his wacky inventions satirizing modern technology. In fact, his name is synonymous with the outlandish ideas and highly specialized products of today's world.

6. Some strips even had movie-inspired titles—for example, E.C. Segar's *Thimble Theater Starring Popeye,* Ed Wheelan's *Minute Movies,* and Chester Gould's experimental *Fillum Fables.*

7. James Steranko, *The Steranko History of Comics* (Reading, Pa.: Supergraphics, 1970) I, p. 3.

8. Of course, some comic strips defy categorization and cut across more than one area or even several areas. My plan here is merely schematic for the purpose of demonstrating the visual-nostalgic import of the popular comic strip.

9. *Little Nemo*'s format remained the same over the years, also. Each Sunday's page showed Nemo dreaming another episode in his continuing Slumberland saga only to be abruptly awakened at a critical moment by the last panel of each page.

10. Incidentally, the animated cartoon's relatively short history is filled with examples of media crossovers. Walt Disney, as a pioneer in this field, appears to have been always in the right place at the right time respecting successful crossovers in the media of film, comics, and television. Even though the Disney name has had a tremendous collective impact on popular culture, there were individuals of consummate talent who have deserved credit and recognition but were literally buried in the production system of the Disney corporation—for example, Floyd Gottfredson, who developed the newspaper comic-strip image of Mickey Mouse, and Carl Barks, who should be credited with creating the familiar harassed figure of the Donald Duck comic-book character and its spinoffs.

11. Maurice Horn, "Little Nemo in Slumberland" in *The World Encyclopedia of Comics,* ed. Maurice Horn (New York: Chelsea House, 1976), p. 458.

12. In contrast, observe the work of Cliff Sterrett in *Polly and Her Pals,* whose Sunday pages by the late 1920s had developed into highly whimsical examples of a distinctively modern art style.

13. Coincidentally, Gray worked on Sidney Smith's famous strip as a letterer in the early 1920s, and although Gray's drawing became more polished over the years, we can still observe the influence of Smith's style and manner in his work.

14. For the complete Jack Boot story, see *Arf! The Life and Hard Times of Little Orphan Annie* (New Rochelle: Arlington House, 1970). The story covers the period March 9—September 29, 1936.

15. The popular success of the Broadway musical, *Annie,* attests to the nostalgic durability of Harold Gray's appealing character and her world, promising further exposure in the movies and on television.

16. This situation, of course, offers further evidence of the fact that each medium of popular culture learned a great deal from the other respecting visual inspiration.

17. Compare the bleak manner of the American painter, Edward Hopper, in depicting the city as a place of isolation and deserted streets, symbolic of the human condition in an urban setting.

18. Upon Gould's retirement in the late 1970s, after drawing the strip for over forty-five years, a new artist and story consultant have collaborated to recreate the strip's earlier characterization and atmosphere. For an in-depth feel for the earlier *Dick Tracy,* see *The Celebrated Cases of Dick Tracy* (Chelsea House, 1970) and *Dick Tracy: The Thirties, Tommyguns and Hard Times* (Chelsea House, 1978).

19. *Terry and the Pirates* was continued by George Wunder in 1947 when Caniff began his work on *Steve Canyon.* Wunder himself chose to discontinue *Terry* in the 1970s.

20. The mystique has reasserted itself in 1979 with the release of

Glen A. Larson's production, *Buck Rogers in the 25th Century*, originally scheduled for television but released for nationwide theater showings.

21. Ray Bradbury, introduction to *The Collected Works of Buck Rogers* (New York: Chelsea House, 1969), p. xii.

22. McManus is supposed to have drawn ten different strips and outlined thirty more possibilities before conceiving *Bringing Up Father* in 1913; it eventually became the oldest strip drawn continuously by one man.

23. Only the most knowledgable of comic-art students can recall that in 1905 and 1906 McManus, in one of his experimental moods, was turning out a satirical piece after McCay's *Nemo* called *Nibsy the Newsboy in Funny Fairyland.*

24. King's strip began in 1921 and Young's in 1930.

25. That the market for vintage comic books is sizable is attested by *The Buyer's Guide for Comic Fandom,* a weekly tabloid averaging 100 pages that goes to over 10,000 subscribers from its headquarters in East Moline, Illinois.

26. Many adults who grew up on comic books also credit them with improving their ability to read in spite of educators' incessant attacks on the medium. Others, like psychologist Frederic Wertham **in the 1950s, felt their influence to be morally corrupting. Wertham's** book, *Seduction of the Innocent* (New York: Rinehart and Co., 1954), led to a Congressional investigation of the effects of comic books on youth. Today television has assumed the role of villain in the undermining of educational and moral values.

27. *Action Comics,* in June 1938, was the first comic book to feature Superman, who became the superhero model for a multitude of imitations. This comic book was also the prototype of the familiar comic-book image that most fans came to know.

28. Nye, *op. cit.,* p. 237.

29. Yet the movies have never had to contend with a problem like that faced by the popular horror comics of the 1950s. Feeling that the stories in these comic books went way too far in visualizing readers' psychic dreads, critics sparked a Congressional investigation which resulted in a publishing code and the demise of the horror comics. Observe, however, the content of only a few of today's drive-in movies for a general audience to see to what extent the movies have gone to visualize our so-called psychic dreads.

30. Certainly the Jerry Siegel-Joe Schuster character of Superman could be considered here as among the comic book's most influential mythmaking sources, but so much has been said already about the Superman mystique (and will continue to be said in the wake of the *Superman* movie spectacular) that I feel it more appropriate to my purpose to discuss two other major influential characters created by artists of superb technical skills.

31. Steranko, *op. cit.,* II, p. 88.

32. A case in point occurred when the extremely popular Captain Marvel character created by C. C. Beck brought on a lawsuit by the Superman people, who felt that Captain Marvel was a direct imitation of their character. Comic book fans knew better, however. To them, there was really no basis for comparison between the straight world of Superman and the tongue-in-cheek world of Captain Marvel.

33. In 1974 the Warren Publishing Company brought back *The Spirit* in a magazine of its own, which was to be published on a regular basis. As editor-in-chief, Eisner was to contribute an original story for each issue, and the magazine would also carry reprints of earlier stories.

34. The innovations of Orson Welles appear to have been especially influential. See the section on film.

35. Steranko, *op. cit.,* p. 116.

3

The Nostalgic Vision in Film

What was different about the movies in the 1930s
was not that they were beginning to communicate
myths and dreams—they had done that from the beginning—but that the moviemakers were aware in a
more sophisticated way of their mythmaking powers, responsibilities and opportunities.
                                —Robert Sklar,
                                Movie-Made America

From its beginnings in the silent era but especially during those thrill-filled Saturday mornings
and afternoons at neighborhood theaters all over
America during the 1930s and 1940s, the movie
serial acted out the fantasies and daydreams of millions of adolescents, and adults, too. The serial's
action-packed sense of visual movement, which sacrificed serious characterization and plot development to the basic tastes of the ten-year-old mind,
represents a significant link between the nostalgic
flavor of the comic-character world and that of the
movies. This situation was particularly apparent in
the kind of visual action that characterized the serials produced during the period between 1935 and
1945. It was action that fairly exploded on the
screen and that frequently mirrored the daring exploits of a superheroic character. Appropriately

enough, no less than twenty heroes of the comics
were brought to life in the chapter-plays of this era,
a fact which tells us as much about the fantasy
obsessions of the time as it does about the movies
as a popular form of entertainment. According to
the editors of a recent chronicle of the sound-era
serials, "The importance of comic strips in our lives
(to a youngster of the thirties and forties) can't be
overestimated, and in the serials we actually saw in
action the people we read about in the comics."[1]
The obsession for visual expression of dynamic
movement and the mania for the sensational event,
both needs which were fed by the comics as well as
the motion picture, were more dramatically realized
through the medium of the serial than through any
other film genre. Although the serial is not considered to be among the finer achievements of the film

industry, it does afford us a graphic insight into understanding our fantasy-nostalgia relationship with the movies as well as their mythmaking powers.

Like the creators of other successful forms of popular expression, the writers, producers, and directors who collaborated on a serial seemed to know instinctively what audiences of their time wanted in the way of visual entertainment. Accordingly, it seems, serial fans desired to see their favorite heroes from the comics engaging in a veritable orgy of thrill-a-minute action. Opportunely, the individuals involved in the business of producing serials were capitalizing on the fact that, by and large, fiction, radio, and the comics had already invented appealing characters that an audience readily recognized. All that remained was to project them in a teasingly exciting series of perilous predicaments that sought to outdo preceding episodes in tempo and action, but that wound up dramatizing strained variations on the same "cliffhanger" situation.

To a ten-year-old living in a world devoid of tele-vision, the serial offered not only a means of fantasy identification but a unique weekly escape from the grown-up world of threats and demands. Still, one wonders just how many grown-ups "escaped" from their workaday world through indulging their fantasies in the serial of the Saturday matinee. As an oasis of pure escape in a chaotic world sitting on the edge of disaster, the movie serial of the 1930s and 1940s was probably the most indulgent form of fantasy fulfillment that the popular eye has ever been subjected to. In visually dramatizing a kinetic kind of action that had its hero continually at the point of annihilation, the serial stumbled onto the dramatic key that could sustain fan interest over ten to fifteen episodes. Actually, the feature movie exploits of a

The serial or chapter-play was the purest form of escapism ever produced by the movie industry. These ads for some popular serials during the heyday of the medium tell us that Republic Studios was the most prolific in production and that on occasion a real-life hero like football star Sammy Baugh might crash the lineup of comics-related characters, the most popular single source for serial subject matter.

In this 1936 photograph, billboards of coming movie attractions tell of a fantasy world of escape from the grimy reality of a Depression-era neighborhood, thus symbolizing the purpose of the Hollywood film from its inception. "Billboards and frame houses, Atlanta, Georgia, March, 1936"—photograph by Walker Evans in A Vision Shared. REPRINTED BY PERMISSION OF ST. MARTIN'S PRESS, INC.

contemporary character like James Bond had already been realized, although in a more elementary fashion, by serials like *Tim Tyler's Luck*, *The Phantom*, or *Captain Midnight*. Even though the serials viewed on those long-ago Saturdays, now seem, in a nostalgic sense, to be part of another time, another place, it is my contention that the serial form is still with us, that it keeps finding ways to express itself even in our more sophisticated day. It is our peculiarly American sense of visual experience as dynamic movement culminating in the sensational event which emphasizes character and place and contributes to a unique kind of nostalgic vision in the movies.

One of the most popular and elaborately made serials ever released exemplifies this observation.

Universal's *Flash Gordon* (1936), with its harmonious blend of character, exotic locale, and thematic continuity, represents what many believe to be the only quality serial.[2] Admittedly, much of *Flash Gordon* appears hokey and contrived by present film production standards. Yet a screening today can reveal a brand of nostalgic appeal that tells us a great deal about the kind of escapism people of the 1930s were looking for. Looking back on the great fantasy films in *Cinema of the Fantastic* (1972), Chris Steinbrunner and Burt Goldblatt say of *Flash Gordon* that "It was the sort of epic for which we hungered."[3] Such a statement refers directly to the fantasy hunger and quest for wish fulfillment that pervaded the 1930s. Even so, the troubled times of the Depression, when people looked for vicarious fantasy identification wherever they could find it, have their parallel today in our continuing search for fantasy experience. The earlier sections dealing with pulp and "hard-boiled" fiction and the adventure comic strip reveal the nature of the escapism of the 1930s, but nowhere was this fetish borne out more explicitly than in the masses' love affair with the movies. In *Flash Gordon* the fantasy wishes of the 1930s found focus, visualized in such a manner that they reveal the movies' special response to what I have termed the nostalgia neurosis.

Like the comic-strip version of *Buck Rogers,* the movie version of *Flash Gordon* derives its dramatic intensity from the uncertainty of the times that inspired it. This situation is graphically illustrated at the serial's beginning when Earth is depicted as being on a collision course with another planet. In closely following the origin story of Alex Raymond's comic-strip, the film offers a ray of hope in warding off this impending catastrophe by introducing us to the athletic, handsome heroic type of the 1930s—blonde Flash Gordon who, accompanied by the beautiful Dale Arden, falls in with Dr. Zarkov, an eccentric scientist who has invented a rocket ship with which they hope to fly to the planet Mongo to avert its course and save Earth. But on Mongo they are confronted by Ming the Merciless, ruler of the planet and the personification of evil, or at least what the mind of the time thought evil to be —oriental, sly, scheming, and bent on controlling all civilization, a character modeled after the fiction and movie composite of Fu Manchu and the pulps' Wu Fang.

With the entrance of these four character types, the stage is set for a dramatic buildup through the technique of segmented continuity, and there follows a series of thirteen episodes unified mainly by a sense of dynamic movement. The episodes exist as variations on a single, simple theme—the clash between good and evil, symbolized in the characterizations of Flash, played by Larry "Buster" Crabbe, and Ming, played by Charles Middleton, whose appearance and performance established him as one of the all-time movie villains. With Ming's decision to destroy Earth another time, the elementary plot takes a turn more familiar to audiences of the time: it deals with the problems of an oppressed people under a despotic ruler. Thus the single-minded determination of Flash to free the people of Mongo from their oppressor is melodramatically presented through the variety of perilous predicaments from which Flash must extricate himself. Chapter titles like "The Destroying Ray," "Flaming Torture," "Shattering Doom," and "Fighting the Fire Dragon" suggest the kinds of ordeals our hero is subjected to; yet no matter how cunningly contrived the situation, Flash always manages to escape Ming's elaborate traps and perpetrations.

Flash Gordon *(Universal, 1936), with its emphasis on dynamic movement punctuated by rising and falling action, is one of the best examples of the American film tradition's preoccupation with escapism expressed as pure action. The translation of comic-strip characters to the screen often fell short of the mark in physical appearance, but Buster Crabbe as Flash was about as perfect a casting as there ever was in the serials. Here he is dressed in nineteenth-century Prussian officer's garb about to bail out of a futuristic rocket ship with an airplane parachute! Such anachronisms never seemed to bother fantasy-hungry audiences, however.* PHOTO FROM THE AUTHOR'S COLLECTION.

Although *Flash Gordon* was designed primarily for a youthful audience, there was an adult sexual attractiveness not only in the character pairings, but in the dramatic development of each chapter as well. Each episode's air of dynamic movement featured action rising to a peak, only to subside and begin anew with the next episode, which in turn would culminate in a sensational happening designed to lift the viewer out of the ordinary into the realm of exotic, or if you will, erotic experience. Actually, *Flash Gordon* itself was rife with sexual implications what with the lecherous Ming's persistent pursuit of Dale's favors while Ming's daughter, Princess Aura (played by Priscilla Lawson, who was physically appealing enough to be the subject of one of today's magazine centerfolds) made her feelings toward Flash quite plain. Some forty years later, an X-rated film entitled *Flesh Gordon* made the most of the sexual innuendos that pervaded its classic forerunner.

Whatever the reason for its popularity, *Flash Gordon* was unadulterated escapism at its best, a perfect blend of those essential ingredients that would stimulate a viewer's nostalgic identification for years to come, yet a type of fantasy experience that would redefine itself for each succeeding generation, one of the most recent examples being the much-acclaimed film, *Star Wars* (1977), whose astounding success ensures an abundance of spinoffs and sequels in the tradition of the serial form's sensational climax that entices the viewer back to watch further development. *Flash Gordon* itself inspired two more sequels, *Flash Gordon's Trip to Mars* (1938) and *Flash Gordon Conquers the Universe* (1940), but they were never as popular as the original, which somehow managed to radiate the appeal of both fantasy identification and exotic-erotic experience. Like the nostalgiac turned on by his intimate relationship with a sense of character and place, anyone who has ever had the pleasure of seeing the original *Flash Gordon* in his or her younger days will retain a nostalgic affinity for it throughout life.

The tradition of the movie industry in America reveals an obsession for dramatizing the kind of sensational experience that has the widest audience appeal for its particular time. This obsession is evident throughout the history of film, in an archetypal film like Edwin S. Porter's *The Great Train Robbery* (1903), in the elaborate and grandiose epics of D. W. Griffith and Cecil B. DeMille, and in such recent spectacles as *The Exorcist* and *Jaws,* both successful enough to demand sequels in the tradition of the serial.

As we have seen in our examination of popular fiction and comic-strip art, reigning popular tastes for certain kinds of film can reveal important psychological and sociological information about the period that demands such experiences. Regardless of time, though, all viewers expect what they see on the screen to be charged with a special sense of movement that will involve them as though they were participants in the experience, thus enhancing their susceptibility to the nostalgia neurosis. Films fail or succeed according to how well they fulfill this requirement, and all one has to do to comprehend what I mean by a "special sense of movement" is to compare the American tradition of filmmaking with the more statically visual manner of the European

film or others of international background. Little wonder, then, that it would become customary over the years for Americans to refer to film or cinema as the "movies."

Yet within the tradition in American film of movement for movement's sake, there developed a genre that catered to an audience's hunger not just for pure action and the remote or exotic, but for the familiar and the formulaic. These were the "series" films, whose popularity, like that of the serial, also peaked in the 1930s and 1940s and whose range of visual experience was as diverse as the domestic scene and the jungles of Africa. Even though series were classified in most cases as B movies, they were extremely popular with the masses for the same reason that today's television viewers tune in a favorite program week after week. Seeing a familiar character performing in an expected role is somewhat like greeting a longtime friend, and as James Robert Parish reminds us, "It is reassuring for audiences to have a recurring group of familiar performers going through their paces in well-explored plot routines in expected genres."[4] Here again, a popular creative form has contributed immeasurably to our susceptibility to the nostalgia neurosis.

The source for the series movies, which unlike the serials were complete stories in themselves of approximately one hour's duration, can be found in the one- and two-reel series shorts that were pioneered by Mack Sennett and Hal Roach during the 1920s, but that reached their greatest popularity in the 1930s and 1940s. The series short was usually built around a comedian like Harry Langdon or Harold Lloyd, around team characters like Laurel and Hardy, or even around groups like the appealing kids featured in Our Gang comedies. The substance of the short itself was slapstick comedy in the tradition of Charlie Chaplin, the Keystone Kops, and Buster Keaton. The fabulous "chase" scenes of these comedies, in which the central character, usually an innocent, finds himself recklessly but relentlessly pursued by apparently hundreds of lawmen or other establishment types, stand out as the visual epitome of our peculiar zest for dynamic movement on film.

The series movies, although they might retain elements of the short's feeling for comedy and action, could afford to be more expansive and inventive with respect to plot and character development. That these movies were often built around characters already familiar from fiction, radio, or the comics not only helped script writers in their characterization and plot development, but it also

D.W. Griffith had an intuitive sense of what audiences wanted to see in a movie, and in Intolerance *(1916) he staged what is probably the most visually-oriented mass scene in film history in the Babylonian episode. Overwhelming, yet captivating viewers through its immensity and sweep, this kind of scene not only spoke to the American sense of action as dynamic mass movement, it established the visual prototype for movie epics to follow.*
CULVER PICTURES

conditioned audiences to know what to expect from series like Blondie, Mr. Moto, or Jungle Jim.

Of the multitude of series films produced, some, of course, stood out both in perennial popularity and quality of production, the latter trait somewhat rare in these assembly-line productions. One fine example was MGM's Andy Hardy series, which focused on a type of close-knit family relationship that appears to have vanished from contemporary society, and is therefore a situation that greatly enhances the nostalgic attractiveness of these films. Judge Hardy (Lewis Stone) attended to the "psychiactric" needs of son Andy (Mickey Rooney) in a

most unique manner by today's standards of parental behavior, and in most films in this series, their interrelationship culminated in an obligatory scene of communicative understanding. Although the gruff Lionel Barrymore as Dr. Gillespie in MGM's Dr. Kildare series appeared to dominate the action, there were other interesting characters in this other quality series which was really the prototype of today's hospital fare on television. A high level of production standards also marked the Warner Brothers' films in which juvenile delinquency was considered a social problem and in which this problem was dramatized through the experiences of the Dead End Kids in movies like *Angels with Dirty Faces* (1938). This film looked ahead to the social-conscious films of the 1960s while also generating the nostalgic aura of the period that inspired them.[5]

The various Western series outproduced all others in sheer number if nothing else, but the Hopalong Cassidy films, despite their competition from

Cecil B. DeMille may have followed suit, but his inclination was toward satisfying the inner, hidden feelings of an audience, as the sexually oriented scenes of his Biblical epics appear to do. Erotic expression pervades the films of DeMille (here, The Sign of the Cross—Paramount, 1932) almost as though he has recognized the dark and repressed Puritanical side of the American psyche.
CULVER PICTURES

Gene Autry and Roy Rogers, two of the most popular Western stars of their day, were far superior to their many competitors simply because of the inventiveness of their plots and their sense of meaningful action in a field in which action was, in many cases, its own excuse for being.[6] Much of the credit for the success of the Cassidy series should go to the casting of William Boyd in the title role as a convincing portrayal of the strong, self-assured cowboy that most Western fans admired. His manner allowed for no romancing and singing roles; rather he was deadly serious, yet personable in the business of tracking down cattle rustlers and other range crooks. The acid test of Boyd's effectiveness as an actor is that in the sixty-six films in this series, it is difficult to imagine anyone else performing in the title role other than Boyd himself.

By the same token, who could have played Sherlock Holmes more expertly than Basil Rathbone? The same question might be posed about Warner

Oland as Charlie Chan, who had both predecessors and successors in the role of the Oriental detective, but who somehow seemed to best project our visual conception of such a role. The detective film probably tested the ability of an actor to portray a typecast role like Ellery Queen or Philo Vance more demandingly than any other assignment in movie series, and as a consequence only a few stand out as having presented a convincing visual image of such a role: for example, Warner Baxter in the Crime Doctor series, Tom Conway as the Falcon, and William Powell as the Thin Man.

Visualized conceptions of famous characters on the screen rarely ever measured up to their fictional

THE SERIES MOVIE: FAMILIAR IMAGES FOR MOVIEGOERS

Some of the more popular series films reveal that their appeal is derived from their ability to project familiar characters in expected situations: For example, Andy Hardy's family and courtship problems, the Dead End Kids' anti-establishment attitudes, and Sherlock Holmes's intuitive reasoning to resolve crime cases. PHOTOS FROM AUTHOR'S COLLECTION.

Whether together in a musical or in the Andy Hardy series, the appearance of Judy Garland and Mickey Rooney conditioned audiences to expect that the boy-girl relationship would be at the heart of the plot.

Angels with Dirty Faces *(Warner Bros., 1938) set the stage for the exploration of ghetto-delinquency problems through the characterizations of the Dead End Kids, here seen with James Cagney.*

Moviegoers of the 1940s knew there was only one Hopalong Cassidy and his real name was William Boyd, a solid, self-assured actor who played this role in over sixty films.

SWORN...
TO BRING BACK TARZAN'S BODY
For Her Fiendish Jungle Rituals!

Edgar Rice Burroughs'
TARZAN
AND THE
Leopard Woman

SEE beast-clawed leopard men prey on fellow-humans!

MEET their beautiful high priestess, pledged to kill!

THRILL to weird pagan rites of horror!

SHUDDER as lovely maidens are trapped by fierce savages!

BEAUTY VEILS HER LUST FOR HUMAN BLOOD!

R K O RADIO PICTURES

STARRING
JOHNNY **WEISSMULLER**
BRENDA **JOYCE** • JOHNNY **SHEFFIELD**
WITH **ACQUANETTA** • Produced by **SOL LESSER** • Associate Producer and Director **KURT NEUMANN**
Original Story and Screen Play by CARROLL YOUNG Based Upon the Characters Created by EDGAR RICE BURROUGHS

The most popular movie Tarzan was Johnny Weissmuller who was a far cry from the original Edgar Rice Burroughs character, but audiences had their own visual expectations of Tarzan and turned out for these films in droves.

The roles of Sherlock Holmes and Dr. Watson have never been better cast in a visual sense than by Basil Rathbone and Nigel Bruce respectively.

or comic-strip counterparts, but naive audiences of the thirties and forties rarely ever challenged the visual conception that was presented them. The overall result, other than to reveal the powerful influence of the movies on popular taste, was that most series fans really did not care if characters like Tarzan failed to meet the descriptive standards set up by the Edgar Rice Burroughs' novels and the syndicated comic strip, so masterfully drawn by an artist like Harold Foster and, later, Burne Hogarth. The movies, after all, were providing fantasy entertainment for the viewer, and if the image of Johnny Weissmuller, from the dozen or so who played the role, was visually compelling enough that most people who saw the series were to always imagine Tarzan as the barrel-chested, world-class swimmer that Weissmuller was, then what we have is further evidence of the movies' capacity to satisfy the fantasy wishes of the mass mind.

In this relationship of the viewer with the film medium lies a central fact of the nostalgia neurosis that controls and directs the individual's attitudes toward what he expects and actually gets from his fantasized images of life. In fact, the Tarzan series, as produced by Metro-Goldwyn-Mayer during the heyday of its popularity from the late thirties on into the forties, will serve well to exemplify what I mean. Generally, as we have seen in the case of the serial, the collaborative efforts of the movie people demonstrated vividly enough what it was that audiences of popular movies were after—escape—but, in many cases, the kind of escape that one could readily identify with, and the most successful series films seemed to abide by this formula. The exotic settings of a Hollywood-made Africa are the very stuff of escape all right, but the fact that most Tarzan movies of this period depict the title hero as a devoted family man kept this pleasing blend of fantasy and reality on such a level of audience identification that attendance at movies like *Tarzan Finds a Son* (1939), *Tarzan's Secret Treasure* (1941), and *Tarzan's Desert Mystery* (1943) were often a family affair. In fact, the Tarzan movies were so eagerly anticipated by family moviegoers of this time that I can recall seeing whole families I never saw together any other time sitting in the audience of our neighborhood theater on a Friday or Saturday night awaiting a showing of the latest Tarzan picture.

We didn't realize it at the time, of course, but this kind of experience represents one of the first examples of popular entertainment that would evolve into the shared experience of television. Yet in viewing the Tarzan movies again as television reruns, most of us find it difficult to recapture our nostalgic feeling for them simply because of the impossibility of recreating the audience conditions under which the films were initially viewed. In seeing a favorite old movie once again, then, it becomes evident that what we really yearn for is not so much the unfolding of the movie's story as it is the times that produced it, a situation which accounts for our realization that most movies, when viewed later in life, never are as good as they once seemed. Obviously, the escape flavor of a movie is generated by the times that inspired it, and an appreciation for this feeling is about as close as we can ever come to recapturing a movie's background period in a nostalgic sense.

Series that promoted a similar reaction were the classic horror films of the thirties and forties, which on viewing today do not seem so terrifying after all, but rather comic or pathetic, sometimes even silly, especially after the producers came up with their seemingly endless spinoffs which served to transform originally interesting characters like Dracula, Frankenstein, the Wolf Man, and the Mummy into film clichés. Again, what nostalgic flavor is generated by these movies is due primarily to the period attitudes which produced them and to the fact that what may have frightened us one time is now nostalgic because it reminds us of earlier, more innocent times. Audiences were in agreement that, surely, there could hardly be a more hair-raising sight than Frankenstein's first stirrings of life in the initial film of the series, or Bela Lugosi's Dracula arising from his coffin. But somehow the impact of these scenes has been tempered over the years by time's passage as well as by different audience expectations as to what a horror movie should do.

Although a film like *Frankenstein* (1931) inspired a visual influence that is still being felt in contemporary movies of the horror genre, its classic ingredients of mad scientist, evil henchman, gothic castle, and man-made monster have been modified over the years to satisfy the growing obsession with sex and violence. As pointed out in the fiction section dealing with the pulp magazines, sex and violence have always been identified with popular entertainment of the horror stripe. Perhaps this situation developed simply because it is the one mode of popular entertainment in which the conventional trappings easily allow for such goings-on, and the stereotyped image of the monster and the girl or the vampire and his victim is really the outgrowth of our subliminal desire to behold the abominable act, whether sexual or violent or both. Today it is the tradition of the vampire film that functions best in visualizing ambiguous physical relationships which approach the sensitive area of pornography, and the films in which Vincent Price portrays a psychotic mind reflect the limits that can be realized in combining all the horror trappings with liberal doses of sex and violence. Such films frequently use Edgar Allan Poe's name in an authorial sense when he actually had little or nothing to do with the film's story, and this custom attests once again to the powerful image the Poe name wields for the popular creative forms that attempt to fantasize the horrific experience. That part of the nostalgia neurosis which springs from our fear of the future or the unknown also finds visual expression in the large number of science-fiction films that seem to derive their inspiration from the cataclysmic potential of the atomic bomb which was so dramatically unleashed on the world in the mid-forties. Ironically enough, films like *The Thing* (1951), *Them* (1953), and *Creature from the Black Lagoon* (1954) have stimulated a nostalgic following all their own whenever they show up today in television time slots allotted to vintage movies, a phenomenon that we will examine in the final section of this book.

The topical and period flavor that we find in the classic one- and two-reel shorts of the thirties and forties—those films that featured Laurel and Hardy, the Our Gang troupe, Edgar Kennedy, and Leon Errol and which are comparable to the comic-strip medium in their ability to capture visually the popular tastes of their times—can also be perceived throughout the mob gangster and social-issue film canon, particularly in the Warner Brothers films of the period. Although actors like Paul Muni and John Garfield were to turn in highly creditable perfor-

SEX IN THE HORROR FILM

When monster met maiden, the screen fairly crackled with sexual implications. In fact, the genre always invited such situations, and fans have reveled in them ever since the Lon Chaney films of the silent era like The Phantom of the Opera *(1925). Today the tradition is carried on by movies of vampirism and the occult much more graphically than these scenes from classic horror films convey.*

The menacing presence of Bela Lugosi in prototypal films like Dracula *(Universal, 1930) hinted at dishonorable and devious plans for any woman who happened to be around. The woman in this case is Helen Chandler.* PHOTO FROM THE AUTHOR'S COLLECTION.

Lon Chaney, Jr. in the title role of The Wolf Man *(Universal, 1941) lusted after Evelyn Ankers but never quite succeeded in winning her cooperation.* PHOTO FROM THE AUTHOR'S COLLECTION.

In The Bride of Frankenstein *(Universal, 1935) the idea was to create a mate (Elsa Lanchester) for the lonely monster (Boris Karloff), but as it turned out she would have none of him and the match was off.* PHOTO FROM THE AUTHOR'S COLLECTION.

Horror movie producers seem to believe that one of the best ways to sell their movies is to credit Edgar Allan Poe, since a sensation-seeking public has been conditioned to equate Poe's name with the horrific experience. Undoubtedly Poe's body of work has had a tremendous influence on the development of the horror genre in all media, but about the closest the movie version of The Haunted Palace comes to being a Poe tale, is the title's allusion to one of Poe's poems by the same name.

A TRILOGY OF SHOCK AND HORROR...A NEW CONCEPT IN MOTION PICTURES!

AMERICAN INTERNATIONAL presents
EDGAR ALLAN POE'S

TALES OF TERROR

in PANAVISION and COLOR

"...and there was an oozing liquid putrescence ...all that remained of Mr. Valdemar." --POE

"I had walled the black monster up within the tomb!" --POE

"The winds of the firmament breathed but one sound within my ears and the ripples upon the sea murmured evermore...MORELLA" --POE

STARRING
VINCENT PRICE · PETER LORRE
BASIL RATHBONE SPECIAL GUEST STAR **DEBRA PAGET**

Produced and Directed by ROGER CORMAN Screenplay by RICHARD MATHESON
Executive Producers JAMES H. NICHOLSON · SAMUEL Z. ARKOFF

mances in criminal roles, the inspirational credit for the popular image of the gangster in American film has to be accorded to Edward G. Robinson, James Cagney, and Humphrey Bogart for their 1930s films, *Little Caesar, The Public Enemy,* and *The Petrified Forest,* respectively. These movies, with their realistic rendition of the criminal mind as well as of the social behavior of their day, conditioned both audiences and moviemakers to a sensitive awareness of the visual image of the gangster on film. We have only to witness the cold-bloodedness of a Robinson, the upstart brashness of a Cagney, or the calculating cynicism of a Bogart to realize that with these three the portrayal of crime on film had its strongest dramatic influence on the acting tradition of crime movies.

Paradoxically, though, the social disorder that these movies dramatize so vividly projects a nostal-

THE BIG THREE OF GANGSTER FILMS
During the 1930s and on into the '40s, Edward G. Robinson, James Cagney, and Humphrey Bogart established the lifestyle image of the movie "mobster" of the era. Each was inimitable and unique in his contribution to an acting tradition still evident in films and on television.

James Cagney. PHOTO FROM THE AUTHOR'S COLLECTION.

Edward G. Robinson. PHOTO FROM THE AUTHOR'S COLLECTION.

Humphrey Bogart. PHOTO FROM THE AUTHOR'S COLLECTION.

gic aura in a way that no other film genre can. Perhaps the fact that social unrest mirrors the times that produce it more conspicuously than any other force is the real reason for the nostalgic affection we attach to such movies. The stylized manner of the *Dick Tracy* comic strip of the same era shows up in the gangster film's depiction of the times through patterns of dress and slang expressions as well as through individual and group behavior. Thus the social realism that inspired the crime movie made it more accurate in recording and visualizing the life-style of a period than any other mode of popular culture.

On the other hand, those propagandistic films of World War II, like *Sergeant York* (1941), *Wake Island* (1942), *Bataan* (1943), *The Purple Heart* (1944), and *Pride of the Marines* (1945), to select one of the better films for each year of this genre's heyday, reveal the patriotic fervor and system of values of a time that today come across as basically unreal. As Judith Crist expresses it in her introduction to a book on the films of the period, "For my generation, the trashiest of the films of World War II are worth looking at, if only in their recall of a time of innocence, of a purity of morality that has vanished. . . ."[7] She concludes that most of these films tell us little about the war, but a great deal, beneath the surface, about the American people of the time.

Her contention lends credence, of course, to my interpretation of the nostalgia neurosis as it affects our understanding of the American movie and its popular influence. Despite whatever bad moments we may have endured in the past, we will continue our love affair with it simply because it is closer to our youth, the finer moments of our lost innocence. No matter how harsh or unsettling the subject, whether crime or war, the Hollywood movie had a way of seeing things the way we wanted to see them, of visualizing for us our innermost fantasies, dreams, and wish fulfillments as they might be experienced, in many cases, through the popular image of a single individual.

John Wayne, whose career spans the origin and development of the sound film, is probably the most classic case of the Hollywood star system devised to meet the changing demands of popular taste. Even though Wayne's reputation could survive solely through his portrayal of the Western hero, many of us prefer to remember him as a lusty, brawling military man taking on the enemy in hand-to-hand combat in *Sands of Iwo Jima* (1949) and a raft of other war pictures. In the spirit of the comic books' Captain America, the movies' John Wayne not only functioned effectively in a propagandistic sense, but, like the comic book heroes, conditioned audiences to a scathing brand of racial prejudice, one that suggested eventual victory over our enemies through racial superiority. Hadn't Wayne in a burst of patriotic verve in one of his films referred to the Japanese as "bug-eyed monkeys"? The upsurge of nostalgic interest in World War II in the late 1970s can be attributable in large part to a fascination with the unreal, naive attitudes fostered by the war movies which a generation had viewed over thirty years before, and which were Hollywood's way of letting people fantasize in order to exorcize their fears during an extremely trying and uncertain era. For anyone who saw *Thirty Seconds over Tokyo* in 1944, for example, viewing this film again can indeed be a nostalgic experience because of the highly emo-

HOLLYWOOD AND WORLD WAR II: *Film Images That Helped Win the War*

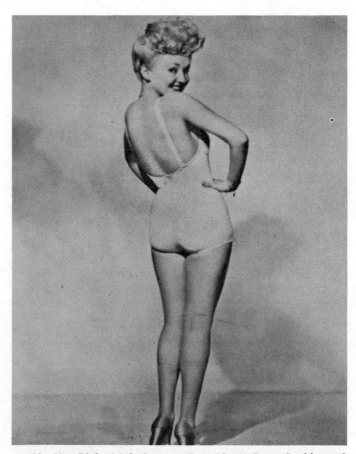

In Pin Up Girl *(20th-Century Fox, 1944) Betty Grable established this sexy pose that probably did more to boost the morale of servicemen than any other inspirational source.* PHOTO FROM AUTHOR'S COLLECTION.

Audiences knew that the enemy was in for a rough time if a movie had John Wayne in it. Making the transition from Westerns to war pictures with effortless ease, Wayne found a huge fan following in movies like Flying Tigers *(Republic, 1942). Whatever the branch of service, his image seemed to generate the kind of confidence needed at the time.* PHOTOS FROM AUTHOR'S COLLECTION.

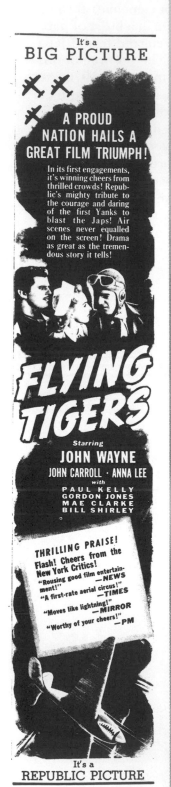

It's a
BIG PICTURE

A PROUD NATION HAILS A GREAT FILM TRIUMPH!

In its first engagements, it's winning cheers from thrilled crowds! Republic's mighty tribute to the courage and daring of the first Yanks to blast the Japs! Air scenes never equalled on the screen! Drama as great as the tremendous story it tells!

FLYING TIGERS

Starring

JOHN WAYNE

JOHN CARROLL · ANNA LEE

with

PAUL KELLY
GORDON JONES
MAE CLARKE
BILL SHIRLEY

THRILLING PRAISE!
Flash! Cheers from the New York Critics!
"Rousing good film entertainment!"
—NEWS
"A first-rate aerial circus!"
—TIMES
"Moves like lightning!"
—MIRROR
"Worthy of your cheers!"
—PM

It's a
REPUBLIC PICTURE

GREAT GUY! GREAT GAL! GREATEST ROMANCE SINCE "TEST PILOT"!

SPENCER TRACY
AND IRENE DUNNE
IN VICTOR FLEMING'S SPARKLING PRODUCTION
A GUY NAMED JOE

AN **M-G-M** PICTURE WITH

VAN JOHNSON • WARD BOND • JAMES GLEASON
LIONEL BARRYMORE • BARRY NELSON • ESTHER WILLIAMS
Screen Play by Dalton Trumbo • Adaptation by
Frederick Hazlitt Brennan • Directed by VICTOR
FLEMING • Produced by EVERETT RISKIN
A Metro-Goldwyn-Mayer Picture

Casablanca (Warner Bros., 1942), one of the all-time screen classics, had a variety of ingredients going for it, but Humphrey Bogart's role as the cynical cafe owner personified for many the kind of attitude needed to hold up under the War's duress. Here he is with singer Dooley Wilson and co-star Ingrid Bergman.
PHOTO FROM AUTHOR'S COLLECTION.

tional atmosphere in which this film was once promoted.

How Hollywood allowed us to fantasize both the past and our dream world can best be illustrated by two classic films from that vintage year of great movie productions—1939.[8] Both *Gone with the Wind* and *The Wizard of Oz* are, in their own way, super fantasies that have retained their popularity because they speak to something elemental in our fantasy makeups, which enables these films to go on year after year creating a wider range of nostalgic fascination for anyone who has ever seen them. It would be redundant to enumerate here the legendary superlatives that have come the way of *Gone with the*

Wind since its world premiere in Atlanta toward the end of Hollywood's biggest year. It is my feeling, though, that what contributed most to the the film's astounding success and popularity was the collaborative effort that sought to incorporate into one film almost every ingredient that would endear it to the mass audience of its day. Ever since the days of D. W. Griffith, lavish movie spectacles had been produced on a grandiose scale with much attendant ballyhoo, but not until *Gone with the Wind* had there been such a magnificently concerted effort on the part of every component figuring in a movie production, all aiming at one major objective: to create the best movie ever made, or at least "the best" by the popular standards of that time. A curious contrast of romanticism, as expressed in the idyllic plantation scenes of the old South, and realism, as revealed in the scenes of the burning of Atlanta, *Gone with the Wind* set out to outdo itself right from

THE HOLLYWOOD STAR SYSTEM

The Hollywood star system—the business of publicizing a screen personality for public adulation—has paralleled the development of the motion picture since the silent era. Creating fantasy images for public consumption, the system was recognized by Hollywood as the most dependable method of promoting and selling a movie.

The image of the virile male was pioneered by Rudolph Valentino, particularly through his role in The Sheik *(1925). Peaking with the choice of Clark Gable to play Rhett Butler in* Gone with the Wind *(1939), the system still expresses itself through the various lifestyles of male stars like Burt Reynolds and Robert Redford.*

A starlet adorning the cover of a magazine has been among the most time-tested publicity techniques, and this 1915 Green Book *cover proves that Mary Pickford was the Farrah Fawcett-Majors of her day.*

the beginning with its introduction of rolling title credits rendered by the most magnificent projection process ever invented up until that time. The technicolor images presented to awed audiences were audibly enhanced by the full, melodic sweep of Max Steiner's brilliant score, whose familiar themes continue to echo over the years.

Gone with the Wind is that film rarity which was not only as phenomenally successful as its book version; it is also a faithful rendering of the novel that inspired it. A finer example of a successful crossover from one popular art form to another could hardly be found, and because of this achievement, both the movie and the novel persist as classic examples of the nostalgic principle that haunts popular American culture: the conflict between a secure past and an uncertain future. Margaret Mitchell may or may not have had the movie medium of expression in

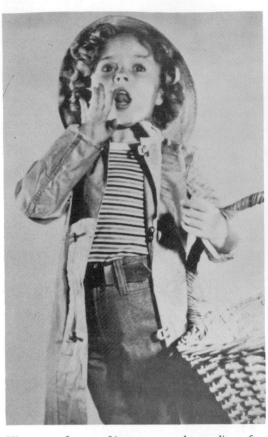  

Women as figures of innocence and sexuality—from Shirley Temple to Marilyn Monroe—have played a major role in the system. Other influential variations on the theme were Bette Davis and Jean Harlow.

A natural spinoff of the system was the endorsement of commercial products by stars readily recognizable to the public as, for example, Edmond O'Brien and Lucille Ball in this 1941 Pepsi Cola ad.

mind when she wrote *Gone with the Wind*, but we realize that her dramatically visual sense of what was right for a novel about the Civil War—the tragedy of the Southern cause as symbolized in general by the demise of a way of life and personified in particular by the frustrated love affair of the central characters—translated admirably onto the screen. There is probably no more nostalgic subject in American social history than the idealized picture of this vanished world—the *ante bellum* South, rife with magnolia-scented plantation scenes of crinoline-attired belles; tall, straight-backed suitors; and their devoted black servants, field and house workers alike, laughing, singing, and apparently loving their routine existence, all this played out in fairy-tale innocence within and before a white-columned mansion of gleaming elegance. Before writers like William Faulkner and Erskine Caldwell shot it

down, such was the popular stereotype of the old South, and many writers sought to pen this image in fiction, but few were as successful in a popular sense as Margaret Mitchell.

The key to Mrs. Mitchell's success was her ability to create flesh-and-blood characters to set within the fictional trappings of the conventional historical novel. The vivid characterizations of Rhett Butler and Scarlett O'Hara, which were brought to life on the screen in the persons of Clark Gable and Vivian Leigh, were portrayals that convincingly visualized their fictional counterparts to the extent that Rhett and Scarlett have become part of American folklore. The Hollywood star system that originated in the 1920s with the creation of public images like Rudolph Valentino and Gloria Swanson reached its zenith in the furor leading up to the choice of both Gable and Leigh for the lead roles in *Gone with the Wind*. Never again would there be such mass interest in determining who would play a particular movie role. It was a situation that plainly pointed out the predominant influence that movies exerted

Errol Flynn, in movies like Captain Blood *(1935) and* The
Sea Hawk *(1940), perpetuated the swashbuckling heroic image
that Douglas Fairbanks, Jr. had begun during the silent era. The
image lives on today in the womanizing, cool-mannered figure of
the James Bond mold.*

FROM THE DEPTHS
OF AN EVIL MIND
CAME A DIABOLICAL
PLAN OF TORTURE.
INCONCEIVABLE...
UNBELIEVABLE!

AMERICAN
INTERNATIONAL
presents

BORIS KARLOFF IS THE TERROR
COLOR

NO ONE WILL BE ADMITTED WHILE
THE COFFIN IS BEING OPENED!

The face of Boris Karloff, whether heavily made up in his classic roles as the Frankenstein monster and the Mummy, or in more conventional roles like this 1963 ad, dominated movie villainy from the 1920s to the '70s. He is the most prominent and remembered performer of this kind of film role.

on the mass mind in the late 1930s, a period in the history of the movies never to be realized again.[9]

Thus the achievement of *Gone with the Wind* as popular film art rests in large part on its fortunate choice of visually suitable players for the main roles, particularly Clark Gable, who had created in the American popular mind a particular image of maleness. Another reason for the movie's success was its effective use of innovative photography to visualize for us the most nostalgic of subjects—that which the movie's title suggests—the tragedy of an idealized world lost forever to those of us who revered it and

Transcribing Margaret Mitchell's Gone with the Wind *(MGM, 1939) to the screen was accomplished in such convincing fashion that many of the novel's characters have since become a part of American folklore. Here are some of the principals whose acting helped enhance the impact of this classic film: (from left to right) Olivia De Havilland (Melanie Hamilton), Ward Bond (Yankee captain), Clark Gable (Rhett Butler), and Leslie Howard (Ashley Wilkes).* PHOTO FROM AUTHOR'S COLLECTION.

what it stood for. Rhett Butler may have had the last word on Scarlett, but our real feelings lie with her and the world she represents, a victim of relentlessly changing times and forces beyond individual control—those very things that contribute to what I have identified as the nostalgia neurosis.

Thanks to television, *The Wizard of Oz,* that other favorite dream-world fantasy, keeps coming back at us as an accepted national ritual for viewing each time it is shown, thereby instilling new generations of devotees with a nostalgic affection for what is probably the film fantasy of fantasies—the story of a dream within a dream. Like Little Nemo, the child-hero of the magnificent comic strip discussed in the last section, Dorothy experiences a dream journey to the Land of Oz and there encounters all the wondrous and nightmarish episodes that dreams are made of. As a result, Dorothy's dream is fraught with the inconsistencies and contradictions that comprise all our fantasy wishes and by extension our nostalgic affinities. In fact, the literal meaning of *nostalgia* is homesickness, and Dorothy's entire dream is directed and controlled by her desire to return home. This desire provides a framework for the story and symbolizes the wish fulfillment or desire in us all to identify with meaningful experience. Consequently, Dorothy's return to the homespun reality of Kansas, as expressed through her relieved awakening, is more than a necessary rounding off of the story and a reminder that "there's no place like home," as Dorothy says. It is also a nostalgic reinforcement of a simpler, more innocent way of life common to an earlier, younger America, a way of life that is no more and therefore more nostalgically entrancing.

Combining a supreme sense of fantasy with a delightful musical score, The Wizard of Oz *(MGM, 1939) is one of the screen's great achievements. In adapting itself to meet the demands of a popular audience, this classic has outdone itself in each of its forms of expression: fiction, film, and television.* PHOTO FROM AUTHOR'S COLLECTION.

The stereotypes of the mid-American rural scene around the turn of the century—the three farmhands, the eccentric spinster, and the itinerant fortune teller—were character images of their time, lending both nostalgic and dramatic emphasis to their counterpart roles in the dream portion of the movie. Thus the most familiar and influential characters in Dorothy's home life direct and define her dream quest to find a way to return home, but not before confronting the unexpected obstacles that are a necessary part of the unfolding of any quest story. The Wicked Witch of the West as the epitome of the evil that stands in the way of all purposeful quests serves to heighten the movie's dramatic impact and, ironically, to add much to our nostalgic fascination for it. Although the movie is filled with memorable characters, the Witch, as played by Margaret Hamilton, is probably the most remembered character of the film for much the same reason that villains stand out in other media, as earlier sections of this work have pointed out. Along with Charles Middleton's Emperor Ming in *Flash Gordon,* Miss Hamilton's Wicked Witch has to rate among the all-time movie villains.

The Wizard of Oz is one of the best examples, too, of both the collaboration and interaction of cultural forms that help to reinforce the nostalgic mood of this movie each time it is shown, once again highlighting a premise which I have established for this book. Although the 1939 movie version superseded most children's visual interpretation of the story's main characters, attesting once again to the movie medium's dominant role in perceiving for us, L. Frank Baum's inspired story and W. A. Denslow's whimsical drawings were the visual inspiration for

Along with the direction of Busby Berkeley, the dancing performances of Fred Astaire and Ginger Rogers in movies like Top Hat *(RKO, 1935), are considered among the supreme achievements of the Hollywood musical.* PHOTO FROM AUTHOR'S COLLECTION.

the film; theirs was a happy combination of text and illustration which contributed in no small way to the polishing of the final movie script. Harold Arlen and E. Y. Harburg's musical score, introducing such a perennial favorite as "Over the Rainbow," was also highly instrumental in triggering our nostalgic response to the movie's thematic scenes. In *The Wizard of Oz,* music, story line, and performance function as an organic whole to create a nostalgic masterpiece that undoubtedly will go on for years recreating nostalgic experience for new audiences.

Music as a form of popular expression does not fall into the purview of this book, of course, but we are aware that it has a unique power to evoke nostalgic feeling and visual identification and that this capability has not been overlooked by the film industry. Because the silent film era seems so far away from us today, it is difficult to imagine a movie that would attempt to achieve dramatic effect without benefit of background music. Yet even the silent film's sense of action and movement was punctuated by the emotionally charged arpeggios and crescendos of music hall pianos and movie palace pipe organs and orchestras that echoed across the country in the 1920s. Even with the advent of sound in the late 1920s, musical scores at first were not totally integrated into a movie production as they later would be; the visual stimulus of film and the sound stimulus of music were initially thought of as being separate and distinct modes of perception with each having little to do with the other in projecting a unified dramatic effect.[10] It remained for an innovator like Busby Berkeley to show what could be achieved with song and dance (dance being understood as the visual interpretation of music) in the mode of popular film expression that came to be known as the "Hollywood musical."

The heart of the Depression, 1933, was a year that produced three of Hollywood's most impressive and influential musicals—*42nd Street, Gold Diggers of 1933,* and *Footlight Parade.* These films were outstanding not because of their stories, which were often hackneyed beyond credibility, but because they revealed to popular audiences and critics alike what a director with imagination and initiative could accomplish with a movie camera. When Berkeley was at the helm, as he was in all three of these films, it was obvious that the only restrictions on his creative ability were those imposed by the budget he had to work with. The visual impact of Berkeley's 1933 films, with their veritable fireworks display of pretty chorus girls converging in mind-boggling

dance routines, can be traced through all the musicals that were to follow, especially those highlighted by the spectacular performances of Fred Astaire and Ginger Rogers and the cleverly coordinated routines of Shirley Temple and Bill "Bojangles" Robinson, a dancing team which endeared itself to the moviegoers of that decade. In retrospect, many of Berkeley's spectacular dance arrangements may appear somewhat fanciful, overdone, and even ridiculous by today's standards of realism, but taken within the perspective of the times in which they were produced, they have to rank among the movies' all-time technical feats.

Berkeley's elaborate adaptations of the popular tunes of the day to the dancing and singing of stars like Ruby Keeler, Dick Powell, Joan Blondell, and James Cagney were both visually and audibly complementary in creating an atmosphere of escape in the 1930s. In fact, because of their unique blend of sound and sight, the Berkeley musicals represent the most self-conscious attempt at fantasy escape of any movie genre, and herein lies their real nostalgic appeal, even for younger audiences who may never before have been exposed to this kind of entertainment. To help audiences forget whatever cares and problems they may have left at home, these musical extravaganzas obviously tried to create a baroque effect that sought to outdo itself with each new film. The real key to appreciating Berkeley's total achievement is found in his freeing the camera from its moorings so that it becomes a moving, searching, probing instrument—almost a character with a visually perceptive role all its own.

Even though the freedom of expression that the camera assumed in these movies is our most outstanding visual inheritance from them, we should note several other basic characteristics which are important to my thematic purpose because they set the pattern and tone for the nostalgic appeal of the later Hollywood musical. Beyond the fantasy effects projected through the synchronization of song and dance, Berkeley's films attempt to reflect the manners and attitudes of a time and place. At the same time, the rendering of a real place like New York City, for example, comes across as a fairy-tale world where people involve themselves as characters from a fairy tale do. Also, the simple, skeletonic plots of these films usually forego the psychological problems of in-depth characterization and rely on the superficial problems of organizing and putting on a show ("the-show-must-go-on" syndrome).

These traits evolve and manifest themselves in

one form or another in the more sophisticated musicals of the forties and fifties. These films were produced by Twentieth Century-Fox (*Springtime in the Rockies, Coney Island, Tin Pan Alley,* and *Sweet Rosie O'Grady*—vehicles for crowd-pleasing stars like Alice Faye and Betty Grable) and, most lavishly, by Metro-Goldwyn-Mayer (*Meet Me in St. Louis, An American in Paris,* and *The Bandwagon*). One of the best of the MGM musicals, and one that will best serve our intent here of illustrating Hollywood's version of the nostalgic vision, is *Singin' in the Rain,* a 1952 film starring Gene Kelly, Donald O'Connor, and Debbie Reynolds. The 1950s saw the first upsurge of interest in the 1920s, and *Singin' in the Rain* sought to dramatize this feeling for the period by being both satirical and nostalgic about the Hollywood myth of pampered stars, temperamental directors, and idealistic hopefuls who overcame all obstacles to achieve stardom. The irony of these stereotyped situations is that we are now far enough away from the time of a movie like *Singin' in the Rain* that the film itself has created a nostalgic following; and even though it draws on some of the greatest tunes of the 1920s ("All I Do Is Dream of You," "You Were Meant for Me," "You Are My Lucky Star," and "Singin' in the Rain") to capture the flavor of the period, what we really remember more than anything else about this movie are those unique scenes that give it a period class of its own. In fact, two of the greatest one-man exhibitions in the history of the movies are from this film, both unforgettable to anyone who has seen them: Gene Kelly's brilliant and exhilarating song-and-dance routine to the title song in a rain-splashed street, and Donald O'Connor's fantastic, plastic gyrations done to the ebullient "Make 'Em Laugh." Another significant factor enhancing the nostalgic flavor of an MGM film like this one was the high quality of its color, a process that created a spectacular world of its own in contrast to the rather mundane interpretation of other studios. Yet in spite of all the technological advances that the movies cashed in on over the years, it would be difficult to forget the old black-and-white musicals of the classic Busby Berkeley period, which in their special way created a fantasy world of their own.

Because of its power to recreate both the visual and auditory feel and flavor of an era, the movie is the medium of visual expression that has contributed most significantly to our nostalgia neurosis. In film, the provocative ingredients of nostalgia —character and place, which call forth a particular time—are more dramatically compelling than they are in any of our popular media. There are hardy souls, for example, who either stay up or set their clocks for some early morning hour to get up and relive some meaningful part of their past through watching an old Busby Berkeley musical on television. Although the movie musical with its special ability to generate the characteristic sounds of its day has tremendous fascination for the nostalgiac, the comedy genre has a similar propensity to reveal how we were.

The comedic tradition in movie-making is as old as the industry itself, and in many of the best films of the silent greats—Charlie Chaplin, Buster Keaton, Harry Langdon, Harold Lloyd, and the team of Laurel and Hardy, all of whom performed when the comedic effect depended entirely on visual expression and interpretation—there is a timelessness that

Although there were a number of talented comics in the silent era like Buster Keaton, Harry Langdon, and Harold Lloyd, the figure who exerted the widest influence on the visual development of screen comedy was clearly Charlie Chaplin. His inimitable talent was based on perfect timing, a unique sense of visual presence, and a capacity for enlisting sympathy for the underdog. These characteristics in one form or another were the key to success for all later screen comedians, both individuals and teams. PHOTO FROM AUTHOR'S COLLECTION.

In a long career spanning both the silent and sound eras, the team of Stan Laurel and Oliver Hardy established the pattern of comedic relationship between straight man and fall guy. In such a situation the straight man may appear to have the upper hand, but his partner's natural innocence usually wins out in the end.
PHOTO FROM AUTHOR'S COLLECTION.

transcends period atmosphere. When comedy, like tragedy, speaks to something elemental in human nature, it takes on a classic function, reminding us of our essential humanity through pointing out our weaknesses and follies as humans. This observation holds true for later comics and comedy teams of the sound era, of course, but of all the many performers who tried their hand at this most difficult of the popular forms of expression, only a few succeeded in making us laugh in both a nostalgic and classic sense. In this category, we certainly have to reserve a place for the Marx Brothers.

The films of the Marx Brothers have had a history of mixed receptions. Some of their movies that were panned at first have since become recognized as classics of comedy, and others that were highly thought of when they first appeared have since been relegated to the mediocre category. Their movies of the 1930s now appear to be their best, and those of the 1940s seem weaker. Probably the main reason

for the popular following of the earlier films today is that they reveal to us the absurdities of a madcap world in a way that no other medium of popular expression could. This special zaniness, so representative of the Marx Brothers movies made prior to World War II, seems to reflect the uneasiness of a society precariously poised btween the lingering effects of a disastrous Depression and the uncertainties of an increasingly ominous world situation, or from another point of view, the conflict between an older, more traditional way of life and the hectic, misdirected lifestyles of modern life. As though to combat a growing feeling of bewilderment concerning the world's state of affairs, the humor of the

Marx Brothers was based on its capacity for ridiculing society, the establishment, and anything smacking of organized deceit or political humbug.

Functioning as comedic versions of the nostalgia neurosis, the Marx Brothers films of the 1930s exhibit a special appeal of their own today. Visually their comedy routines harken back to the days of vaudeville and of the broadway revue in which the Brothers learned their trade. Early films like *The Cocoanuts* (1929) and *Animal Crackers* (1930) were really movie versions of their broadway counterparts, a fact which may help explain why it took a while for the Brothers to overcome the dominant influence of the stage on their screen performances and adapt to a medium that demanded a different approach to visual interpretation.

But adapt they did, and the films made during the period between 1930 and 1935 reflect this development; they also show how the movies' propensity for satisfying the American desire for a sense of dynamic movement exerted its influence on this development. *Animal Crackers* revealed the boys on their way to breaking away from the constraints of the stage by adapting their natural talent for "winging it" to the more expansive medium of film; *Monkey Business* (1931) saw them engaged in some of their wildest chase scenes; and *Horse Feathers* (1932) and *Duck Soup* (1933) were vehicles that allowed them to satirize the educational system and the totalitarian state, respectively. It all seemed to peak beautifully in *A Night at the Opera* (1935), a production noted for its series of big comedy scenes, particularly the classic stateroom fiasco, but a film whose scenario was tried out on the stage before it was filmed. This project designed to test audience reaction, revealed more convincingly than anything else just how far along the two entertainment modes of stage and screen had evolved at this time. What the stage could never capture, film certainly did, and if we still laugh at the antics of the Marx Brothers after nearly half a century, it may be because of their mastery of a visual medium of comedic expression which achieved the level of the timeless in those seemingly impromptu escapades that reflect the unpredictable and absurd moments of life. It is their special way of "seeing" these things that has contributed to the nostalgic aura surrounding the Marx Brothers films.

Unlike their predecessors, Bud Abbott and Lou Costello produced a kind of humor that was only right for the frenetic years of World War II, the times that inspired the most characteristic of their movies. Products of the straight man–stooge comedy act of burlesque and radio, their movie routines made the most of Lou Costello's role of the put-on innocent at the mercy of Bud Abbott's schemes and diatribes. There was something appealing about this situation in a time when the little man had been put down often enough, and it pleased the audience no little to see the blundering but well-meaning Costello somehow manage to get the better of the crafty, devious Abbott. Even if he didn't, fans always seemed to derive satisfaction from naturally identifying with the underdog role of Lou Costello during the uncertain, demanding years of World War II. Even though Abbott and Costello were to go on and make a great number of films after the war ended, they never quite caught up with the zany ebullience and spontaneous brand of comedy that made a movie like *Buck Privates* (1941) such a crowd pleaser in its day and a nostalgic reminder today of a period that could dramatize military experience in a lighthearted, comic manner, a visual interpretation that was shortly to change.

Also in contrast to the humor of other comedy teams, that of Bob Hope and Bing Crosby in their "road" pictures generates a kind of nostalgia that is not necessarily as much a part of their times as it is of the exotic places and unexpected situations their movies depended on for audience appeal. Taking off for places like Singapore, Zanzibar, Bali, and and even a mythical Utopia kept Hope and Crosby embroiled in a magical kind of screen action that was peculiarly of their own making. Of course, Hope and Crosby both had secure enough reputations on their own, but when these two came together in the "road" pictures, audiences were treated to a type of visual comedy not found in any other team of comics before or since. Hope's "loser" image was always offset by the effortless performance of Crosby, and this happy combination paradoxically added to the stature and reputation of each as an entertainer. As a result, much of the nostalgia of this series is derived from the recognition of two familiar character types caught up in amusing, though contrived, situations in places that may have had real geographical names, but that were really fantasized dream worlds. The Hope and Crosby films could easily have been dubbed the "Road to Oz" series because of their unabashed attempt to visualize for us a world that never was.

On the other hand, the films of W. C. Fields are sufficiently realistic in that their humor is based on an irascible individual's quarrel with society, and

The Marx Brothers, four of them at first and then three, utilized their vaudeville training to bring to the screen a brand of zaniness that has never been equaled. Here are, from left to right, Chico, Harpo, and Groucho. PHOTO FROM AUTHOR'S COLLECTION.

Bud Abbott and Lou Costello's slapstick, burlesque-style humor was descended from Laurel and Hardy but was mainly typical of the times that produced it, the War years of 1941–45. PHOTO FROM AUTHOR'S COLLECTION.

Whether playing with Bing Crosby in their "Road" series or just playing it on his own, Bob Hope has been a popular favorite for over forty years. He has also consistently held his own in both radio and television. Here he is with Martha Raye in one of his early films, College Swing (Paramount, 1938). PHOTO FROM AUTHOR'S COLLECTION.

their nostalgic attraction generally stems from the mirroring of the social habits of their day. Fields's comedy method depended on the conflict between accepted lifestyles or conventional behavior and his flouting them in order to expose the underlying hypocrisy and sham of social convention. His visual technique or sense of stage presence is vaudevillian in manner, an inheritance from his many years on the circuit and one of the main reasons for the method of delayed timing that contributes so much to his brand of humor. Although the free rein given Fields's manner in such classic shorts as "The Fatal Glass of Beer," "The Dentist," and "The Barber" is more controlled in most of his feature films, his presence in a movie always alerted audiences to the fact that plot development would probably be sac-

rificed to any flights of whimsy Fields might come up with. His sense of stage action predominated in such situations, and his roles as a foil to the sexual innuendos of Mae West provide us with concrete evidence of this fact. In *My Little Chickadee* (1940), for example, Fields is his usual opinionated, philandering self who, whenever he appears to be getting the short end of the stick, seizes on the opportunity to improve his community image at the expense of whatever social custom might dictate, whether he is mooching a drink, cheating at cards in the town saloon, or carrying out his sham marriage with the two-timing Flower Belle played by Mae West. In playing opposite such a forceful personality as Mae West, Fields wisely chose to perform his role so that their relationship was a complementary one, each contributing to the stage presence of the other. The result is a striking visual impression that persists long after an audience has seen these two unique personalities in action; hence

The male-female confrontations of W.C. Fields and Mae West in films like My Little Chickadee *(Universal, 1940) sometimes baffled moviegoers of a more naive time, but audiences nevertheless recognized theirs as a unique, different kind of humor.* PHOTO FROM AUTHOR'S COLLECTION.

our high susceptibility to the nostalgic atmosphere of character and place in the movies in which Fields and West appear together.

Like the Marx Brothers, W. C. Fields has become a visual institution in the tradition of American film comedy, and his movies are periodically revived, particularly on college campuses, for reasons, it is inferred, other than just nostalgia. For college students too young to have experienced the times of the Fields films and therefore unable to connect nostalgically with them, Fields's disrespectful and iconoclastic humor has achieved more relevance in today's hectic, polarized world than when it first appeared during a time of a more naive and innocent way of looking at experience. The victims and targets of Fields's vitriolic barbs really represent those persons and institutions who continue to function as part of a more conventional or simpler way of life, yet one that was rapidly disintegrating. Although the viewer of a Fields film recognizes the difference in these antithetical ways of looking at life, the humor of the situation lies in the fact that the victim does not. The 1930s were a time in our social history when audiences as a rule identified and sympathized with the victimized, and this may account for the lukewarm reception Fields's movies received in less sophisticated areas like small-town or rural America, which were the conservative strongholds of traditional lifestyles.[11] Generally, movie comedies of the thirties and forties supplied fare that was either purely escapist or which showed the world as a better or more interesting place than it actually was. However, the W. C. Fields films may enjoy a more popular reputation today in a nostalgic sense for a different reason than, say, the Abbott and Costello movies which were big box-office hits during the war years because they were exactly what audiences of the time wanted in the way of comedy, zany and screwball enough to offer moviegoers both a taste of fantasy and a degree of escape.

The term "screwball," though, had more direct application to a brand of comedy that was contradistinctive to that of the popular comedians of the time, although it also, in its own way, created a fantasized, escapist existence out of contemporary reality. In fact, it was the so-called sophisticated type of screwball comedy that contributed to a whole new way of interpreting reality through dramatizing the absurd and unpredictable side of human relationships. It was this kind of screen entertainment that evolved into television series like the *Mary Tyler Moore Show,* the *Bob Newhart Show, Maude,* and even *All in the Family.* As diverse in in-

tent as they are, the common inheritance of all these programs from the screwball comedy tradition of the movies is a manner of projecting and honoring the established system for what it is. Despite life's unexpected situations and ridiculous predicaments, these programs seem to be saying that it is really true love, marriage, family, and the American way that count in the long run. Because the things these programs celebrate are so much a part of the woman's world, she plays a dominant role in such comedies.[12]

The seminal source for much of contemporary television comedy can be found in movies like *My Man Godfrey* (1936), *The Awful Truth* (1937), *Holiday* (1938), and *The Philadelphia Story* (1940), to name a few of the more successful films of this genre. In these movies much of the action turns on misunderstanding and lack of communication between individuals, usually husband and wife or two lovers attempting to resolve their differences before marriage. After a series of wacky, improbable events seemingly designed to show the world as one crazy, mixed-up place, a resolution is brought about at the film's end, and the world or social order is seen in a new, harmonious light. Apparently the lead couples in screwball comedies lived happily ever after, certainly a popular misconception that not only contributed to the nostalgic attraction of these movies, but to a viewing audience's possible misinterpretation of American lifestyle as well.

Accordingly, these were the kinds of movies that led audiences to believe that there must be much more to life than it was their destined lot to endure. This feeling is still with us as an example from contemporary television will illustrate. With the show's demise, a nostalgic affection has grown up around the *Mary Tyler Moore Show* for the simple reason, I think, that this series was built around believable characters who, despite their personal problems, came across to viewers as belonging to a structured, well-ordered existence, something that many fans of the show had little of in their personal lives. Apparently, then, the seeds of the nostalgia neurosis are inherent in contemporary television programming—a condition we shall examine in more detail in the next section—and its visual influence can be traced to the screwball comedies of the 1930s. Robert Sklar, in his social history of American film, *Movie-Made America,* has pointed out that even though these comedies ". . . never challenged the social order, the pictures gave audiences a whole new vision of social style, a different image of how to be a person. . . ."[13] This revolutionary new image many

Americans sought to emulate was that of the individual dedicated to the pursuit of pleasure and the good life, a lifestyle that has made a distinctive visual impression on the popular mind since the 1930s and one that has since become more accessible to the masses because of improved economic conditions. But there were other kinds of movies produced by Hollywood, many of a more serious nature, that were imbued with this same "new vision of social style."

For example, the movies directed by Frank Capra, which were structured not so much to make you think as they were to make you feel good, set out to show that the good life was in reach of everyone, rich and commoner alike, provided your values were put in proper perspective. In fact, for millions of moviegoers in the thirties and forties Capra's films functioned as the movie counterparts of the inspirational novel of the time. Even in *It Happened One Night,* the 1934 Academy Award winner and his one film that most nearly approaches the "screwball" genre, Capra's understanding of the American people's manner of fantasizing about the good life is appealingly visualized through the relationship of rich girl (Claudette Colbert) with a handsome young man of average means (Clark Gable). Audiences all over the country readily identified with Gable's affable manner of initiating a pretty but spoiled rich girl to the accepted public rituals of the masses: taking a trip on a Greyhound bus, hitching a ride, and staying overnight in a motor court, for example. Gable's winning Miss Colbert's hand in marriage at the end of the film was not only a triumph for the role itself, but his acting won an Academy Award. This happy ending, both on the screen and in real life, also marked Capra's way of identifying with and carrying out the wish fulfillment of the masses. Gable, in particular, caught their fancy as a symbol of American naturalness, and Frank Capra went on to direct a series of popular films whose heroes were all characters that the people could identify with because they were of them. Films like *Mr. Deeds Goes to Town* (1936), *Mr. Smith Goes to Washington* (1939), and *Meet John Doe* (1941), which starred Lincolnesque actors like Gary Cooper and James Stewart, unwittingly contributed to our susceptibility to the nostalgia neurosis by comparing the virtues of the established way of life with the false philosophies of those who would undermine or destroy it.

In movies like these, Frank Capra appears to be inspired by the same vision that motivated Harold Gray, the comic-strip artist *(Little Orphan Annie)*—to create dramatic situations that were really visual metaphors for a way of life the masses could comprehend. The dramatic situation in which a central character, usually a quixotic but courageous sort in the face of adversity, must single-handedly overcome what seems to be overwhelming odds is one that the American popular mind has always appreciated. Such a situation had even greater appeal when this character achieved what he set out to do, thus perpetuating the myth of American self-actualization and resourcefulness while expressing a theme designed to speak to the common good of all men.

Because of the Capra film's special sensitivity to the dream wishes of the mass mind, it is easy to understand why his films attained such a high level of popularity. In reality, Capra was a master at visualizing and then transcribing the ingredients and conventions of successful popular fiction to the screen. The result was that audiences enjoyed an even closer identity with imagined characters once they became "real" people on the screen. In a popular sense, then, it was only natural that the hero of a Capra film took on the appearance and manner of a small-town or country boy. The image of the naif who is really smarter than he appears to be is generically American, and every now and then, someone in the area of popular culture comes along who instinctively perceives the significance of the Huckleberry Finn archetype and what to do with it to project meaning for the mass mind, as Capra did with his heroes. Thus, in viewing a film like *Mr. Deeds Goes to Town,* we are witness to the neurotically nostalgic side of the Mark Twain vision that not only creates a nostalgic mood for us today, but must have provided instant nostalgic identification for many of those who first saw this movie, simply because the role of the symbolically named Longfellow Deeds, as played by Gary Cooper, reflected a kind of pastoral innocence that in its time was fading and would soon be lost forever. In the mid-1930s there were many city dwellers who were still close to the simpler plain of existence in the small towns or rural areas of their origins, much like the background of Longfellow Deeds whose "grassroots" spirit pervades the movie. When Deeds inherits a fortune and heads off for the Big City to claim his inheritance, which he plans to share with poor farmers, audiences recognized the sincerity of his intent and rooted for him to show up those who stood in his way—the crafty, devious city types they all recognized. Accordingly, Deeds not only turns the tables on his natural enemies by establishing his sanity at the trial, the movie's highpoint in both a symbolic and dramatic sense, but he also wins the love of the girl reporter who had been assigned the task of depicting him as nothing more than a small-town bumpkin. Throughout the film, though, Deeds's honest, straightforward manner proves to be infectious among the people with whom he comes in contact, and through the theme of human solidarity and a happy ending, the movie established itself as one of the most popular of its day.

In our day, however, the nostalgia of a movie like *Mr. Deeds Goes to Town* affects us differently than it did audiences of 1936 when much of the innocent charm of the hero's background was still physically evident. Ours now is a nostalgic feeling for a period of our social history as remote and irrecoverable as the half-light atmosphere of the "dream palaces" in which these fantasized daydreams were shown. We who happen to watch these same films today over the television set in the familiar snugness of our den or living room can never hope to recapture the magic aura of the old movie theaters within whose spacious and glittering confines the fantasies of millions were portrayed in such a way that the individual could pursue his own private dream fantasies while sitting next to a stranger engaged in the same act. The real nostalgia involved in viewing vintage movies today is compounded of the fact that in their case film and theater were inseparable, and the ingredients necessary for recreating this condition have passed away forever.

However, there are some things among our visual inheritance from the movies that keep renewing or recycling themselves in one way or another as if to keep sensitizing us to the infinite varieties of expression still available to the medium of film. There have been many pioneers in the development of innovative film techniques, of course, but we have Orson Welles to thank for uniquely synthesizing the achievement of his predecessors to condition us to new ways of viewing cinematic action, thereby enhancing the possibilities for the creation of nostalgic moods in film. Orson Welles, as both director and actor, is exemplary of the creative person who can instinctively recognize the most meaningful moments of experience, and as such he is an intensely visual person. *Citizen Kane* (1941) is a repository of the sensitive perceptions of this visual person who, in line with the major premise of this book, sought to find a way to see or visualize character and place for us. Undoubtedly, the movie director is one of the few visually oriented people in contemporary society who is in a real position to see and evaluate experience as it relates directly to human concerns. In *Citizen Kane*, Welles's direction attempted to visualize the life of one man as the sum of all his experiences, and the central irony of this film is that for all Welles's intended realism in depicting the life of Charles Foster Kane, example of the American success story, the action turns on a nostalgic reference to his childhood—the "rosebud" motif. Nostalgia, as I have continually pointed out, is a powerful and pervasive ingredient in the popular expression of all American cultural forms. It plays a significant role in *Citizen Kane* in that Welles has integrated the nostalgic motif as the key to understanding the makeup of his complex protagonist.

Appropriately, Welles discovered that the camera was a marvelous device for creating atmospheric effect. In fact, the vision of Orson Welles operates on the premise that it is not so much what we see that affects personal emotions as it is how we see. Thus his first film, *Citizen Kane*, stands as a tour de force in the use of visual techniques to reinforce meaning and purpose. Of these, the most impressive is the reliance on deep-focus photography to visualize the interrelationship of physical details and characterization. As the novelist or poet works with words to generate descriptive atmosphere, so Welles utilizes the subtleties of deep-focus camera expression to enable background to contribute to character development. Such a method approaches the poetic in that it suggests much more than is actually stated. It is also a method that contributes to the nostalgic feel of a particular era, an effective technique in Welles's overall intent since Kane's story is told through a series of flashbacks, all from the varying points of view of acquaintances in his life. Revelation of character, place, and emotional mood are further expressed through Welles's use of angle shots, dissolves, and shock images, all visual features that made a lasting impression on not only the filmmaking industry but on all popular graphics forms. Although Orson Welles went on to direct and act in other memorable films, he never again surpassed the visual achievement of *Citizen Kane,* a film that still stands as a veritable grammar of visual language for the movie camera.

If *Citizen Kane* explored to what extent the camera could visualize human relationships in the so-called real world, then *King Kong* (1933) was that movie which did the most with special effects in order to avoid the real world and transport mass audiences toward a wish-fulfillment world of fantastic adventure. In a visual sense, *King Kong* was the epitome of the unique ingredients that went into the making

Among the all-time technical achievements of the movies is the 1933 production of King Kong *(RKO) that functioned both as pure entertainment and moral fable by dramatizing a situation in which the natural is overcome by technological forces. As a popular film* King Kong *has probably been seen by more people than any other movie.* PHOTO FROM AUTHOR'S COLLECTION.

of the fantasy worlds of the pulp magazine and the adventure comic strip, territory expansively explored, as we have seen, in the fiction of Edgar Rice Burroughs. But never before had such experience been so dramatically visualized—or since, as many would have it, despite the technical accomplishments of the 1976 Dino de Laurentiis *Kong*. Actually the popularity of the original movie and the growing nostalgic affection for it over the years since its release can be attributed to its artless synthesis of the following fantasy conventions: the mysterious quest, the lost civilization or alien world, the comparing or contrasting of the world as we know it with that of the alien or exotic, and a central figure of mysterious origin and wondrous powers who

dominates the action. Before *Kong,* movies had attempted, of course, to incorporate several or all of these ingredients in their quest to visualize the ultimate fantasy experience, but the basic difference between them and *King Kong* is the latter's manner of showing a human side of the forty-foot ape that is its central figure by expressing emotional qualities that the audience identified with. Frustrated in expressing his love for the tiny creature (Fay Wray) he adores and misunderstood by the masses who come to gape at him in captivity, Kong as a character generates a direct empathy with movie audiences of any era that has beheld him. The de Laurentiis version is still proving this. In fact, some forty-five years after its initial release, *King Kong* is still among the most popular reruns on television; yet there is something more than just the appeal of the "beauty-and-the-beast" formula that sets this film apart as one of the most popular of all time. The key to *Kong*'s appeal is really the same thing that Edgar Rice Burroughs projected through his creation of the Tarzan character and which contributed so much to the popularity of its transcription to the screen, even though the movie versions frequently strayed from the original characterization and thematic purposes of Burroughs. For a people who carved a unique civilization out of a virgin wilderness in so short a time, the dramatic contrast of life in a natural state with that of a man-made or artificially created one strikes a responsive chord in the American psyche, and Tarzan's bitter reaction to the great urban centers of the world as well as Kong's rampage among the skyscrapers of New York are graphic metaphors for what happens when man becomes divorced from the "Garden." *King Kong,* then, is another of our exemplary film versions of the nostalgia neurosis because it not only reminds us where we have been; it suggests

Humphrey Bogart might possibly be the most influential American actor respecting a sense of visual presence and, ultimately, nostalgic impact. These advertisements for Bogart films extend from his popularity as a supporting actor in the 1930s to his many versatile roles that have been repeatedly presented through film festivals and on television.

what might befall us in a world of our own making.

In conjunction with what I have said about the most visually influential films that Hollywood has produced, whom might we nominate as the star whose dominant personal image has contributed the most to visual inspiration and nostalgic affection? And which is the director whose perceptive skills have resulted in productions with which the masses could most readily identify? From the literally thousands of movie character images that have been exposed to the popular mind during this century, I would select Humphrey Bogart as the star.[14] I would be more hard pressed to choose a director from the astronomical number of quality films that have been produced in this country, but my choice over the long run, for reasons we will look into here, is John Ford.[15] Both the presence of Bogart and the touch of Ford in a film guaranteed a special kind of movie magic that was uniquely American in flavor and manner, and it is this sense of a special style that their movies project which has contributed primarily to the proliferation of nostalgia cults devoted to their films.

The test of Humphrey Bogart's acting ability lies in the fact that he rose above the stereotyped role of the gangster to turn in some of the most varied, honest, and naturally acted performances in the history of American film. Other than his roles in some of the more popular gangster movies during their heyday, most notably *Dead End* in 1937, Bogart performed creditably in the Western (*The Oklahoma Kid*, 1939), in the sociodocumentary drama (*Black Legion*, 1937), in the soap-opera vehicle (*Dark Victory*, 1939), in the horror-oriented film (*The Return of Dr. X*, 1939), in the military role (*The Caine Mutiny*, 1954), and as a private investigator (*The Big Sleep*, 1946). These isolated examples from the many roles Bogart actually played are named here to convey an overall picture of this actor's amazing versatility, but if he had appeared in only four films his tremendous achievement as a film actor would have been ensured as well as his versatility in handling diverse roles, not to mention their contribution to Bogart's stature as a nostalgic image.

In fact, when we think of Bogart the actor, we visualize a sense of presence that is an amalgamation of his roles in the following four films. In *The Maltese Falcon* (1941), Dashiell Hammett's laconic, self-styled Sam Spade comes to life on the screen in the person of Bogart's cynical and tough characterization. Here was a manner of acting that not only set the style for Bogart's later film roles, but it dramatized an attitude, lifestyle, and a whole new way of looking at existence for thousands of fans, particularly males who found it increasingly difficult to be self-assertive in an increasingly absurd and indifferent world. Bogart's self-actualized manner, which dared fate and any other external force, achieved its most characteristic visual interpretation in *Casablanca* (1942), considered by many to be among the finest American films ever made. Here again the movies made the most of joining music and mood to create dramatic effect. Who, for example, can forget the closeup of Bogart's agonized face, suggesting the most profound inner torment, as he listens to the haunting strains of "As Time Goes By"? Both from a nostalgic and a psychological point of view, most Bogart fans feel a regeneration and revitalization of their inner being upon watching a screening of this film. Perhaps the most striking example of this fact has been visualized in the Woody Allen play, *Play It Again, Sam*, later a movie itself, which had its anti-hero attempting to overcome the emotional crises of his own life through identifying with Bogart's key scenes in *Casablanca*—an example of movie nostalgia as psy-

chiatric therapy! Although Bogart took on character roles in *The Treasure of the Sierra Madre* (1948) and in *The African Queen* (1952) that called for ignorant drifter types—the gold prospector Fred C. Dobbs in *Treasure* and the river rat Charlie Allnut in *Queen*—he still managed to inject into these roles something of the Bogart acting trademark—a personal defiance and expression that stamp even the lowliest person as an individual supreme within the confines of his own narrowly realized world. Such an experience, when visualized as effectively as it was in these two films, can have great import in our nostalgic fascination for them.

Since his production of Sinclair Lewis's *Arrowsmith* in 1931, the major interest of John Ford as film director has been to project and mythologize through the film medium the varying shades and dominant colors of the American experience.[16] The varying shades were captured in movies like *Young Mr. Lincoln* (1939), *The Grapes of Wrath* (1940), *Tobacco Road* (1941), *Mr. Roberts* (1955), and *The Last Hurrah* (1958). The dominant colors shown forth in Westerns like *Stagecoach* (1939), My *Darling Clementine* (1946), *She Wore a Yellow Ribbon* (1949), and *The Alamo* (1960). The fact that a star like John Wayne got his first big break in *Stagecoach* and went on to appear in a number of Westerns directed by Ford is an important clue to understanding Ford's intent as a director and his handling of the Western genre to focus on the essence of the American experience. Ford was quick to recognize in the unbridled, rawboned appearance of the young John Wayne something that reflected the kind of spirit he wanted to capture on film, and as the masses of moviegoers soon discovered, John Wayne in a Ford Western spoke to something elementally American. Here was the kind of character who physically represented the very qualities they wanted to believe distinguished the American experience from all others. Rugged, unflinching in the face of adversity, just and equitable in his dealings with others, John Wayne as Western hero was nevertheless firm enough to take matters into his own hands if he felt the situation called for it.

As Ford controlled and directed it, the John Wayne image was the personification of our respect for traditional values and of what happened when these values were threatened by alien forces. As such, the nostalgic image of John Wayne as Western hero contains the essential ingredients of character and place that make the mass mind so susceptible to the nostalgia neurosis, and as such this image would rank somewhere near that of Humphrey Bo-

Walter Wanger Presents

STAGECOACH

A New Kind of Picture About the American West

A strange adventure that befell seven oddly assorted travelers who start out by stagecoach for Lordsburg, New Mexico in the year 1885. Each has his own personal reasons for wanting to get there. Then strange things begin to happen. The telegraph is mysteriously cut... the way station burned to the ground. Danger grows steadily more menacing, until...

As conventions break down, the lives of the travelers are tangled together ... you live with them this strange adventure... tense, full of action... deeply moving...

★ ★ ★

(Due to the tremendous suspense developed in "Stagecoach," we recommend that you get to the theatre for the start of the picture.)

Directed by JOHN FORD

ACADEMY AWARD WINNER, DIRECTOR OF "SUBMARINE PATROL," "THE HURRICANE," "THE INFORMER," ETC.)

with CLAIRE TREVOR • JOHN WAYNE

ANDY DEVINE • JOHN CARRADINE • THOMAS MITCHELL • LOUISE PLATT
GEORGE BANCROFT • DONALD MEEK • BERTON CHURCHILL • TIM HOLT

Released thru United Artists

"BUCK"
...the stage driver

"CURLY"
...the marshal

The Seven Oddly Assorted Strangers Who Started for Lordsburg

FRONT SEAT

BANKER
Why so careful of the little black bag?

WIFE
"We must go on—I've got to find my husband!"

MAN of MYSTERY
A strange whim—something from the past—forced him to go.

BACK SEAT

DOCTOR
It took 12 cups of coffee to sober him in time.

DANCE-HALL GIRL
Nothing mattered but a man she'd never seen before.

TRAVELING-SALESMAN
"I'm a married man—father of five—I insist we go back."

ON THE FLOOR

CONVICT
He gave himself up in order to be taken to Lordsburg; where three men waited to kill him.

The team of John Ford as director and John Wayne as actor has produced some of the movies' most "American" films, particularly those of the Western genre like the classic Stagecoach *(United Artists, 1939). Ford had a genius for visualizing the American sense of action and movement, and Wayne was the actor who best represented Ford's heroic vision.*

Appearing in Western films over a period of nearly fifty years, John Wayne seemed as durable as the Western genre itself. PHOTO FROM AUTHOR'S COLLECTION.

gart as the most dominant and pervasive movie-star image to stimulate the visual sensibility of the popular mind. Because of his genius for combining the heroic role with an organic sense of action and movement—that basic characteristic that has always distinguished the American film and endeared it to the masses—John Ford, more than any other film director, perpetuated the movie version of the nostalgic vision through his understanding of what popular audiences wanted to see in a movie. The popular success of his movies speaks for itself.

At a time when the movies appear to be devoting much of their energies to a mood of fantasy for fantasy's sake (further evidence of where the public mood exists today), it would be appropriate to round this section off with a look at the achievement of Walt Disney, animated cartoons, and their effect on our nostalgic vision. If, as I have asserted throughout this section, the American film has always been controlled and directed by a special sense of movement, then by its very definition the animated cartoon stands as the most characteristic

form of this movement. Its necessary ingredients—music, sound effects, and action—all blend to create a total visual effect on audiences. Like most of the creative innovators mentioned in this book, Disney grew up with the technological discoveries in visual communications of this century, and his real genius in working with the animated cartoon lay in his ability to exploit what had already been done technically and to make it uniquely his own. Even though a precedent had already been established for the animated cartoon in the work of Winsor McCay and although there would be other approaches to the animated form of film production, such as Max Fleischer's, Disney's strong business sense and knack for diversifying his enterprises (comic-strip adaptations of his characters, merchandising toys and products, live movies, television, and the theme amusement park) have made his name synonymous with the most pervasive visual influence on popular culture in the twentieth century.[17]

The animated cartoon was Disney's apprenticeship for whatever he was to achieve in later years, and it is his handling of this medium that we must examine if we are to understand his dominant influence on the nostalgic vision in popular culture. As early as the short cartoon feature, *The Three Little Pigs* (1933), we can spot basic elements of the Disney philosophy that reflect his attitude toward traditional American values, such as resourcefulness and hard work, which is exemplified in the pig who built his house of brick, and a cheerful optimism in the face of adversity, which is expressed by the song, "Who's Afraid of the Big Bad Wolf?" Depression-era audiences loved this cartoon, and today it stands as one of the most popularly received productions in the entire Disney repertoire. In retrospect, it appears that a better morale-building statement than this simple tale could hardly have been devised during a time when the future loomed dark and foreboding for most people. Thus the conditions for nostalgic identification with Disney's work were evident right from the beginning.

The moral fable side of Disney continued to express itself in other short cartoons, evolving eventually into the first feature-length cartoon, *Snow White and the Seven Dwarfs* (1937), which is considered by many to be the finest work of its kind and to be among the greatest film achievements of all time. In this fairy-tale allegory of good versus evil, we see Disney's optimistic outlook surfacing in the character of Snow White who, in spite of the magical machinations of the wicked Queen, wins her longed-for Prince. Even though the appealing dwarf

THE AUDIO-VISUAL IMPACT OF WALT DISNEY

Indicative of a pioneer spirit that looked ahead to the television age, the Disney Studios conducted numerous experiments with the union of sight and sound during the 1940s. Films like Saludos Amigos *(1943),* The Three Caballeros *(1945), and* Song of the South *(1946) depended on a combination of animation and live action (for example, a "live" Uncle Remus conjuring up animated versions of Joel Chandler Harris's animal characters in* Song of the South*), but some films like* Make Mine Music *(1946) had animated characters cavorting to the "live" voices and music of well-known personalities of the time.*

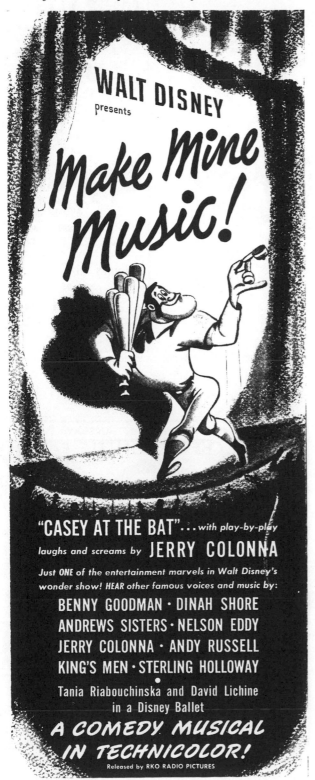

These two ads for Snow White *and* Fantasia, *presented forty years apart (1938 and 1978 respectively), reveal that the Disney image has maintained its spell on the mass eye and that experimentation is still going on in order to project "the ultimate experience."*

GOING TO THE MOVIES IN 1938
If you were interested in going to the neighborhood or down-town movie theaters in 1938, here are some of the choices you had as advertised in the newspapers and magazines of that day.

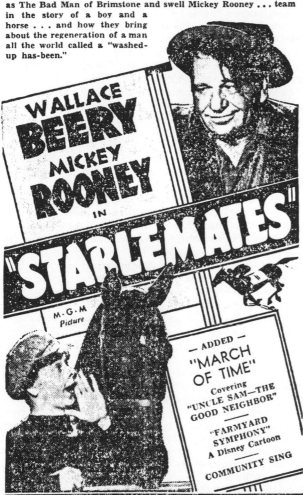
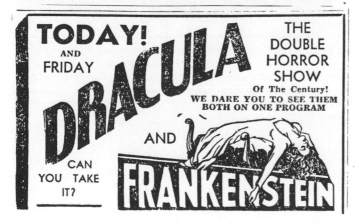

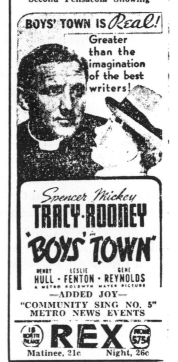

characters are given unique, individual personalities, they all stand united on the virtue of work as espoused in the songs, "Heigh Ho, It's Off to Work We Go" and "Just Whistle While You Work," and they all rally to the cause of their beloved Snow White. Inherent in the interrelationships among the characters in *Snow White* is a positive attitude toward existence that appeared again and again throughout the Disney canon, but this was the feature-length cartoon which was the most visually effective in getting the Disney message across to viewers.

The most technically ambitious of the Disney cartoon features was *Fantasia* (1940), advertised as the "ultimate experience" in sight and sound, and as such highly relevant to our discussion here. As a kind of experimental tour de force of what the animated cartoon experience could be, *Fantasia* sought to recreate in visual terms the marriage of sight and sound in order that audiences might cultivate a deeper appreciation for classical music. Even if this had not been a primary mission, the overall result would have been the same for popular audiences never before exposed to the augmented sounds of composers like Bach, Tchaikovsky, Beethoven, and Stravinsky in a delightful, exciting visual approach that made it quite evident what these highbrow composers were about.

The example of *Fantasia* proved that the so-called classical experience can be nostalgic provided that the identification is visually intense enough. Popular audiences of this film always remember that after the Moussorgsky sequence dealing with the devil and his cult, the film ends on a typical Disney note with the reassuring sounds of Schubert's "Ave Maria" accompanied by the symbolic procession of cowled monks moving toward some assemblage of meaningful significance. In fact, Walt Disney's experiments with the union of sight and sound in a film like *Fantasia* not only reinforce what is meant by the nostalgia neurosis, they anticipate the most visually compelling and influential medium of mass behavior and popular culture that we have yet encountered—television.

Notes

1. Ken Weiss and Ed Goodgold, *To Be Continued . . .* (New York: Bonanza Books, 1972), p. ix.

2. There are those who would nominate Republic's *The Adventures of Captain Marvel* (1941) for this distinction. Starring Tom Tyler as the title hero, this serial was produced by the studio that did turn out more quality serials than any other.

3. Chris Steinbrunner and Burt Goldblatt, *Cinema of the Fantastic* (New York: Galahad Books, 1972), p. 131.

4. James Robert Parish, *The Great Movie Series* South Brunswick: A. S. Barnes and Co., 1971), p. 13.

5. The Warner Brothers films evolved into Monogram's East Side Kids and Bowery Boys series, a parody of the earlier films, yet suggesting a nostalgic flavor all their own.

6. The Western is the film genre which is most conducive to capturing and conveying our peculiar understanding of spatial movement as it relates to character and place. See the fiction section dealing with Zane Grey for further discussion of the popularity of the Western.

7. Joe Morella, Edward Z. Epstein, and John Griggs, introduction, *The Films of World War II* (Secaucus, N.J.: Citadel Press, 1973), p. 7.

8. Some other popularly acclaimed films of 1939 were *Goodbye, Mr. Chips, Union Pacific, Mr. Smith Goes to Washington, Destry Rides Again, Stagecoach, Gunga Din, Beau Geste, Dark Victory, Babes in Arms, The Hunchback of Notre Dame, The Roaring Twenties, Juarez,* and *Of Mice and Men.*

9. The movies would continue their influence on our sexual attitudes, however, particularly through the creation of love goddess symbols like Jean Harlow, Betty Grable, Rita Hayworth, Marilyn Monroe, and Elizabeth Taylor.

10. Note that *The Jazz Singer* (1927) was a silent film except for the singing sequences in which Al Jolson performed. Evidently, it took a while for the movie industry to adjust to the impact of sound on visual expression.

11. Ironically, though, the very way of middle-class life that Fields's humor satirized inspired a Norman Rockwell kind of nostalgia which in itself has contributed to the spread of the nostalgia neurosis.

12. By contrast, women also played the major roles in a type of movie that revealed life and its problems as the outgrowth of human vagaries and weaknesses, the forerunner of the "soap opera" genre. Witness films like Joan Crawford's *A Woman's Face* (1941) and *Mildred Pierce* (1945) and of course Bette Davis's *Jezebel* (1938) and *Dark Victory* (1939).

13. Robert Sklar, *Movie-Made America: A Social History of American Movies* (New York: Random House, 1975), p. 188.

14. Strong cases could certainly be built for the following, too: Bette Davis, James Cagney, Henry Fonda, Katherine Hepburn, Spencer Tracy, and John Wayne. My choice of Bogart is based on the peculiarly American flavor he imparted to every role he played.

15. John Huston, with films like *The Maltese Falcon, The Treasure of Sierra Madre, Key Largo, The Asphalt Jungle, The African Queen, Moby Dick, The Misfits,* and *The Night of the Iguana* could qualify for this honor; however, Ford, because of his characteristically American interpretation of his subject matter, is closer to the premise of this book.

16. Even during the silent era, Ford had been laying the foundation for his myth of the American West with an epic film like *The Iron Horse* (1924).

17. Fleischer created one of the more memorable characters of the animated cartoon in Betty Boop, who first appeared in 1931, but his work on Popeye the Sailor and Superman was more popular. As delightful as his feature-length cartoons were *(Mr. Bug Goes to Town* and *Gulliver's Travels),* Fleischer could never match the business acumen of the Disney organization and consequently faded from the scene.

4

The Nostalgic Vision in Television

Television is actually a *blind* medium. We may think of it as visual, recording a world "out there." But it really records a world within. Sight surrenders to insight, and dream replaces outer reality. Television, far from expanding consciousness, repudiates it in favor of the dream.

—Edmund Carpenter,
from an interview

With the coming of network radio and the attendant growth of the recording industry in the 1920s, sound as a characteristically expressive medium of popular communication began to make a significant impact on American popular culture. From an imaginative viewpoint, these media forms afforded a degree of opportunity for the listener to identify visually with what he heard. But, as we have seen, it was not until Walt Disney's experimentations with the animated sound cartoon in the 1930s, resulting in the first feature-length cartoon, *Snow White and the Seven Dwarfs,* and later a landmark film like *Fantasia,* that the masses began to comprehend the unlimited possibilities of sound and its bearing on visual experience. For example, when the popularly misunderstood music of the masters was visually interpreted through the animation genius of Disney's staff in

Fantasia, many people grasped for the first time what a composer like Moussorgsky probably intended in the enchanting and wildly dissonant "Night on Bald Mountain." As a result, the animated cartoon's happy combination of sight and sound was an achievement of such consequence that the popular visual sense would be henceforth conditioned by this combination.

The musical track of the Hollywood movie also capitalized on its ability to play on an audience's emotions by matching appropriate mood music to certain dramatic scenes. But ultimately, in a later day, the medium of television synthesized the cultural contributions of all popular art forms in a sight-and-sound experience that projected the nostalgia of character and place in a way uniquely and peculiarly its own. The climax of this process in our

By conditioning listening audiences to the imaginative qualities of sound, popular radio of the 1930s–40s was the medium that prepared us for the visual dominance of television. These ads for popular radio shows reveal how home listening patterns and habits were being established by radio programming, a harbinger of things to come in the television age.

day is the creation of a readily accessible, all-enveloping daydream experience for the masses. Accordingly, the animated sound cartoon pioneered by Disney and Max Fleischer has found television expression in the factorylike productions of studios like Hanna-Barbera for the Saturday morning cartoon shows, and in the adult-slanted commercial, which is really the ultimate fantasy experience of sight and sound as conceived by the medium of television. Even though the nature of the medium is commercially committed to the visual revelation of the reality in which we exist, we realize that, like other forms of popular expression, televi-

sion has learned to relegate itself to fathoming the currently popular fantasies and wish fulfillments of its audience. A look at some of the implications and repercussions of this commitment will lead us to a better understanding of the mythmaking powers of contemporary television.

To further substantiate my contention that the modes of pop-culture expression are derivative of and interdependent on each other, we find that all the cultural forms discussed in this book have discovered extended creative expression through the medium of television. Examples abound: works of popular fiction like Irwin Shaw's *Rich Man, Poor Man* enjoy highly successful television productions; comic-strip characters are given new life in the animated Saturday kid shows and the live-character "Wonder Woman" and "Spider-Man" series; and an astronomical number of Hollywood-produced movies fill prime time as well as other time slots.

The Griffith-DeMille vision climaxed in movie spectaculars like Caesar and Cleopatra (United Artists, 1946), whose advertising copy instructed viewers that they would SEE all manner of sensational activity for the price of admission.

Although Edgar Rice Burroughs was aware of his many imitators, as in this 1936 Ka-Zar *pulp, he would have been pleasantly surprised to find that first-edition copies of his works are highpriced collectors' items today. Like other subject matter of popular interest, Burroughs's books were read and frequently discarded, a factor that contributed to the rarity of certain volumes and their ultimate worth on the buyer's market.* Ka-Zar COVER REPRINTED BY PERMISSION OF ODYSSEY PUBLICATIONS, INC. ANTIQUES JOURNAL COVER REPRINTED BY PERMISSION OF PUBLISHER. © 1975.

the ANTIQUES JOURNAL

K48134

JUNE

1975

$1.00

ART OF THE ESKIMO

DOWER CHESTS

STONEWARES

NOVELS OF EDGAR RICE BURROUGHS

THE FROST GARRISON COMPOUND

EARLY TELEGRAPHIC APPARATUS

During the war years many studios turned out movies like Stage Door Canteen *(United Artists, 1943) in which well-known movie people and other entertainment personalities appeared briefly in a kind of morale-boosting effort. Needless to say, plot was practically nonexistent in such films.*

FROM SUPERMAN TO WONDER WOMAN: the Comic Book Comes to Television
From the fabricated backgrounds for the TV series Superman *(starring George Reeves in the 1950s) through the campy version of* Batman *in the 1960s (Adam West as Batman and Burt Ward as Robin) to the more realistic portrayal of Wonder Woman by Lynda Carter in the 1970s, there is much to tell us about the technical accomplishments of the television medium during that period of time. Superhero types, presented both live and animated, have always had a popular reception on television. Lately the trend is toward shows with an adult slant featuring anti-heroes like Spider-Man and the Hulk.* PHOTOS FROM AUTHOR'S COLLECTION.

The flexibility and adaptability of the television medium have made of it our most reliable means for reexperiencing many of our most nostalgic moments of identification with popular forms of expression. As a result, television enjoys a multiple function today as a repository of all the forms of visual media; but in contrast to the other forms we have examined, it provides us with a persistent source for nostalgically relating to popular experience in mainly a shared sense. When millions of contemporary television viewers annually watch the classic film *The Wizard of Oz,* they are participating in a mass ritual that is diametrically opposed, in total visual effect, to that undergone by those earlier generations who first had the 1900 book and then the 1939 movie to relate to. To observe our gradual transition from the print experience through the film to television is to realize in a nutshell how our popular visual sense has evolved and how this de-

velopment has affected us as a people.

Even though the more individualized experience of reading a book or even viewing a film in a theater may still be accessible to us, the dominant impact of television on our visual sense has compelled us all, it seems, to relate to the once uniquely personal habit of reading a novel as a communal experience. Now, as we read, we often visualize how the print experience might come across on film or television. As the Hollywood movie made us into self-appointed casting directors, acutely sensitive to personalities who seemed qualified to play special dramatic roles (Clark Gable as Rhett Butler or Claudette Colbert and later Elizabeth Taylor as Cleopatra), so television in contrast to film's dependence on the dominance of personality, has made us more aware of raw experience itself as subject matter that subjugates the personality of a character to it. Archie Bunker may be the dominant character of the "All in the Family" series, but his actions are controlled to a great extent by what happens around him in a society that has grown increasingly permissive toward wide variations in social behavior.

Our day's sensitivity to experience for experience's sake apparently accounts for the overemphasis on sex, violence, and the sensational in the various forms of popular expression, but these are areas of experience in which the characters function more as victims than as doers and thus offer further evidence of the "diminished self" in today's society. Regardless of how we may realize our personal relationship with these forms, the fact remains that television has created a new fantasy realm for us, one that has extended our daydream options and consequently the range of our nostalgic vision—and, it might be added, our susceptibility to neuroses other than those produced by the conditions of the nostalgia neurosis. Because of this predicament, television has made us more aware of the anxieties and concerns of our inner selves than we ever thought it would.

If the nostalgic vision is derived from our affinity for daydreaming and fantasizing, as I have reiterated throughout this book, then the shared experience of television may be responsible for a new and different kind of daydreaming and ultimately a unique kind of nostalgia experience. Harry F. Waters, in a February 21, 1977 *Newsweek* article exploring the effects of television on children, points out a trend that, if it continues, will probably have more wide-ranging neurotic consequences than any of the sociological or psychological conditions that we have confronted thus far. According to a fourteen-

The annual ritual of viewing The Wizard of Oz *on television illustrates how a popular classic can successfully adapt itself to the demands of any media form. Since the appearance of the original story in 1900 to its being televised in the 1980s, our visual expectations of this delightful fantasy have dramatically evolved.*

PHOTO FROM AUTHOR'S COLLECTION

year-old quoted in this article, "Television is perfect to tune out the rest of the world." As one nine-year-old puts it, "I'd rather watch TV than play outside because it's boring outside. They always have the same rides, like swings and things."[1] If these are typical attitudes, then we may be witness to a generation of fantasists who find most television fare to be more real than reality itself. We would agree, I think, that to actively fantasize is one thing, but to actively avoid reality through fantasizing is quite another. If, as I have suggested through the metaphor of the daydream that controls the thematic organization of this book, the visual experience of daydreaming has always been at the root of our fantasy and nostalgic affinities, we appear now to have arrived at a point in our visual history at which we can indulge in as much fantasy experience as we please, compliments of the packaged daydreams of the ubiquitous television tube. Even though television has been referred to as a "drug," unlike the drug-related experiences that induce dreams to expand the imagination, television in its role of functioning visually for us—as a literal extension of our own eyes, as Marshall McLuhan observed—controls the imaginative process to the extent that in many people it has atrophied or even disappeared. Radio may have received its share of criticism when it was at the peak of its popularity, but programs like "I Love a Mystery", "Lum and Abner", and "Inner Sanctum" captured the imaginative fancies of a national listening audience simply because the listener was induced to visually imagine what he heard coming over the airwaves, an experience that in time would markedly contrast with the visual dominance of television.

It would appear, then, that the television viewing experience has contributed to a whole new way of perceiving reality and subsequently a different way of responding to the televised event and its revelation of character and place. Whereas an individual's nostalgic reaction to popular fiction, the comic strip, the movies, and even radio demands more of an active, self-assertive visual role on the part of an audience, television, as today's predominant media form, pacifies and numbs our visual senses to the extent that whatever nostalgic identification we may have through this medium can only be realized in a sense of shared experience, that is, in identifying with a televised event as a communal happening in contrast to the more individualized experience of reading a favorite novel or comic-strip series, or viewing a vintage movie in a theater setting. How, we might ask, did this situation come about?

Like the other visual forms of popular expression, television was awkward and crude in the beginning, so much so that in the late 1940s a viewer of special events, panel programs, and live dramatic productions participated in a uniquely primitive visual experience in comparison to that of watching the movies of that time or today's sophisticated, well-polished color programs that are constantly beamed our way. It is this thirty-year evolutionary process that has subtly beguiled and conditioned our popular visual sense to be highly dependent on the ritual of the publicized or shared television event, ranging from the thoroughly researched news documentary and ballyhooed sports event of the real world to the situation comedy and late-show movie designed primarily as pure entertainment. In a shorter period of time, television has prepared us to expect more from it than we have from any other medium of popular expression, and we are just now beginning to understand how and why this situation came about in a society that has always prided itself in being dynamically active.

In looking back to the late 1940s and a more innocent time when the traumas of World War II had been put behind us, we can now see that American social behavior had finally developed to the point where it was generally receptive and conducive to the advent of a communally realized medium of visual expression like television. First of all, with a standard of living that allowed more families than ever before to purchase homes on liberal mortgage plans, the country took an important step toward creating the appropriate atmosphere for home television. Then, too, the conditions created by a higher educational level among the masses as well as a variety of revolutionary technological achievements undoubtedly contributed to a heightened visual sensitivity to and interest in contemporary events and various elements of popular culture. Consequently, societal conditions at this time were ripe for the masses to indulge themselves in a kind of visually shared fantasy feast, the likes of which previous world societies had never known. In the long run, though, this communal feast would develop into a gorging experience resulting in a homogenization of lifestyles as well as a continuously expanding realm of fantasy expectations.

By going back to the beginnings of commercial television and tracing its effects on us through the popular acceptance of particular personality types and the development of certain trends in the medium, we may obtain a better understanding of what I mean by the "shared" visual experience of televi-

Like the movies, early television thrived on comedy. Some, like Red Skelton, had already established successful images in the media of radio and the movies; others, like Milton Berle and Jackie Gleason, became primarily known through their television roles; Berle as his own show's "Uncle Milty," a man of many roles, and Gleason as Ralph, the frustrated husband and busdriver, in The Honeymooners, **here pictured with the other principals of the show.** PHOTOS FROM AUTHOR'S COLLECTION.

Red Skelton

Jackie Gleason

Milton Berle

sion in contrast to the uniquely verbalized (fiction), democratized (comic strip), and dramatized (film) experiences of the other three popular forms that I have previously discussed.

In looking back to television's infancy, we detect the start of a pattern of mass behavior that has persisted right up until today—the giving over to or organizing of an entire evening, or afternoon in the case of most sports events, around watching a popular televised event. At first, these attractions consisted mostly of viewing the weekly antics of comedians like Milton Berle, Jackie Gleason, or Sid Caesar. Like the early movies, television in its early years offered a heavy fare of comedy, and it wasn't long before the more established figures of other entertainment media like film and radio—Bob Hope, Jack Benny, and Red Skelton—came over to television to enhance the established pattern. Consequently a common habit among family members during these years was their spurning of outside activities to stay home and watch the zany shenanigans of a comic like Milton Berle or Red Skelton, two of the most popular and influential television comedy stars in the history of the medium.

Although we did not realize it at the time, the thing that was happening to us because of our special attention to the live televised events of these early years was the creation of a sense of visual immediacy or ultrasensitivity to current experience that would begin to undermine, however subtly, whatever traditional conception or understanding of the past we might have had. In fact, the past became now, and the end result after some thirty years of constant exposure to this phenomenon has been a totally unique way of examining experience and consequently a singular way of experiencing nostalgic feeling. Whereas the movies had opened up vistas on new fantasy experiences for mass audiences in the rather impersonal surroundings of the theater (the person sitting next to you, for example, might be a total stranger), television conjured up for us at the touch of a button and within the familiar confines of our living quarters its peculiar vision of the real world as well as the fantasized interpretation of reality that popular audiences have always craved. The fact that television viewing was subject to the viewer's control made it that much more fascinating. Ironically, though, its visual attraction was so powerful that it soon began to exercise more control over the viewer than he did over it.

In further contrast to the movies, which had made us all celebrity conscious in a remotely detached sense so that most movie personalities seemed unapproachable in real life, television conditioned

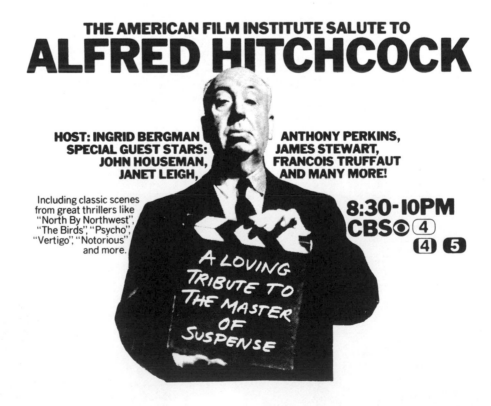

Television attracted movie personalities to its fold right from the beginning, and many of them retained and enhanced the identity that movies had built up for them. Even a director like Alfred Hitchcock, for example, who had established a name for himself as a master of suspense dramas like Notorious! *(RKO, 1946), could become even more popular as the macabre host of* Alfred Hitchcock Presents, *beginning in 1955.*

us to expectations about and private identifications with its specially created personalities in a directly engaging, more familiar manner. Hollywood had created public myths like Rudolph Valentino, Jean Harlow, and Clark Gable for the masses' fantasy adulation and enjoyment, but it was the coming of television that humanized the Hollywood star and brought this mythical creature down to the level of personal identification. Thus movie personalities who had made a name for themselves in countless films—stars like Douglas Fairbanks, Jr., Adolphe Menjou, Loretta Young, Ronald Reagan, Dick Powell, and even a director like Alfred Hitchcock—endeared themselves to millions of television viewers as real down-to-earth people by introducing popular series shows in television's earlier days. Others who started out in other media became household names because of their TV success—Ed Sullivan, Arthur Godfrey, Dave Garroway, Jack Paar, and Johnny Carson, to name a few of the more outstanding host personalities. Actually, the popular success of this latter group was directly dependent on how familiar a personal image they could project to audiences. A colorless personality like Ed Sullivan, whose real genius lay in his ability to recognize the pervasive visual powers of television for entertainment purposes and to adapt his manner to its unique demands, became widely known not for any special talent of his own but for his perceptiveness and timeliness in promoting celebrities who had claim to fame in either the pop- or high-culture scene.

One of the most peculiar attributes of the familiar television images of this stripe and one that points out a necessary requisite for success in a medium noted for its high casualty rate is an ability to perform effectively within the medium and yet not dominate a show in the way a Hollywood star might dominate a film. The long-running popularity of both an awkward Ed Sullivan and an urbane, witty Johnny Carson came about primarily through the viewer's visual expectations of one host's shortcomings and the other's minor triumphs: Sullivan's clumsy manner contrasted in most cases with the more polished air of his guest performers to create an unintentional humorous effect, and Carson's calculated demeanor is designed to size up his guests' unguarded moments for conscious humorous effect. Both approaches served to enhance the visual images of these two classic television personalities in the eyes of the viewer. Whenever there is a nostalgic rerun of television scenes which reveal these two at their characteristic best (or worst), we

The long-running popularity of a personality like Johnny Carson on NBC's The Tonight Show *attests to the visual power of television, and that success in the medium is not necessarily dependent on the visual dominance of an individual but rather on his pervasive adaptability to it.*   PHOTO FROM AUTHOR'S COLLECTION.

A commanding figure like Frank Sinatra, for example, has dominated the recording industry and the movies since the 1940s, but he has never really achieved any significant success as a television performer.   PHOTO FROM AUTHOR'S COLLECTION.

are usually presented scenes of them engaged in situations like just described. Television audiences delighted, it seemed, in watching star performers make mistakes and react in an offbeat manner. In fact, the medium seemed made for the kind of activity which humanized performers by making them essentially part of the viewing audience, whether at home or in the studios. Carson himself has always been one to go out into the studio audience and directly identify with those in attendance. Thus, from a nostalgic point of view, the informal talk show, which was pioneered in the early 1950s by a zany late-night production called "Broadway Open House" and passed on in the form of the "Tonight Show," has always been a favorite with television viewers.[2] Steve Allen, Jack Paar, and finally Johnny Carson each brought his own whimsical flavor to this show. Hosts of daytime TV programs like Mike Douglas discovered that time of day mattered little to audiences who loved to hear people talking about themselves and/or about other people and that it mattered little whether those interviewed were celebrities or just ordinary people. The medium of television has surely capitalized on this fact of human nature, not only informally in its talk-show format, but dramatically in the genre of the soap opera, an increasingly popular mode of entertainment which closely mirrors social changes.

There is another interesting phenomenon that supports my contention that the most successful television performers are not those with dominant personal images but rather those who appear familiar and accessible: the most successful musical stars of television have mainly been those who, comparatively speaking, have had only moderately successful careers in radio, films, and the recording industry. Bing Crosby and Frank Sinatra, who enjoyed huge followings in radio, movies, and records, never achieved the consistent television appeal of performers like Perry Como, Dinah Shore, and Lawrence Welk, basically because the star images of Crosby and Sinatra were too expansive for the medium of television. By contrast, Perry Como and Dinah Shore's easygoing, folksy personalities kept their personal images unobtrusive and comfortably assuring to viewers who visually identified with television almost as they would with a familiar piece of furniture, which indeed it is.

But of all the musical performers with any lasting appeal on television, Lawrence Welk best epitomizes the medium's peculiar interpretation of what I mean by the nostalgia neurosis that permeates the visual forms of popular culture. Whatever we may say critically of Welk's own stylistic approach to musical production, we must admit that his is a unique visual image whose popular success is based on its sight-and-sound appeal to an older age group. By playing on this age group's susceptibility to the nostalgia neurosis—the lure of the past as idealized by its popular music and in pointed contrast to the music of today's youth—Welk's company of singers and musicians stage thematic medleys that inspire pleasant memories of the apparently better times that the tunes were a product of. The shared experience of the moment is enhanced, too, by Welk's allowing couples from the studio audience to come forth and dance on camera. Although these dancers have the advantage of participating in a live event, home viewers, in a nostalgic sense, are also in a reciprocal position to share the experience in terms of whatever the tunes may personally mean to them. In the televising of a Lawrence Welk musical rendition, we sense an air of nostalgic remoteness existing in an overall atmosphere of "nowness."

Thus a prevalent characteristic of the television medium is that, unlike other media forms, it can express these environments simultaneously. The unique binary visual outlook of television stems in the main from its outward dedication to reporting

The Lawrence Welk Show

WITH HIS WHOLE

CHAMPAGNE MUSIC FAMILY

Saturday 6:00 p.m.
WJHG-TV 7
Panama City, Florida

"The Lawrence Welk Show" exemplifies the musical side of the nostalgia neurosis through its sight-and-sound appeal to an older age group. In a Welk production, the attractiveness of the past is idealized through its musical hits.

what it sees now as well as its underlying zeal to fathom the fantasy wishes and daydreams of its audience. These characteristics of the medium, which have been evident since the days when television drama was presented live, can tell us as much about our currently dominant psychological circumstances as can the characteristics of any of the popular forms examined in this book.

By the early 1950s, with the growing popularity of television, the conditions were set for a universal acquiescence to the effects of immediate experience as visualized through the medium of television. However, in the early days there was not yet an effective method for playing back or reshowing a televised event at a later time; as a result most of what was seen on live television has been lost to the ether waves. With the advent of the videotape recording process, the medium came up with a revolutionary system for storing the television experience and responding to the potential nostalgic identification of the viewer.

Even before the introduction of videotaping, however, there was evidence of how our nostalgia for a time and place could distort our perception of specially remembered events, particularly in the case of what we may have thought were the greatest live moments of early television. Ironically, though, many of these dramatic moments are among those that are most difficult to recall since the nature of the medium does not allow for the spectacular effects of the big-screen movie theater, nor does it give us sufficient time to savor or absorb the impact of the dramatic moment.[3] As great as they were in their time, the ephemeral quality of superior live productions like "Marty" (1953), "Patterns" (1955), and "Requiem for a Heavyweight" (1956) would be as evident today as that of most vintage Hollywood films, provided we were again to view the original productions. It was the one-time viewing experience that conditioned audiences of series like *Playhouse 90, Kraft Television Theater,* and the *Hallmark Hall of Fame* to look for mistakes in both the acting and the technical coordination. The fact that viewers were occasionally rewarded for their alertness further exemplifies the humanizing side of television and in itself establishes a basis for nostalgic identification with early television. It was the experimental nature of most dramatic productions during this time that made these productions an excellent testing and training ground for actors and actresses who later made names for themselves in the movies.[4] As if in response to television's special needs, the new breed of actors the medium turned out revealed a down-to-earth quality that answered the increased demands for heightened realism in the Hollywood film, which by the end of the 1950s had reconciled itself to having to outdo the competitive threats of the television medium in order to survive.

While many would-be stars who had received the bulk of their experience in the dramatic productions of television were packing for Hollywood, an even greater number of established performers who had gotten their start in the golden years of Hollywood were heading for the television cameras to ensure even longer careers. This condition was particularly applicable to the situation comedy of the 1950s which attracted faces already familiar to millions of movie-goers: Lucille Ball in "I Love Lucy," George Burns and Gracie Allen in their own show, Phil Silvers in "You'll Never Get Rich," Walter Brennan in "The Real McCoys," Robert Young in "Father Knows Best," and Ann Sothern in "Private Secretary." Although audiences appeared to take an indiscriminate delight in seeing longtime favorites of the movies cast in a variety of television roles that grew increasingly familiar each week, television producers, quick to capitalize on any noticeable trend, as our mythmakers have been throughout the history of popular culture, seemed sold on the image of the family or the married couple as one of the most popular means for selling a program. Families, after all, comprised the majority of television's viewing audience anyway.

It all started in 1949 with a series about a Jewish family, "The Goldbergs," which built its situations around the minor problems of family and neighborhood relationships.[5] As the popularity of television mushroomed, the trend expanded rapidly in the 1950s with programs, in addition to those above, like "Amos 'n' Andy," which was criticized and finally taken off the air for its allegedly stereotyped portrayal of blacks, "Ozzie and Harriet," and "Make Room for Daddy," to name only a few of the more popular shows. The family situation, whether Jewish, black, or white, appeared to contain a solid formula for success with television viewers. Variations of the theme continued on through the 1960s with "My Three Sons," "The Andy Griffith Show," and "Family Affair," novel series which featured male-run households; "The Beverly Hillbillies" and "Green Acres," shows that carried on the rustic tradition of "The Real McCoys"; and the best of them all, "The Dick Van Dyke Show," a well-scripted series about a young married couple. Hanna-Barbera studios even came up with an animated cartoon version of a prehistoric family called "The Flintstones." The genre continues to manifest itself in the 1980s in sitcoms that reflect a more liberal interpretation of the mores of our day ("All in the Family," "Maude," "The Jeffersons," and "Good Times") or a nostalgic identification with the past ("Happy Days" and "The Waltons"). There appears to be no letup in sight; in fact, two late 1970s

As obviously disparate in depicting lifestyles as these popular situation comedies were, they commonly projected much of their humor through family problems and situations that audiences could identify with.

series, without any beating around the bush, labeled themselves simply "Family" and "Soap," the latter a no-holds-barred takeoff on the family complications that arise in the soap-opera genre.

The spectacular reception of the television version of *Roots,* which inspired millions to take an interest in family ancestral ties, ensures even more spinoffs and variations for years to come, each lending to that nostalgically communal aura that only the social group known as the family can generate. Even today, to view once again in syndication many of the family shows that we may have watched in the 1950s and 1960s is to be reminded of how we may have planned and directed our evenings at home

In the 1950s the zany acting of Lucille Ball found full expression in I Love Lucy, *a series built around the misadventures of a married couple, Lucy and Ricky Ricardo (Desi Arnaz). Support comedy was provided by their neighbors, played by Vivian Vance and William Frawley.* PHOTO FROM THE AUTHOR'S COLLECTION.

With an all-black cast, Amos 'n' Andy was a 1950s series that got many of its laughs from the relationship of the Kingfish (Tim Moore, standing) with his wife, Sapphire. The leads were played by Spencer Williams as Andy (left) and Alvin Childress as Amos (right). PHOTO FROM THE AUTHOR'S COLLECTION.

The 1960s introduced The Dick Van Dyke Show, *a more sophisticated version of the situation comedy in which Van Dyke plays a TV writer married to Mary Tyler Moore. Miss Moore, of course, was to go on to her own show which many viewers came to look upon as the ultimate experience in television situation comedies.* PHOTO FROM AUTHOR'S COLLECTION.

The cliche-ridden Western movie with stars like William Boyd (Hopalong Cassidy) and Gene Autry, as well as series like The Lone Ranger *(starring Clayton Moore and Jay Silverheels) was quick to adapt to the popular demands of television in the late '40s and early '50s, either in reruns or original productions. With the advent of shows like* Gunsmoke *in the mid-fifties, however, the genre took on a decided adult slant by dealing with problems of psychological impact.*
PHOTOS FROM AUTHOR'S COLLECTION.

during that seemingly long-ago time. If Lucy's predicaments don't seem to be as funny the second or third time around or the problems of Fred McMurray's sons don't appear to carry the poignancy they used to, then perhaps our times don't seem as funny or as poignant anymore. As our examination of the film medium has reminded us, our real nostalgic tie with the past is in the visual reminder of a place and time to which we can never return.

Actually, television, with its built-in capacity to see everything for us, has brought us visually closer to everything, to the remote as well as the familiar. When we watched newsreels in the movie theaters of the past, there was both a distance and time factor affecting our reaction to the scenes we saw, whether they were of World War II, a natural disaster, a beauty contest, or a sporting event. With the coming of television and concomitant developments in technological fields affecting factors of

time and space, the psychological conditions were set for our visual acceptance of and identification with an actual or imagined event as though it were happening now, perhaps somewhere in our own town or neighborhood, even though in reality the event was being transmitted by satellite from a point halfway around the world. Much has already been made over television's contributing as much as any other force, if not more, to the American people's growing revulsion toward the Vietnam war, whose combat scenes proved to be visually unpalatable in most of the living rooms of America.

By contrast, the function of delivering the remote event into our homes was more entertainingly presented in program series of the early 1950s like Edward R. Murrow's "See It Now" and Walter Cronkite's "You Are There." The very titles of these programs that dealt with current issues, as Murrow's did, and key historical events (Cronkite) caught the psychological significance and impact of the contemporary television viewing experience perfectly, and it soon became apparent that the documentary contained the ingredients for what was to become some of television's most triumphant moments. Here was a visual format that could provide in-depth investigation into an unlimited variety of subjects, no matter how remote or specialized, as long as the subject being spotlighted could be made visually familiar to a popular audience. Ironically, the technical advances of television, especially the appearance of the color set in the 1960s, could make the least interesting of subjects appealing to a mass audience. As a result, many viewers discovered themselves conditioned to watching programs in which they had no real interest. Because of its pervasive power to see for us and convert all experience, even that of the past, into an overwhelming sense of "nowness," television could even convey to us on occasion a fantasized sense of reality itself. One recalls the on-camera assassination of Lee Harvey Oswald, the ghetto riots of the 1960s, and the first-man-on-the-moon telecast in 1969. Paradoxically, though, the contrived situations of adventure series like the TV Western, for example, could seem more realistic than these real-life events whose surprisingly fantasied air can be attributed to the television medium's uncompromising zeal to report unblinkingly what it sees.

What really made the televised Western seem so real to adult audiences for whom it was designed was its dependence on psychological problems and even sociological issues that people could identify with. Beginning in 1955 with the long-running "Gunsmoke," the adult Western reacted against the cliché-ridden films of popular movie heroes like Gene Autry and William Boyd (Hopalong Cassidy) who had transferred their B-movie successes to the television screen in the late 1940s. Ten years later, shows like "Wagon Train," "Maverick," and "Bonanza" were still supplying grist for the mill to enhance America's perennial love affair with a genre that has cut across all forms of popular culture. "Bonanza," whose popular success was inherently ensured by its dramatization of family-group solidarity against any outside foe, was particularly good at supplying a mass audience with the kind of Western story it desired. Once again, television producers were investing in the medium's power to fuse both a sense of remoteness and contemporaneity to create a popular series.

If, like the other popular media that we have examined, television has always sought to measure and evaluate trends in popular taste in order to come up with the entertainment formula that has the greatest appeal for a certain time, then in retrospect the 1950s come through as the period when television as a medium of mass entertainment was in search of itself. Thus a number of pacesetters for ensuing trends in television programming were very much in evidence. "The Millionaire" depended on a way-out gimmick—the donation of $1,000,000 by an unknown benefactor to a specially selected individual in order to dramatize the effects of sudden wealth on people with whom the audience could identify.[6] "Perry Mason" set the pace for a deluge of courtroom drama series, and Jack Webb's portrayal of a curt-talking police detective in "Dragnet" established the tone and atmosphere for dozens of such shows.

In a paradoxical sense, programs with controversial social issue themes proved to be highly entertaining fare to a mass audience probably because of the psychic distance between TV viewer and program character. We know that psychologically, it is more pleasurable and satisfying to watch the special problems of others if those problems are not essentially our own and sometimes, as the success of the daily soap operas attest, even if the problems are our own. Hence the popular reception of a hospital series like "Medic," forerunner of the even more popularly received "Dr. Kildare" and "Ben Casey" of the 1960s. Accordingly, in the 1960s, a series like "Peyton Place," a spinoff from the bestselling novel of the same name, found a liberal attitude toward its dramatization of sexual escapades and an assorted variety of other scandalous behavior in a small New England town. Its inspirational roots could be traced to examples of the soap opera genre like "As the World Turns" and "The Edge of Night," both among the most popularly received of this form. "Peyton Place" was also an early example of another unique trend in television programming: the direct transcription of fictional material to television, a practice which became much more pronounced in the 1970s.

If television contributed to the death of Hollywood as it existed in the thirties and forties, there also is a great deal of evidence revealing that television has kept it alive. Undoubtedly, the Hollywood movie has found its widest and longest-lasting audience through television. Any hour of the day, prime time or otherwise, throughout the land, we can watch a Hollywood-made film on television, and these broadcasts offer something to suit everyone's

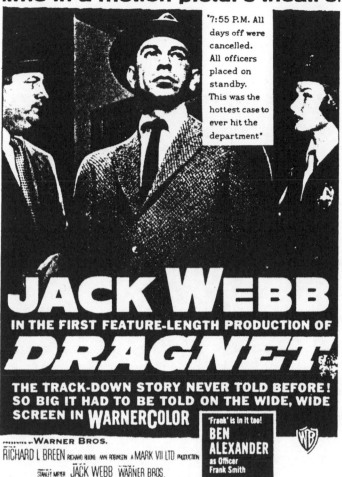

SGT. JOE FRIDAY for the first time in a motion picture theatre!

"7:55 P.M. All days off were cancelled. All officers placed on standby. This was the hottest case to ever hit the department"

JACK WEBB

IN THE FIRST FEATURE-LENGTH PRODUCTION OF

DRAGNET

THE TRACK-DOWN STORY NEVER TOLD BEFORE! SO BIG IT HAD TO BE TOLD ON THE WIDE, WIDE SCREEN IN WARNERCOLOR

'Frank' is in it too! BEN ALEXANDER as Officer Frank Smith

WARNER BROS.

RICHARD L BREEN A MARK VII LTD PRODUCTION

JACK WEBB WARNER BROS.

The year 1952 saw the beginning of a realistic police drama called Dragnet. *It starred a curt-talking Jack Webb as a plain-clothes detective, and it was to influence a host of crime dramas to follow. The fact that* Dragnet *was made into a feature movie in 1954 points out the impact that television was having on the movies at the time. In 1959 the crime drama and nostalgic feeling for the 1920s were combined to produce* The Untouchables, *starring Robert Stack as the legendary Elliott Ness who waged what seemed a one-man war on the booze runners of the 1920s.* PHOTO FROM AUTHOR'S COLLECTION.

taste, ranging from the old B movies of the 1930s offered at 2 o'clock in the morning to more recent releases and even to movies made specially for television and slated for an 8:00 P.M. prime-time slot. Right from the beginning, local station programmers realized the advantages of scheduling movies as fillers at certain times of the day, and after the performance rights to an astronomical number of old Hollywood movies were resolved, the practice of scheduling old movies in designated time slots, especially late at night became a reality.

As a result, instant nostalgia was available at the touch of a button through "theater" series that thematically programmed horror and science-fiction films, the B Western, and the "classic" movies of the major studios. Even series shorts like *Our Gang (The Little Rascals)* and *The Three Stooges* were revived, primarily for a children's audience, but it is generally known that many an adult has renewed his moviegoing youth through watching these reruns with a defensive air of nostalgic indulgence. The

viewing atmosphere might not have been the same in a nostalgic sense, yet the visual fascination has remained; and younger generations, many of whom have never even been in a movie theater, have grown up absorbed in a daily diet of what their parents were able to see only on a Saturday afternoon. This experience in itself may be a major reason for the diluted effect of television nostalgia as opposed to the pure, concentrated reaction one remembers from the moviegoing habit of an earlier time. But doubtless the primary factor contributing to the diffused experience of television viewing has been the periodic breakup of visual continuity into chunks of commercial messages designed for the specific groups that make up a mass audience.

Even though the television commercial had the disarming habit of interrupting a story at the most inopportune moment, we all realized that were it not for a product or company's sponsorship, the program would not even exist for our mutual entertainment. So we endured, and in that spirit of en-

Designed primarily for a juvenile audience, popular movie series like The Little Rascals *and* The Three Stooges *discovered new generations of viewers through television, but many an adult rediscovered his movie-going youth by watching the antics and escapades of these short features that seem to project an endless appeal for viewing audiences.*
PHOTOS FROM AUTHOR'S COLLECTION

Television may have altered the habits of a theater-going movie audience, but the Hollywood film still lives on via television through an endless round of showings of the best, and sometimes not-so-good, that Hollywood had to offer.

durance, we not only acquired further acclimation to the unique "now" sense of television, but our lifestyles became conditioned to and permeated with the economic priorities of our capitalistic system.[7] Consequently, waves of children growing up under the visual influence of television have been materialistically indoctrinated into a level of fantasy expectations that, in many cases, has been exceptionally difficult, if not impossible, to live up to. Because of its power to create a fantasy world of its own, whether using live actors and actresses or animated figures, the television commercial has generated a unique visual nostalgia of its own that has had a continuing subliminal effect on both children and adults. It has often been observed in family viewing situations that when adults converse during a commercial break, children who have been ignoring the story that interested the adults often find the commercial attractive enough to watch, a situation which tells us a great deal about not only the intelligence level for which these messages are designed, but about their visual methods for attracting attention as well.

Never given to using a highly specialized manner in advertising, television, with its eye ever directed toward mass taste, has taken a cue from the type of magazine advertising illustrated near the beginning of this book. Wherever possible, television has sought to make use of familiar faces and characters from all areas of media and entertainment. Thus movie stars, sports heroes, and comic-strip characters abound in television endorsements of commercial products. Because these are figures created for and by the masses, selling campaigns visually featuring them usually bring highly lucrative returns. It seems that Madison Avenue, too, is keenly sensitive to television's peculiar visual ability to relate to the masses by making the remote familiar: through the sales pitch of a personal image we readily recognize, a once unfamiliar product becomes readily recognizable and thus salable. Yet for all its effective selling powers, television advertising, by its very intrusion on our private sensibilities, represents another way in which this medium has helped catalyze a visual split in our temporal awareness.

Paradoxically, the dichotomy of "nowness" and "remoteness" that television has sensitized us to has resulted in the most pervasive synthesis of popular culture forms that we have yet realized. As if to emphasize its special role and unique identity in today's society, television cuts deftly across the media of print, comic art's live and animated forms,

and film. As a result, we cannot say that the medium of television, at least as we recognize it today, is more dependent for its expressions on any one form of popular culture than any other. It therefore can be considered a repository of our visual forms of popular culture and as such advantageously draws upon those forms which are best suited for a particular kind of communication.

For example, a contemporary program like CBS's "Sixty Minutes" is structured around a format of investigative reporting that depends on both print and film to express its viewpoints on current issues and problems. Numerous other programs that have taken on a magazine format illustrate television's special ability to synthesize the modes of print and picture in a unique blend of all the media forms that have preceded it. As our most synthetic visual medium of popular culture to date, television communicates with the masses through its dependence on print, animation, and sound to visually enhance both its program and advertising content. In short, it makes use of those communicative forms that are most familiar to the masses. The result is a medium of expression highly sensitive to the current fantasies, anxieties, and perplexities of our society, whether they are visualized through the dramatic movie made especially for television or through the investigative documentary. In televising Alex Haley's marvelous "detective story" about his black ancestry, *Roots*, television achieved one of its most magnificent moments simply because this production contained strong elements of both the feature movie and the investigative documentary, the form that television is best capable of producing. The payoff was the largest audience ever to watch a televised event. Although it possesses the power to alert us to issues and concerns of immediate urgency, television has provided us with our most dependable source for reliving the past in a shared experience. Again, the televised version of *Roots* serves us as a clear example of the duality of nowness and remoteness that controls the television viewing experience.

Although, from its earliest days, television has provided us with a source of instant nostalgia in the reissuance of movies from Hollywood's golden age, it has recently begun to reveal a nostalgic consciousness of its own through the syndicated reruns of series shows that were popular in the 1950s and 1960s. Programs like "Gilligan's Island," "Gomer Pyle, USMC," "Bewitched," and "Hogan's Heroes" seem destined to the fate of endless reruns in low-

Like the movies, television has created a nostalgic identity of its own through the syndication of once-popular series shows, some from as long ago as the 1950s. These are ads for some of the shows that seem to crop up in endless reruns around the country.

One of the most popular rerun series has been **Star Trek,** *a space saga based on more fantasy than fact, but one that has inspired a national cult of fan support since its inception in 1966. This stylized picture includes the show's three principals: Deforest Kelley as ship's doctor McCoy, William Shatner as spaceship commander Kirk, and Leonard Nimoy as the show's most popular character, Mr. Spock.* PHOTO FROM AUTHOR'S COLLECTION.

keyed time slots. At the same time, television's growing nostalgic consciousness has resulted in entertaining documentaries like the 1977 CBS production, "When Television Was Young," which exemplified much of what has been said here, underscored by a *TV Guide* ad for the show that promised "Great Faces, Moments and Issues from Television's Early Days." Those who happened to see this program were reminded in the true nostalgic sense of times that appear in retrospect to be a lot less complex than the present and reminded, too, that the nostalgia derived from television viewing is communal and inseparably interrelated with the open-ended experiences of domestic or leisure-oriented activities of an earlier day.

Compared with the special-event atmosphere that the moviegoer of the thirties and forties enjoyed, the familiar surroundings of today's television viewer, whether they be the family den or the local tavern, can never emulate the magic aura of the downtown movie palace or even the old neighborhood movie theater. The air of expectancy with which movie audiences of another day awaited the curtain's opening and that first stab of light from the projector announcing the newsreel indicates an intensity of experience which has since faded because of our visual saturation in television over the years.

Accordingly, the window on the world that television has provided for us has psychologically conditioned us to the feeling of being everywhere at once, a subtle but prevalent visual orientation of our time that dilutes whatever personally realized viewing experience we may obtain from this medium. Although the personalized identification that we might have derived from the reading of a book in our youth or from active contact with other visual forms of popular culture may still be with us in a nostalgic sense, television watching has subjected us to a mood of increasing passivity and an inordinate fascination with nostalgic experience because we find it easier to yield to an all-encompassing visual power that can see for us. The overall effect on the mass mind—or mass eye, if you will—since the advent of popular television some thirty years ago has been an increased awareness of the world around us but an accompanying loss or impairment of our ability to communicate with or relate to each other, even within the same family group. Nevertheless, as the climactic result of over two hundred years of interaction between the creative expression or nostalgic vision of the popular artist or mythmaker and the fantasy needs of his audience, televi-

sion exists as the mythmaking medium of a technological age with much the same function that earlier dominant forms of cultural expression had for their times: to satisfy the fantasies and wish fulfillments of the masses who set and demand the standards of popular taste. Thus the argument over whether or not television should present explicit scenes of sex and violence is not really so much a recent problem to contend with. In fact, the history of popular fiction is rather full of instances of controversial works that have offended and outraged the establishment because of their graphic portrayal of sex, violence, or whatever subject matter might not have been acceptable to the tastemakers of the period. A parallel situation runs through the chronology of other popular media forms as well. The real difference between the psychological and sociological effects of earlier forms and that of television on our visual sense lies in the overwhelming pervasiveness of television as opposed to the comparatively restricted nature of a form like eighteenth-century fiction, for example, which was accessible to only those who could read it and then only to those who could afford to purchase it. Today the lowliest rental home in a big-city ghetto may boast of a television set serving the same purpose that popular art forms have always done over the years: to appease the fantasy hungers of those who have always craved and needed this kind of satisfaction.

If the medium of television has made such a tremendous impact on our visual sense in the relatively short time that it has been with us, what lies ahead for those of us who will confront the visual onslaughts of undreamed of forms of expression? What variations will either add to or detract from the individual's visual understanding of the world around him while responding to those fantasy needs that lead to nostalgic patterns of identification? There are already signs of revolutionary developments in television's pervasive influence on individual behavior. The expansion of cable television and the proliferation of such technological wonders as the increasingly inexpensive home video cassette recorder, which enables anyone to create his own library of television nostalgia, are already increasing the viewer's options. In fact, there are probably sufficient enough examples around today for us to conclude that the future is already here.

Although the documentary format pioneered by Murrow did much to make us aware of serious topics within the framework of television's trite and

The individual and group success of popular images like Elvis Presley and the Beatles was based on the union of sight and sound, a TV-inspired marriage that has pervaded all the popular media forms in which these entertainers performed. The overall result has been the creation of a passive attitude on the part of the popular culture consumer and also an extension of the nostalgia neurosis with respect to the memory of these performers. Note the nostalgic moods that have already built up around Presley after his death, and the Beatles, after their demise as a group. PHOTOS FROM AUTHOR'S COLLECTION.

Tune In The Good Life With Cox Cable T.V. of Pensacola's Window on the World via Our Satellite Receive Station

If you had our Window on the World you could see a whole lot more including

Major Movies

Night Club Acts

SEC Games

Starting Jan. 4, 1978
Metro 7 Conference
Starting Jan. 7, 1978

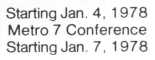

Perhaps the answer to creating a more active sense of participation on the part of the consumer of popular culture is to provide more opportunities for selectivity and diversity of choice through media forms like cable television, as this advertisement seems to suggest. Regardless of whatever new forms through which popular culture may choose to express itself, the nostalgic vision that has pervaded the development of popular expression in this century will no doubt continue to direct the fantasy needs of a mass audience. RE-PRINTED WITH PERMISSION OF COX CABLE TV OF PEN-SACOLA.

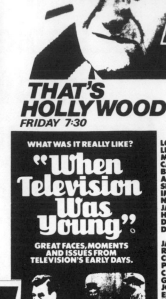

Here is plenty of contemporary evidence that the nostalgia neurosis is still with us and probably will be for some time to come: advertisements for a film made for theater release as well as one made expressly for television; a biopic of a classic movie comedy team; a classic animated cartoon comedy team; a program dealing with the golden age of Hollywood; a documentary treating the early days of television; the serial genre in both a classic and an updated version; and underscoring our need for all these forms, a series called 60 Minutes, *which informs us of current happenings in such a manner that the past seems much more pleasant than the present and/or the future.* 60 MINUTES AD REPRINTED COURTESY OF CBS-TV.

trivial program fare, it also made us more susceptible to the nostalgia neurosis or daydream experience by making us more future conscious. As we have seen, it is a fear of the future and what it might hold in store for us that has driven us back in upon ourselves and upon the nostalgic fantasies and daydreams that our popular culture forms have created for us. Accordingly, there are those who would rebel against the future's hold over us by predicting that today's dominant purveyor of dreams, television, will drive us all back to the prototypal popular-culture habit of reading books. Such self-appointed prophets are apparently unaware that the book publishing business is enjoying its greatest era of prosperity today and that television has played a key role in making the masses more book conscious than ever before.

The interdependent nature of the expressive forms surveyed in this book should help us realize that our demands for daydreams or our nostalgic vision will continue to dictate whatever mythic forms of popular expression may evolve in the future. The inherent greatness of this country may be founded on the American Dream and on our conviction that we have an inalienable right to pursue it; yet the pursuit of this dream has not become any easier over the years, in spite of the technological advances that have made life easier for us. It follows, then, that we must continue to realize our personal daydreams through the forms of popular culture that we know and love, provided we can continue to discern what is real and what is fantasy, for only with the rejuvenation of spirit that comes from indulging in our daydreams can we replenish the vital energies so necessary to continue our pursuit of the American Dream.

Notes

1. Harry F. Waters, "What TV Does to Kids," *Newsweek* 89 (February 21, 1977), 63–70.

2. With spontaneous and obviously unprepared hosts like Morey Amsterdam and, later, Jerry Lester, "Broadway Open House" initiated the format of the show with no format.

3. Because the continuity of sports experience is broken up at periodic intervals, the application of the "instant replay" system to televised sports has aided tremendously in reliving the drama of such events, not to mention its contribution to the resolution of disagreements.

4. Some of the movie stars who acted in the live drama of early television were John Cassavetes, James Dean, Julie Harris, Charlton Heston, Grace Kelly, Jack Lemmon, Steve McQueen, Paul Newman, Jack Palance, Eva Marie Saint, and Rod Steiger.

5. Another 1949 show that had an even longer television run than "The Goldbergs" was "Mama," a series built around a Norwegian-American family. But Molly Goldberg's Jewish "mama" was the more predominant image of early television matriarchs.

6. My theory of television fantasy coming across as real experience to a mass audience strikingly holds up in this case, as a number of viewers wrote to the network asking to be considered for the million-dollar benefaction. Soap opera series have experienced a similar reaction from viewers inquiring about the fate of a particular character as though he or she were a real person!

7. Because the television commercial allows us to actually see a product as it may be utilized or consumed by real people, it has probably stimulated our desires for material things more dramatically than any other form of advertising.

Bibliography

Alger, Jr., Horatio. *Silas Snobden's Office Boy.* New York: Popular Library, 1973.

Armour, Richard. Introduction, *Give Me Liberty.* New York: World Publishing Co., 1969.

Aydelotte, William O. "The Detective Story as a Historical Source," *The Yale Review* 39 (Autumn 1949): 76–95.

Bellem, Robert Leslie. "Labyrinth of Monsters" in *The Pulps.* Edited by Tony Goodstone. New York: Chelsea House, 1970.

Blackbeard, Bill and Williams, Martin, eds. *The Smithsonian Collection of Newspaper Comics.* New York: Harry N. Abrams, Inc., 1977.

Bradbury, Ray. Introduction, *The Collected Works of Buck Rogers in the 25th Century.* Edited by Robert C. Dille. New York: Crown, 1969.

Browne, Ray B. and Fishwick, Marshall. *The Icons of America.* Bowling Green, Ohio: Popular Press, 1978.

Burroughs, Edgar Rice. *Tarzan at the Earth's Core.* New York: Ace Books, 1929.

———. *Tarzan the Untamed.* New York: Grosset and Dunlap, 1920.

Cain, James M. *The Postman Always Rings Twice* in *Three Novels by James M. Cain.* New York: Alfred A Knopf, Inc., 1969.

Cazedessus, Jr., Camille E. "Lords of the Jungle." In *The Comic-Book Book,* edited by Don Thompson and Dick Lupoff. New Rochelle: Arlington House, 1973.

Chandler, Raymond. *The Big Sleep.* New York: Alfred A. Knopf, Inc., 1939.

Couperie, Pierre and Horn, Maurice C. *A History of the Comic Strip.* New York: Crown, 1971.

Crawford, Hubert H. *Crawford's Encyclopedia of Comic Books.* Middle Village, N.Y.: Jonathan David, Inc., 1978.

Dos Passos, John. *U.S.A.* New York: Modern Library, 1937.

Everson, William K. *The Bad Guys: A Pictorial History of the Movie Villain.* Secaucus, N.J.: Citadel Press, 1964.

———. *Classics of the Horror Film.* Secaucus, N.J.: Citadel Press, 1974.

Faulkner, William. "The Bear" in *Go Down, Moses.* New York: Modern Library, 1942.

Feiffer, Jules. *The Great Comic Book Heroes.* New York: Dial Press, 1965.

Fell, John. *Film and the Narrative Tradition.* Norman, Okla.: University of Oklahoma Press, 1974.

Fenin, George N. and Everson, William K. *The Western.* New York: Orion Press, 1962.

Finch, Christopher. *The Art of Walt Disney.* New York: Harry N. Abrams, Inc., 1975.

Fitzgerald, F. Scott. *The Great Gatsby.* New York: Charles Scribner's Sons, 1953.

———. "Winter Dreams" in *Short Story Masterpieces.* Edited by Robert Penn Warren and Albert Erskine. New York: Dell Books, 1962.

Goodstone, Tony, ed. *The Pulps: Fifty Years of American Pop Culture.* New York: Chelsea House, 1970.

Goulart, Ron. *The Adventurous Decade: Comic Strips in the Thirties.* New Rochelle: Arlington House, 1975.

Gould, Chester. *The Celebrated Cases of Dick Tracy.* New York: Chelsea House, 1970.

———. *Dick Tracy: The Thirties, Tommyguns and Hard Times.* New York: Chelsea House, 1978.

Gray, Harold. *Arf! The Life and Hard Times of Little Orphan Annie.* New Rochelle: Arlington House, 1970.

Grey, Zane. *The Arizona Clan.* New York: Pocket Books, 1966.

———. *The U.P. Trail.* New York: Pocket Books, 1956.

Hammett, Dashiell. *The Maltese Falcon* in *The Novels of Dashiell Hammett.* New York: Alfred A. Knopf, Inc., 1965.

Harmon, Jim. *Jim Harmon's Nostalgia Catalogue.* Los Angelos: J.P. Tarcher, Inc., 1973.

—— and Glut, Don. *The Great Movie Serials.* Garden City, N.Y.: Doubleday, 1972.

Hemingway, Ernest. "Big Two-hearted River" in *The Short Stories of Ernest Hemingway.* New York: Charles Scribner's Sons, 1953.

Horn, Maurice, ed. *The World Enclopedia of Comics.* New York: Chelsea House, 1976.

——. "American Dreaming: An Analysis of the Adventure Strip," *Inside Comics* 3 (Fall 1974): 14–21.

Jones, Robert Kenneth. *The Shudder Pulps: A History of the Weird Menace Magazines of the 1930s.* New York: New American Library, 1978.

Kyle, David. *A Pictorial History of Science Fiction.* London: Hamlyn Publishing Group, 1976.

Lewis, Sinclair. *Main Street.* New York: New American Library, 1961.

Lupoff, Dick and Thompson, Don, eds. *All in Color for a Dime.* New Rochelle: Arlington House, 1970.

Lupoff, Richard. *Edgar Rice Burroughs: Master of Adventure.* New York: Ace Books, 1965.

Maltin, Leonard. *The Great Movie Shorts.* New York: Crown, 1972.

Marschall, Richard, ed. *The Sunday Funnies 1896–1950.* New York: Chelsea House, 1978.

McCay, Winsor. *Dreams of the Rarebit Fiend.* New York: Dover, 1973.

——. *Little Nemo 1905–1906.* New York: Nostalgia Press, 1976.

McManus, George. *Bringing Up Father.* New York: Bonanza, 1973.

Miller, Don. *"B" Movies.* New York: Curtis Books, 1973.

Mizener, Arthur. *Scott Fitzgerald and His World.* London: Thames & Hudson, 1972.

Morella, Joe; Epstein, Edward Z., and Griggs, John. *The Films of World War II.* Secaucus, N.J.: Citadel Press, 1973.

Morris, Wright. *The Territory Ahead: Critical Interpretations in American Literature.* New York: Atheneum, 1963.

Nye, Russell. *The Unembarrassed Muse: The Popular Arts in America.* New York: Dial Press, 1970.

Painton, Frederick C. "The Devil Must Pay" in *The Pulps,* Edited by Tony Goodstone. New York: Chelsea House, 1970.

Parish, James Robert. *The Great Movie Series.* South Brunswick: A.S. Barnes and Co., 1971.

Patten, Gilbert. *Frank Merriwell's "Father".* Norman, Okla.: University of Oklahoma Press, 1964.

Perry, George and Aldridge, Alan. *The Penguin Book of Comics.* London: Penguin Press, 1971.

Porges, Irwin. *Edgar Rice Burroughs: The Man Who Created Tarzan.* New York: Ballantine Books (2 vols.), 1975.

Pritchett, V. S. "Cruelty in *The Adventures of Huckleberry Finn,*" *New Statesman and Nation* 22 (August 1941): 113.

Robinson, Jerry. *The Comics: An Illustrated History of Comic Strip Art.* New York: G.P. Putnam's Sons, 1974.

Roth, Philip. "Writing American Fiction," *Commentary* 31 (March 1961): 223–233.

Schorer, Mark. *Sinclair Lewis: An American Life.* New York: McGraw-Hill, 1961.

Sennett, Ted. *Warner Brothers Presents.* New Rochelle: Arlington House, 1971.

Shulman, Arthur and Youman, Roger. *How Sweet It Was.* New York: Bonanza, 1966.

Sklar, Robert. *Movie-Made America: A Social History of American Movies.* New York: Random House, 1975.

Steinbeck, John. *The Grapes of Wrath.* New York: Modern Library, 1939.

Steinbrunner, Chris and Goldblatt, Burt. *Cinema of the Fantastic.* New York: Galahad Books, 1972.

Steranko, James. *The Steranko History of Comics* (2 vols.). Reading, Pa.: Supergraphics, 1970–72.

Thomas, Tony and Terry, Jim. *The Busby Berkeley Book.* New York: A & W Visual Library, 1973.

Trilling, Lionel. "Freud and Literature" in *The Liberal Imagination.* Garden City, N.Y.: Doubleday, 1957.

Twain, Mark. *Autobiography.* New York: Harper Bros. (2 vols.), 1924.

——. *The Adventures of Huckleberry Finn.* New York: Grosset & Dunlap, 1918.

Tyler, Parker. *A Pictorial History of Sex in Films.* Secaucus, N.J.: Citadel Press, 1974.

Umphlett, Wiley Lee. *The Sporting Myth and the American Experience.* Lewisburg, Pa.: Bucknell University Press, 1975.

Vidal, Gore. "Tarzan Revisited," *Esquire* 80 (October 1973).

Waters, Harry F. "What TV Does to Kids," *Newsweek* 89 (February 21, 1977): 63–70.

Waugh, Coulton. *The Comics.* New York: Luna Press, 1974.

Weiss, Ken and Goodgold, Ed. *To Be Continued . . .* New York: Bonanza Books, 1972.

Wertham, Frederic. *Seduction of the Innocent.* New York: Rinehart and Co., 1954.

Wilks, Max. *The Golden Age of Television.* New York: Delacorte Press, 1976.

Wolfe, Thomas. *Of Time and the River* in *The Thomas Wolfe Reader.* Edited by C. Hugh Holman. New York: Charles Scribner's Sons, 1962.

——. "The Story of a Novel" in *ibid.*

Index